PRACTICAL PUBLIC SPEAKING

THE MACMILLAN COMPANY
NEW YORK · CHICAGO
DALLAS · ATLANTA · SAN FRANCISCO

THE MACMILLAN COMPANY
OF CANADA, LIMITED
TORONTO

Practical Public Speaking

A GUIDE TO EFFECTIVE COMMUNICATION

Eugene E. White, Ph.D.
UNIVERSITY OF MIAMI

Clair R. Henderlider, Ph.D.
WESTERN RESERVE UNIVERSITY

NEW YORK

The Macmillan Company

To Roberta and Ruth
for help and encouragement

PREFACE

This book is designed primarily for use in both the beginning undergraduate class and the adult public-speaking course in extension divisions or in industry. It will also provide self-help for the individual not enrolled in a formal course, although best results will be secured under the guidance of an instructor.

Our desire has been to treat concisely yet comprehensively those principles basic to effective speech preparation and delivery. With the student reader foremost in mind, our goals have been ready understandability, practicality, friendly and informal style, and brevity. Although the approach is pragmatic, the reader is repeatedly reminded of the ethical responsibilities which must be assumed by the speaker.

Each of the four divisions of the text is prefaced by an outline. The exercises and problems which follow each chapter are designed to aid the teacher in planning assignments and to help the student in putting principles into practice. To permit the student to prepare and deliver speeches before reading large portions of the book, the fundamentals of speech preparation and delivery are noted briefly in Chapter 1. The detailed treatments of these principles in later chapters can be studied at appropriate times during the remainder of the term.

The text may be adapted to various course outlines. While some may wish to follow the chapter sequence, others who prefer to begin with a study of the techniques of delivery may assign Chapters 1 and 9–13 before Chapters 2–8. If certain speech types or adaptations are to be covered prior to a careful examination of preparation and delivery, selected chapters from Section IV could be assigned early in the course.

We are sincerely grateful to our students in the college classroom and in extension courses for aiding us in our attempt to correlate academic theory with the practical demands of present-day speech making. In particular, we are deeply indebted to three distinguished leaders in the field of speech, each of whom read the entire manuscript and offered invaluable suggestions: Professors C. M. Wise of Louisiana State University, Orville Hitchcock of the State University of Iowa, and Rupert Cortright of Wayne University. Despite the generous assistance of others, errors of fact or interpretation may still remain. For such shortcomings, we alone are responsible.

E. E. WHITE

C. R. HENDERLIDER

Miami, Florida
Cleveland, Ohio

CONTENTS

SECTION I *Developing the Proper Attitudes*

SECTION II *Preparing the Speech*

ix

SECTION III *Delivering the Speech*

SECTION IV *Adapting Basic Techniques to Various Speech Situations*

OUTLINE OF *SECTION I*

Developing the Proper Attitudes

Essential Purpose of Section I: to enable the reader to adopt a positive approach to public speaking by rejecting misconceptions about speech and by adopting sound attitudes which will permit rapid development of effectiveness. Brief discussion of the basic principles of preparing and delivering speeches is included to enable the beginning speaker to complete early speaking assignments before reading the entire book.

CHAPTER 1: *Approaching Public Speaking Positively*

I. Introduction
II. Misconceptions about the study of speech
    A. "You either have it or you don't"
    B. "You cannot trust an effective speaker"
    C. Golden voices and silver tongues
    D. A new personality?
III. A philosophy for the beginning speaker
    A. "I'm scared!"
    B. "Anybody can talk!"
    C. "Who wants to be an orator?"
    D. "I'm willing to learn"
IV. Climbing the ladder to effectiveness
    Handrail One: Your audience and your occasion
    Handrail Two: You and your purpose
    A. Step One: Gathering the materials
    B. Step Two: Organizing the Discussion
    C. Step Three: Discovering and using the supporting materials
    D. Step Four: Developing the Introduction
    E. Step Five: Developing the Conclusion
    F. Step Six: Rehearsing the speech
    G. Step Seven: Delivering the speech

Approaching Public Speaking Positively

INTRODUCTION

So you're going to make a speech! That entails facing an audience, something you may not have done since a childhood appearance in a church Christmas program. You may recall the anxious faces of your parents as their lips moved with your words and their relief when your lines came out letter-perfect. Others will remember an oral book report or a theme read aloud in a high-school English class. Many of you will begin the study of public speaking with mixed feelings. Although possibly disturbed at the prospect of speech-making, most of you will value the opportunity to express your ideas publicly and will want to do it well. Perhaps it strikes you as strange that you should desire an audience and yet fear it.

Why are you enrolled in a course in public speaking? If you are a typical college student beginning a regular college course, you probably recognize the need for effective oral communication in almost any career you may pursue. If you are a business or professional person beginning an evening course for adults, your motivation is probably more specific. Such a class may include (1) a company supervisor who must learn to talk more effectively at employees' meetings; (2) the president-elect of the local chapter of the Federated Women's Clubs, who must deliver an acceptance address and conduct business meetings; (3) an officer of Local 45, United Automobile Workers, whose chances for promotion may depend largely on his vocal contributions in future union meetings; (4) an attorney who hopes to improve his courtroom presentations; and (5) a physician who must address a medical convention on the uses of sodium pentathol. Long hours of work have left him no time for courses in speech until now. He fears his paper will be as poorly delivered as the others, and has a haunting premonition that it may prove to be a better anesthetic than sodium pentathol!

Such motivations are typical of those felt by thousands who enter the beginning course in speech. Common to all of them is the knowledge that man is a talkative animal, that speaking is our most prevalent form of communication. For every word we write, we speak thousands. And each time we talk—on the street, in a neighbor's home, across the conference table, before an audience—we are judged not only by *what we say*, but *how effectively we say it*. In increasing numbers, people are realizing that the ability to talk well may mean greater economic efficiency in a highly competitive world, more rewarding social relationships, increased personal satisfaction, and more responsible citizenship. The development and continued expansion of departments of speech in colleges and high schools, large enrollments in adult evening classes, and the growing number of speech courses organized by business and industry testify to the acute interest of most people in learning to talk well.

MISCONCEPTIONS ABOUT THE STUDY OF SPEECH

Before outlining a positive philosophy for the beginning speaker and suggesting methods for achieving it, several erroneous concepts about the study of speech should be examined and discarded.

A. **"You either have it or you don't."** It is not surprising that many believe speech is not a subject for study. Without remembered effort, most of us learn to talk early in childhood. People who talk frequently, easily, and fluently are labeled "born with the knack." Those with less verbal facility are tagged as "the quiet type." Like blue eyes or curly hair, ability or inability to talk well is accepted as a hereditary trait. Subscribers to this theory point triumphantly to Bill Jackson, who can always say "a few well-chosen words" on any occasion, before any audience, and on any subject. On the other hand, Professor Ellsworth Fox, who talks monotonously to his classes and to women's clubs on his favorite subject, medieval art, lulls most of his listeners to sleep. Fox, it is pointed out, has lectured for fifteen years, is highly educated, and once took a course in public speaking. In contrast, Jackson has had no formal speech training, little education, and had almost no speaking experience until his "talent" was discovered.

Indeed, such evidence exists. Undoubtedly, you can cite similar examples. Because of native ability and accumulated experience, some become adequate and occasionally exceptional speakers. Similar aptitudes are common in music, art, and athletics. A number of renowned authors have never taken a course in composition, and many famous painters have had no formal art training. Nevertheless, those with high aptitudes in these arts usually profit from study. Evidence refutes the claim of some people that speaking ability is easily acquired as a by-product of conversation, committee leadership, or recitation. Most of us need directed study under skilled supervision.

Some never learn to speak well, even with protracted exposure to training. However, a poor speaker with normal intelligence, a desire to improve, and competent guidance can become a good speaker; and a good speaker can become a better one. It happens with encouraging consistency in the classroom, may be readily observed in public life, and has been noted repeatedly in the history of public address.

Although some effective speakers are born, more are made. Accept the fact that you are likely to fall into the latter category and pursue your study of speech on that basis.

B. "You cannot trust an effective speaker." Since the time of Plato and possibly before, some persons have been skeptical of speech training, attacking it upon moral and ethical grounds. They suspect and distrust an individual who is too glib, too confident, too persuasive. When one of the authors was called upon to present a report in a university committee meeting, the chairman good-humoredly warned, "Now be careful of these smooth-talking speech men. They can put one over on you before you know what's happened!" To many, a halting, inarticulate speaker seems more sincere and trustworthy. Possibly many who are skeptical of speaking ability have been deceived by a "slick operator" or a "high-pressure" salesman.

If some of us can be "taken in" by compelling persuasion from a dishonest source, it does not follow that we should abandon speech training as our defense. A sensible alternative is to develop comparable ability on the part of those with honorable causes. Moreover, we can become more critical as listeners and sharpen our awareness of the common techniques of the propagandist. The successful misuse of speech is one of the strongest reasons for intensifying our concern with it as a means to furthering desirable causes.

C. Golden voices and silver tongues. Some people believe that formal training produces a studied, affected, and artificial kind of oratory, replete with bombast, flowery language, and flamboyant gestures. This "elocutionary" style was dominant some generations ago, but today is as outdated as tickets to last year's World Series. Effective speaking is not a "performance" staged to display the ability of the speaker; it is a communicative process designed to stir up particular responses from a particular audience at a specific time and place. More than a skill, speech is an art requiring the effective use of audience analysis, logical and psychological appeals, language and composition, and a host of other rhetorical factors. These precepts and techniques cannot be separated from the materials or content of a talk. Unless we agree that a good speech conveys something worth communicating, we are promoting "small talk" and exhibitionism, but not effective speaking.

Your goals, therefore, will not include the development of golden voices, silver tongues, and the other trappings of the old-fashioned orator "out on display," but rather the study of those principles, processes, and habits which promote effective communication of your ideas to your listeners.

D. A new personality? Promoters of courses in public speaking sometimes make exorbitant claims for the ability of such training to develop personality. Unfortunately advertisements of commercial schools of speech on occasion represent their courses as cure-alls for most personality and adjustment problems. Such claims are not justified. Increased confidence and poise resulting from improvement in self-expression may alter your common behavior pattern; we cannot, however, promise you an entirely new personality as a consequence of speech training.

A Philosophy for the Beginning Speaker

As you approach the preparation of your first speeches, many thoughts may enter your mind. Do you feel inadequate and hope that you won't make a fool of yourself? Are you uncertain about your choice of subject and the response you wish from the audience?

"How shall I prepare? Shall I write it out and read it, commit it to memory, try to talk from an outline, or what? Shall I rehearse? Where? How often? How long shall I speak? Must I begin with a joke? Could I get away with using last week's English theme or a summary of a *Reader's Digest* article? After all, I'm not a professional public speaker. There are others who can do a better job of this than I can. Maybe I can get out of it some way. Should I drop the course? Should I refuse the invitation to speak at Kiwanis?"

These questions are typical. Note that a negative atmosphere pervades them. If you experience similar symptoms of withdrawal and feelings of uncertainty, it may comfort you to know that you share them with thousands.

On the other hand, a bit of successful experience may have conditioned you more positively, in which case your thoughts may be: "How can I improve over last time? Will my initial nervousness again subside quickly? Is my material organized in the best possible way? I wonder if the opening is as good as I think it is." You may even surprise yourself by thinking, "I'm beginning to enjoy this. I'm looking forward to it!"

Our contacts with thousands of students over the years reveal that most people begin the study of speech with one or more of the following attitudes toward it.

A. First attitude: "I'm scared!" By far the most common initial reaction of the beginning speaker is that of *fear*, commonly termed "stage fright." As regularly as classes begin and end, teachers are confronted with students who let trembling hands and knees, perspiring palms, dry mouths, tremulous voices, breathlessness, loss of memory, and "butterflies in the stomach" serve as stubborn roadblocks on the path to improvement. Most of you will not need further elaboration of the symptomatology of this problem. A student recently confessed that until his high-school teacher elaborated on the symptoms of stage fright in vivid detail he had felt reasonably confident about speaking. Upon hearing of the panic felt by some at the prospect of facing an audience, he was in constant fear that a barrage of similar reactions might be forthcoming each time he spoke thereafter. Before any reader reacts similarly, let us leave the symptoms and look for remedies.

Some doctors claim that many of our ills are psychosomatic in origin; they are physical manifestations of emotional disturbances. Many a man whose nervous stomach has not responded to a dozen varieties of pills and diets has found himself miraculously cured upon securing a more satisfying and rewarding job. The primary prerequisite to recovery from emotional disturbances, doctors tell us, is to understand their nature and what brings them upon us.

What is the nature of this emotional disturbance felt to some degree by nearly all of us when arising to speak? It should be clearly recognized at the outset that we are experiencing *fear*. You wonder why you are afraid. You are clearly not in danger. Audiences rarely shoot or lynch speakers, you tell yourself. However, a little introspection will remind you that there are many kinds of fear which are not the result of imminent danger to one's physical person. When we begin to speak, and frequently for some time before a performance, we are feeling *social fear*. Isn't it similar to the sinking feeling you had when the boss called you in "on the carpet" and you had no idea what you had done wrong? Doesn't it remind you vaguely of your first party, when you were so concerned about your appearance and so anxious to please your date that you didn't have any fun? Probably you looked forward to the party with some eagerness; yet you feared the possible disapproval of others who would attend. Similarly, when we face an audience, we do not fear the process of speaking as such, but rather the consequences of it, particularly the possibility of a negative response from our listeners.

When one of the authors delivered his first paper at a professional convention, he was beset with a number of alarming signs of stage fright. Why? He is perfectly at home before a class, and ordinarily experiences only mild nervous tension in speaking to audiences. The convention, however, presented a different problem. There he was talking to professional equals and superiors, whose approval he very much desired. He did not fear speaking, but rather the possibility of unfavorable reaction to his presentation. It is apparent that most of us are victims of a strange paradox—we crave audiences and yet fear them. The tension resulting from the conflict of these antagonistic forces is the problem we face.

What can be prescribed for treatment? First, nervous tension has one desirable result. A certain amount of it is essential in producing a top performance. Just as the successful athlete is "keyed up" before a game, so the effective speaker is emotionally charged to meet the requisites of the speaking situation. Most teachers would rather deal with a student who is excessively tense than with one who is indifferent and lackadaisical. Now that we know a degree of nervous tension is not only normal but essential, the problem is to temper and regulate it so that it works for us rather than against us. How can this be done?

During the preparation period, keep two things in mind. First, it is vital that your beginning speeches be concerned with subjects and materials of interest and importance to *you*. Do not summarize the first article you find in the latest *Reader's Digest*. It is better to search your own mind to find what is important enough and close enough to *you* to warrant passing on to others. In addition to choosing a subject of personal interest, it is essential that you *strongly desire to convey that message to your listeners*. Second, be certain that you prepare thoroughly (preparation of speeches is treated in detail in Chapters 3–8). Do not attempt a speech analyzing our latest diplomatic crisis with a foreign power unless you have made a serious study of our diplomatic relations with that country. To slight preparation is to tempt an excessive onset of tension. In addition to following the foregoing advice, practice mental hygiene by giving yourself four psychological "shots in the arm."

1. *You know more about your subject than your audience.* This is so because of your strong interest in the subject and your long-term and immediate preparation for the speech. In "real life" speaking situations, such is regularly the case. A speaker is rarely asked to appear unless someone is convinced he has special knowledge. If you do not know more about your subject than your audience by the time you are scheduled to speak, you should not speak. If your subject interests you, and if you have prepared conscientiously, you are ready to face your listeners. Confidence born of enthusiasm and meticulous preparation is difficult to duplicate.

2. *You appear more confident than you feel.* It is a truism that we do not see ourselves as others see us. Such is the case when we face audiences. Upon finishing his first speech, a student who had appeared poised and confident told the class with a sigh of relief that he was "glad that was over." He confessed to extreme stage fright and admitted he had doubted he would be able to complete the speech. Although initially reluctant to believe that he had appeared in sufficient control of himself and the situation, he was finally convinced. His attitude then was, "If I can feel that terrible and look that good, I suppose I can put up with tension and fear." Not until later did he realize that through learning of his acceptance by the audience, the major cause of his tension was eliminated and the symptoms markedly reduced in intensity.

Not all instances are as striking as this one, but be assured that "butterflies" are usually well concealed from sight, muscle tremor is so minute it is unnoticeable in most cases, and only a surgeon sees a racing heart. In general, the symptoms of tension are primarily concealed, and those which show are ordinarily not obvious to the audience. If you can convince yourself that you appear more confident than you feel, you will quickly experience a diminution of fear reaction.

3. *Others share your misgivings.* It is said that misery loves company because company reduces misery. To be singled out as the only youngster in the block to come down with measles is an excruciating experience; but if an epidemic strikes and no one can romp and play, a child may not be quite as unhappy at the prospect of being quarantined.

You will be relieved to discover that not only are most of your classmates as tense as you, but that distinguished and successful actors, musicians, lecturers, and athletes are also chronic sufferers. Many of them testify that they have never been without nervous tension in public appearances. Nevertheless, most of them are happy with the vigor and enthusiasm which result.

When you are convinced that you do not differ from a host of others who appear publicly, many of them successful and famous, you have given yourself one of the best antidotes for excessive apprehension.

4. *Audiences are friendly.* In the mind of the novice speaker, the audience he is to face usually becomes the focal point of his fear. This attitude is normal, since we are more apprehensive about the possibility of unfavorable listener reaction than we are about the act of speaking itself. Students frequently claim that audiences look bored and "poker-faced," occasionally seem to smirk, and in other ways noticeably indicate their disapproval. Most of these judgments are imagined by the speaker. Unless the listeners are actively hostile to you or to your subject, they are unlikely to show overt signs of disapproval, although they may be politely bored if you are not careful!

The truth of the matter is that audiences are generally friendly. They want speakers to succeed, and are somewhat embarrassed if they fail. As a listener, test it out yourself. Aren't you happiest and most at ease when listening to a speaker who is well prepared, knows what he wants to say, and says it confidently and enthusiastically? Aren't you somewhat embarrassed when a speaker has prepared hastily and inadequately and delivers his speech falteringly? Don't you wish you could do something to help him? If you will remember that your listeners are silently cheering for you, your fear of them will be reduced.

As you face your audience, *keep your mind on what you have to say rather than on yourself.* As long as your mind is occupied with ideas, there is little chance for a strong fear reaction to set in. Intense intellectual activity tends to reduce emotionalism. When emotionalism gains the upper hand, it crowds out cerebral activity, sometimes to the extent that one is unable to think at all. This explains the mental "blackout" frequently experienced by beginners. Increase your chances for intellectual activity on the platform by choosing ideas you strongly desire to communicate, by preparing carefully, by organizing your points so that they may be retained easily in the mind, and by engaging in enough platform activity to release the tension in antagonistic muscle groups.

What is your prognosis? If you follow the simple principles outlined above, your chances for an early recovery from excessive stage fright are excellent. Remember that the more frequently you speak the easier your adjustment will be.

B. Second attitude: "Anybody can talk!" A professor in another department once asked, "Why do colleges offer courses in public speaking? Except for the rehabilitation of speech defects, I see no reason for speech training. Anyone can talk!" It is true, of course, that the majority of people talk with sufficient volume and distinctness to be understood most of the time. Nevertheless, many such persons are ineffective with audiences because of poor choice of subject, inadequate preparation, faulty audience analysis, mediocre delivery, or ill-chosen language. To limit speech training to the correction of speech defects is as abortive as limiting training in writing to the correction of grammatical errors and then assuming that anyone can write.

Indifference to the value of training in public speaking is also felt by many students, particularly those who are required to complete a course in speech as a prerequisite for graduation. If such students are glib conversationalists, they may enter public speaking courses convinced that they can "talk their way" through the term with little, if any, preparation and with complete neglect of the assigned readings in the text. The legitimate course in public speaking, however, does not concern itself with the ability to "make small talk" on social occasions.

Although almost anybody can talk, most of you will profit from training in selection and organization of ideas, discovery of meaningful supporting materials, use of factors of attention, choice of language, technique of delivery, and a number of other principles essential to effective public speaking.

C. Third attitude: "Who wants to be an orator?" At the conclusion of the first class meeting a student asked if completing the course would qualify him for a series of engagements as a professional public speaker. He was assured that no lecture bureau would consider his services, regardless of his possible skill as a speaker, unless he could attract audiences by an account of unusual experiences or by virtue of some special distinction. The belief that speech courses exist primarily for the training of potential professional orators and lecturers draws a few students to such courses but keeps many others away. Few who read this book will ever become professional public speakers, and the large majority will undoubtedly have no desire to do so. This text is not for professionals; it was designed for those who wish to achieve effectiveness in everyday speaking situations.

D. Fourth attitude: "I'm willing to learn." As you begin your program of speech training, we urge you to be willing to learn. Directed study of the principles herein should point the way to maximum results in minimum time. Prepare each assignment with care, and profit from the criticisms of your instructor and classmates. A word of caution: merely reading this book will not make you an outstanding speaker, any more than reading a book on playing the violin will make you another Heifetz. Only after taking bow in hand and drawing it across the strings are you on the way to becoming a violinist. Likewise, you must face an audience and speak to them before you can begin to climb the ladder to speaking effectiveness.

<h2 align="center">CLIMBING THE LADDER TO EFFECTIVENESS</h2>

The ladder to effectiveness has seven steps and two handrails. A brief explanation of each will guide you in preparing initial speeches without first reading the entire book. In later chapters we shall ask you to linger with us on each step for a more careful and thorough study.

The left handrail on the ladder to effectiveness represents *your audience and your speech occasion.* Before choosing a subject it is necessary to analyze those who will listen. It is desirable to know the age and sex of the group; its size; its educational background; occupations and special groups represented; and the knowledge and attitude of the group concerning both you and your subject. In analyzing the occasion, you will want to know the basic nature of the meeting, what else will be included on the program, and how much time is allotted to you (Chapter 2).

Your other hand grips the right handrail, representing *you and your purpose in speaking.* Is your potential subject within your field of interest? Is it within your range of experience, either real or vicarious? Is it suitable to your personality, reputation, and experience? You must then decide whether your General Speech Purpose is to inform, entertain, or to persuade the audience. Your Specific Speech Purpose is a definite, concise statement of what you hope to achieve in speaking to this particular audience. If your General Purpose is to *inform,* your Specific Purpose may be *to have your audience understand how a gasoline engine operates.* If your General Purpose is to *entertain,* your Specific Purpose might be *to amuse your audience with a description of the unusual individuals one sees on a city bus.* If your General Purpose is to *persuade,* and you have decided to seek action from your listeners, your Specific Purpose could be *to persuade your audience to contribute to the Red Cross campaign* (Chapter 2).

Since you, your purpose, the audience, and the occasion are

fundamental to the preparation and delivery of your speech, they should be kept in mind constantly as you proceed. Keep a firm grip on each handrail, therefore, as you climb the first step.

A. The first step on the ladder to effectiveness is gathering the materials. Although an alarming number of speakers quickly reveal that they have little of significance to say, we advise you to fortify yourself with an abundance of material, certainly more than you will have time to use in the speech. In finding materials, your first move should be to *think*. How much do you know about the subject? Probe your mind for past experiences, ideas, readings, and insight gained from pertinent discussions and college or high-school courses. Possibly your grasp of the subject is greater than you had originally realized. Second, *observe*. If we examine them carefully, our surroundings will often yield materials difficult to duplicate elsewhere. Third, *communicate with others*. Conversations, discussions, interviews, and letters are fruitful sources of information. Fourth, *read*. Do so judiciously rather than indiscriminately. Retain general ideas in your memory, and record specific information on note cards (Chapter 3).

B. The second step on the ladder to effectiveness is organizing the Discussion (sometimes called the Body of the speech). From the materials you have accumulated, jot down the points you want to include in your speech. Derive from this list two to five main headings or major divisions for your speech, under which you will later group supporting points. The main heads may be arranged in any one of six patterns: *Time, Space, Topical, Cause and Effect, Problem-Solution,* and *Proposition of "Fact."* Since the first three patterns are simpler to develop, choose one of them for your initial informative speech. Your choice of organizational pattern is usually determined to a great extent by the subject you select and the purpose you hope to achieve (Chapters 4, 5).

C. The third step on the ladder to effectiveness is discovering and using the supporting materials. Your main points must be explained, clarified, and made interesting. Choose one of the following methods to support each of your main headings: example, comparison, statistics, testimony, and visual aids. To help maintain audience attention, utilize these Factors of Interest when selecting supporting materials: proximity, vivid concreteness, significance, variety, and humor (Chapter 6).

D. The fourth step on the ladder to effectiveness is developing the Introduction. The speech Introduction serves two purposes: to secure favorable attention and to orient the audience to the subject. Favorable attention may be secured by (1) referring to the significance of the subject; (2) using humor; (3) telling an illustrative story; (4) using a stimulating quotation; (5) mentioning common beliefs, interests, and feelings; (6) asking a stimulating question; (7) making a pithy, interesting statement; (8) referring to the occasion or purpose of the meeting; and (9) complimenting the audience. Orientation to the subject may be achieved by (1) stating the POINT of the speech; (2) listing the main headings of the Discussion, and (3) providing necessary background explanation. Avoid apologizing, being long-winded, antagonizing, offending, or using irrelevant material. The average length of the Introduction is about 10 per cent of the entire speech (Chapter 7).

E. The fifth step on the ladder to effectiveness is developing the Conclusion. A speech should conclude rather than just come to an end. The Conclusion should summarize and restate the main points. If you are asking for action, this is your final opportunity to make your plea. Avoid introducing new material, being either abrupt or long-winded, including irrelevant material, or losing the attention of your listeners. The Conclusion usually constitutes about 5 per cent of the entire speech (Chapter 8). Developing the Conclusion completes the preparation of your outline.

F. The sixth step on the ladder to effectiveness is rehearsing the speech. Musicians, actors, and athletes are unlikely to appear before the public without having practiced sufficiently to insure the highest quality of performance. For the same reason, rehearse your speeches, either in isolation or in the presence of friends. Rehearsal should not begin until your outline is finished, and should be completed before the beginning of the program at which the speech is to be delivered. Attempt to fix your outline firmly in mind, and practice until your ideas and supporting materials are thoroughly familiar. Polish your delivery by paying close attention to language, voice, diction, pronunciation, and to such visible factors as posture, movement, gesture, and facial expression. Do not memorize, except for the sequence of points in the outline. Avoid practicing so long at one time that you tire of the speech. How many times should one rehearse? One or two complete rehearsals may be enough for some; most beginners, however, will need from four to eight rehearsals for maximum effectiveness (Chapter 13).

G. The seventh step on the ladder to effectiveness is delivering the speech. Think constantly of your ideas while delivering the speech, and make it apparent that you are eager to convey them to your listeners. If your mind is filled with the content of your talk, there will be little room for worry about how well you are performing and what reaction your audience may have to your techniques of delivery. Use notes if you wish, but keep your eyes on your listeners as much as possible. Try to be lively, enthusiastic, friendly, and sincere. Adjust your volume to the acoustics of the room and the size of the audience. Gesticulate when you feel like it, and change your position on the platform occasionally, if you wish (Chapters 9–12).

SUMMARY

Approach the study of public speaking positively. Accept the inevitability of some nervous tension and make it work for you. Reject misconceptions about the study of public speaking, and develop a positive philosophy that will enable you to acquire effectiveness rapidly.

As you ascend the ladder to effectiveness, keep a firm grip on the handrails: (1) the audience and the occasion; and (2) you and your purpose. The seven steps on the ladder to effectiveness are: (1) gathering the materials; (2) organizing the Discussion; (3) discovering and using the supporting materials; (4) developing the Introduction; (5) developing the Conclusion; (6) rehearsing the speech; and (7) delivering the speech.

EXERCISES AND ASSIGNMENTS

1. What are your present attitudes toward the study of speech? How did you acquire them? Are they good or bad? Write an analysis of your attitudes to hand to your instructor. Be ready to discuss them in class.

2. What misconceptions about the study of speech did you bring to this course? How did you acquire them? Do you anticipate difficulty in eliminating these attitudes? If so, why?

3. What examples of speaking for dishonorable causes are you able to list from your knowledge of history and current events? Did effective speech combat them successfully? If not, why not?

4. Write an inventory of your assets and liabilities as a speaker. Save it, and note at the conclusion of the course whether the list should be altered. How does your list compare with your instructor's evaluation of your assets and liabilities?

5. Introduce yourself to your classmates in a two- or three-minute speech. Include name, age, educational background, major interests, professional objective, work experience, travel, hobbies, and so on.

6. Listen carefully to the speeches assigned in Exercise 5 to discover the nature of the audience you will be addressing during the remainder of the course. Write an analysis of the group, regarding (1) average age, (2) sex ratio, (3) educational background, (4) predominant interests, and (5) apparent biases and predilections.

7. Using the steps on the ladder to effectiveness, prepare a four-minute speech, which may be: (1) A persuasive speech on any subject concerning which you have definite personal convictions. Give three or four important reasons for your beliefs. (2) An informative speech explaining your present job, your reasons for attending college, or an interesting personal experience. (3) A process-inquiry speech, in which you explain a process. During the talk the audience may interrupt at any time to ask questions. Answer each question and then continue your speech until the next question is asked.

OUTLINE OF *SECTION II*

Preparing the Speech

Essential Purpose of Section II: to enable the student to select his speech subject, to gather materials, and to organize and develop his speech in the most effective logical and psychological manner.

CHAPTER 2: *Selecting the Speech Subject*

I. The first step in choosing the subject is to analyze the audience
   A. Age of audience
   B. Sex of audience
   C. Size of audience
   D. Educational background of audience
   E. Occupations represented in audience
   F. Special groups represented in audience
   G. Knowledge of audience concerning your subject and their attitude toward it
   H. Knowledge of audience concerning you and their attitude toward you
II. The second step in choosing the subject is to analyze the occasion for the speech and to analyze yourself as the speaker

   Analyze the speech occasion
   A. What is the basic nature of the meeting?
   B. What else will constitute the program?
   C. How much time is allotted to you?

   Analyze yourself
   A. Is the subject within your field of interest?
   B. Is the subject within your range of experience, real or vicarious?
   C. Is the subject suitable to your personality, reputation, appearance, and so on?

III. The final step in choosing the subject is to select the Speech Purpose

Select the general speech purpose
A. To inform
B. To entertain
C. To persuade
  1. To convince
  2. To stimulate or impress
  3. To actuate

Select the Specific Speech Purpose

CHAPTER 3: *Gathering the Speech Materials*

I. One method of gathering materials is to *think*
  A. What do you already know about your subject?
  B. What materials do you still need to uncover?
II. A second method of gathering materials is to *observe*

Effective observation is:
A. Directed
B. Complete
C. Accurate
D. Objective

III. A third method of gathering materials is to *communicate with others*
  A. Communicate by conversation and discussion
  B. Communicate by interview

  Guides to obtaining an effective interview
    1. Do some preparation on your subject before the interview
    2. Plan the interview
    3. Be alert, poised, friendly, and respectful
    4. Be brief

  Guides to being a good listener
    1. Concentrate
    2. Be open-minded
    3. Be critical
    4. Remember
  C. Communicate by letters

IV. A fourth method of gathering materials is to *read*
   A. What to read and where to find it
      1. Standard references
      2. Books
      3. Magazines
      4. Newspapers
      5. Documents and pamphlets
   B. How to read effectively
   C. How to retain what you read

CHAPTER 4: *Making the Outline*

I. Purpose of the speech outline
II. Rules for the logical partitioning of materials
   A. Show thought relationships by means of some standard system of symbols and indentations
   B. Subordinate points must logically reinforce, develop, or clarify the headings they are designed to support
   C. Coordinate points should not overlap
   D. The outline should cover the subject adequately
   E. Usually every division should have two or more heads
   F. Use parallel phrasing for coordinate heads ·
   G. Avoid compound headings
   H. Novice speakers should write out each heading in the form of a complete sentence
   I. Standard speech organization consists of three major sections: Introduction, Discussion, and Conclusion
   J. An outline of the Discussion should have between two and five main heads

CHAPTER 5: *Organizing the Discussion*

I. Selection of the main heads
   A. First, make an Analysis List
   B. Then evolve two to five main heads from the Analysis List
      1. The main heads should follow a basic pattern or sequence of thought
      2. The Specific Speech Purpose helps determine the selection of main heads

II. Simple patterns for organizing main heads
A. Time Pattern
B. Space Pattern
C. Topical Pattern
III. More advanced patterns for organizing main heads
A. Problem-Solution Pattern
B. Cause-and-Effect Pattern
C. Proposition of "Fact" Pattern

CHAPTER 6: *Discovering and Using the Supporting Materials*

I. The basic forms of verbal supporting materials are:
A. Illustration
1. Detailed factual illustration
2. Undeveloped factual illustration
3. Hypothetical illustration
B. Statistics
C. Comparison or analogy
1. Literal comparison
2. Figurative comparison
D. Testimony
E. Restatement and repetition
F. Explanation
G. Deductive and causal reasoning
II. Visual aids may also be used to support the main heads
A. Nature and purpose of visual aids
B. Rules for the use of visual aids
III. Supporting materials should promote involuntary attention through the use of factors of interest
A. Proximity
B. Vivid concreteness
C. Significance
D. Variety
E. Humor

CHAPTER 7: *Developing the Introduction*

I. The Favorable Attention Step secures the interest of the audience by means of:
A. Reference to the significance of the subject

B. Humor
C. Illustrative story
D. Stimulating quotation
E. Mention of common relationships, beliefs, interests, and feelings
F. Stimulating question
G. Pithy statement
H. Reference to occasion or purpose of the meeting
I. Complimentary remarks

II. The Clarification Step prepares the audience for the Discussion of the speech by:
A. Stating the POINT of the speech
B. Stating the main heads or arguments of the Discussion
C. Providing necessary background explanations

III. The four most common sins of the Introduction are:
A. To apologize
B. To be long-winded
C. To antagonize or offend
D. To use irrelevant material

CHAPTER 8: *Developing the Conclusion*

I. The Summary Step recapitulates the message of the speech by:
A. Statement of the POINT of the speech
B. Formal listing of the main ideas of the speech
C. Informal review
D. Indirect summary by means of quotation, comparison, or example

II. The Action Step helps stimulate the audience to overt response
A. Only speeches to actuate require an Action Step
B. A close relationship exists between the Summary Step and the Action Step
C. The Action Step must clearly indicate the response desired from the audience
D. The Action Step must constitute an effective appeal to the emotions as well as to the intellect

III. The five most common sins of the Conclusion are:
   A. To apologize
   B. To be abrupt or long-winded
   C. To introduce important new points of view
   D. To include irrelevant material
   E. To lose the attention of the audience

CHAPTER 2

Selecting the Speech Subject

Before you can begin to mount the ladder to effective speaking you must select the purpose you wish to achieve with your talk. An appropriate speech purpose is one well adapted to your audience, the occasion for the speech, and yourself as the speaker.

PART I. THE FIRST STEP IS TO ANALYZE THE AUDIENCE

Who are these people to whom you will speak? Psychologists tell us that we are all somewhat different from each other. One man may be a lathe operator with a keen interest in machines; another may be a cab driver who knows every street and alley in the entire metropolitan district; a third may be a high-school teacher who has a master's degree in American history. Some of us root for the Giants, others for the Tigers. Still others care little for baseball but gladly pay scalpers' prices to attend a Stanford-California football game.

Our range of interests is matched by an equally wide gamut of relatively set attitudes and prejudices. We have positive or negative attitudes toward everything which has meaning in our lives. Some years ago, when Henry Wallace was quoted as wishing to give every aborigine in the world a quart of milk, some of us developed an attitude of derision toward Mr. Wallace and his Hottentots. We have definite mental sets toward the Russians, liquor, divorce, free love, Methodists, Catholics, Dwight D. Eisenhower, the C.I.O., the N.A.M., the State Department, coffins, tobacco, women drivers, the vacant lot on the corner overrun with weeds and tall grass, French-style bathing suits, and the gossips next door.

Attitudes which an audience might possess toward the minor things in life probably will not be major considerations for the public speaker, although they make his job more difficult. However,

25

the basic wants and prejudices of an audience are of vital concern. It has been stated frequently that the word "desire" is the key word in human existence. Our "will to believe" on certain issues may be so strong that we become imprisoned within a mental shell, and remain partially or completely impervious to reason. What else could account for the antithetic results men draw from the same basic data? Witness the disharmony among conflicting religious groups, the squabble between advocates of the progressive and of the conservative philosophies of education, the bitter fight between the American Medical Association and the Public Health Service, and the continuing debate between Republicans and Democrats over the proper degree of centralization of government.

The most careful analysis of an audience may not insure complete success in choosing or developing a subject, but you will have a much better chance to deliver a successful address if you understand the interests, desires, and attitudes of your listeners.

FIND OUT THESE EIGHT CHARACTERISTICS OF YOUR POTENTIAL AUDIENCE

A. Age: Although our basic interests probably change little throughout life, our attitudes toward those basic interests do alter considerably. To some extent, greater age means a larger number and variety of life experiences and increased maturity of understanding. Sometimes the maturing influence of experience is vividly evidenced, as in the case of the veteran. Any university professor realizes the difference in mental horizons between the G.I. student and the postwar classroom adolescent. Along with increased maturity, added years bring a hardening of the attitudes and a growing conservatism. The *status quo*, like a pair of well-worn house slippers, becomes comfortable and natural as we become attached to it.

Every age has its particular strains and stresses, ambitions and disappointments. As drill work in audience analysis, think closely for a moment of the problems confronting these individuals of different age groups. Mary, a high-school sophomore, is concerned over her pug nose and myriad freckles. She is self-conscious about her stringbean figure. She wants poise and self-assurance. She wants her "ideal" boy in the junior class to ask her for a date, but he is too busy whistling at other, better-looking girls. She is ashamed of her family because Mom looks a little dowdy, and Dad too well-stuffed. She wishes Dad would get rid of his 1949 Ford and buy a new Oldsmobile like the one Helen's dad bought. She feels frustrated because many of her class friends have television receivers in their homes but her family cannot afford to buy one. Mary's problems of self-adjustment are very vivid to her.

Contrast her problems with those confronting her brother Bill, who is about to graduate from engineering school. Bill, twenty-nine, is a veteran of five years in the army, three of which were spent in Japan and Korea. Married, and with two little boys, Bill finds his G.I. subsistence and income from outside work barely enough to cover the house payments and other essentials. He must get a job as soon after commencement as possible.

Bill has applied for a position with the Johnstone Tool and Die Works in his home town. If hired, Bill's immediate boss will be Mr. Clark, an executive in his early forties. Mr. Clark is pleasant in a dynamic, bustling sort of way. Increasing years have given him new status along with additional problems. He is vaguely concerned about the blackish pouches under his eyes and a duodenal ulcer which he needs to humor. He feels deeply that labor is attempting to exert too much influence in the management of the plant. Honors are beginning to come to him. He has served as president of the Country Club for the past two years, and is the president-elect of the city's Chamber of Commerce. In short, Mr. Clark is a busy, progressive businessman with varied interests and responsibilities, as well as relatively set attitudes.

The father of Mary and Bill is nearing the retirement age of sixty-five. The company will provide him with a limited, though fairly adequate, pension as long as he lives. Much of the bitterness and competition of existence is now behind. With his wife he looks forward to perhaps a score of years of gracious living in the twilight of life, fishing, reading, and gardening.

Although these are only random samplings, perhaps they are illustrative of the different varieties of problems, interests, and attitudes typical of different age groups. As a speaker you need to know what range of age groups will be represented in your audience and what will be the predominant age group. Then your speech purpose will come closer to fitting the needs of your listeners.

B. Sex: Despite the modern trend toward the emancipation of women, it is still essentially a man's world. For instance, at some universities the girls' dormitories are easily recognizable by the encircling "burglar-proof," "kiss-proof" wire fence. Marriage, home, and family still constitute the chief focal points in the lives of most women. Although the interests of career women are similar to those of men in comparable occupations and status in life, there still remain certain basic differences. Psychologists say that women are more conservative than men, more religious, more readily disciplined, healthier, and longer lived. Men tend to be less self-centered, less subject to periods of depression, and less sensitive. Women are more interested than men in the activities of the elite social set, in TV and movie personalities, in the family life of famous men, in people in general, in fashions, in art, in the legitimate theatre, in literature, in the style and appointments of automobiles rather than in their mechanical efficiency, in music, and so forth.

C. Size: Although it is difficult, and sometimes impossible, to estimate the size of the audience before the actual occasion, a consideration of the following principles may be helpful in choosing the subject. Overt mass response is easier to win from a large audience than from a small one. Crowd psychology has little opportunity to manifest itself in a scattering of fifteen or twenty people. Evangelists, politicians, after-dinner speakers, and university homecoming chairmen, among others, capitalize upon this phenomenon. During World War II many persons were so carried away by the in-group feeling at war bond rallies that they subscribed more than they could afford. It is much easier to get an audience of one hundred to laugh, cry, or cheer than it is to evoke such responses from a small group. Inhibitions and self-consciousness tend to decrease as the individuals in large audiences lose something of their individuality and identify themselves with the group. Individual thinking and individual emotions tend to be superseded by group thinking and group emotions. Haven't you seen apparently cultured ladies at ringside scream, "Murder the bum!" or "Knock his head off!" Do you remember the man sitting next to you at the Michigan-Army game, who got so excited that he threw his new snap-brim hat soaring into the air and couldn't retrieve it? Recall how you booed lustily every time your favorite political candidate referred to the opposition during a campaign speech; thousands around you were booing, so it seemed the thing to do. When the speaker made a facetious reference, someone up front laughed, others picked it up, and soon you were laughing too. Later you wondered vaguely what had been so funny; you weren't listening at the moment and hadn't heard the remarks.

A correlation sometimes exists between the size of the audience and the prestige of the speaker. If only a handful of people appear at an open meeting, a person in the audience may reason that the speaker must not be "much good" or more people would have attended. On the other hand, a large assemblage is frequently considered to be a vote of confidence in the worth of the speaker. A person with high prestige can, of course, expect to accomplish more with his audience than can one with lower prestige.

The number of people in the audience in relation to the size of the room also will affect the speaker-audience relationship. Large vacant patches in an audience make the speaker's task more difficult. The in-group feeling will be fostered by having the room filled or overflowing. An aggregation of one hundred auditors will appear to be much larger in an auditorium designed for that number than the same audience in a hall large enough to accommodate five hundred. A large audience closely grouped together will respond more readily than a small, scattered audience to appeals for mass action, such as: to volunteer for emergency Red Cross service, to contribute money, to laugh at the speaker's humor, or to give a stirring welcome to the football coach.

D. Educational background: The amount of formal education one possesses is a rough but suggestive index to his intelligence and mental maturity. In qualification, it should be stated that although an illiterate, a semi-illiterate, or even a grade-school graduate will usually rank relatively low on the intellectual scale, some individuals with limited education may have better minds than many college graduates. Nevertheless, if you are to address an audience of college alumni, you know that they have attained at least a certain minimum standard of intellectual achievement. If you have been asked to speak to the local chapter of the American Association of University Women, you will be reaching minds which *should be* considerably better informed than average. It is probably safe to say that, in general, the better educated the audience, the better equipped it should be to understand your message.

Another consideration is to ascertain whether certain special fields of educational experience will be represented in the audience. That is, will the gathering include significant numbers of engineers, lawyers, school teachers, ministers, physicians, dentists, and so forth? The minds of these people will be especially keen in their specific and related fields, because of their specialized training and experience.

A third point about the educational backgrounds of the audience is that "life" education at times may be even more important than formal education. A cab driver, a night clerk in a large hotel, a WAC, a crane operator, a beautician, or a night club entertainer has had wide "life" experiences of considerable educational value. Even rustic, migrant workers can be extremely shrewd judges of human nature and of appeals to their emotions and intellect. Limited academic training does not necessarily mean limited intelligence.

E. Occupations represented: As the preceding paragraphs have intimated, the occupations represented in the audience are an important consideration to the public speaker in selecting and limiting his subject. For example, the successful industrialist listening to an after-dinner speech in the exclusive Cleveland Union Club is certainly a different individual from the cabinet finisher attending a monthly meeting of the carpenters' A.F.L. local. The occupation of an individual is frequently a fairly reliable indication of his social contacts, economic backgrounds, interests, habits, and attitudes.

Consider the differences in the choice of subject matter and content that would confront you if you were asked to address any of the following audiences: a state convention of primary and secondary school teachers; the graduating class of the local firemen's training school; the yearly meeting of your company's sales force; a conference of the board of directors of Melton Products; a convention of Southern Baptist ministers; a convivial banquet of the Moose lodge. If possible, find out the various occupations which will be present in the audience and the approximate proportion of the audience which falls into each occupation. Then choose your subject and slant your material accordingly.

F. Special interest groups represented: Valuable insight into the interests, desires, and attitudes of your listeners may be obtained by ascertaining their group affiliations, i.e., social, political, religious, business, and so on. Is the light and power company sending its department heads to hear your speech? Will most of the people present be members of the Ipswich Country Club? Will perhaps a fourth of your auditors be delegates to the National Presbyterian Youth Conference, which is meeting in your town? Will significant numbers belong to the Elks, Junior Chamber of Commerce, Rotary Club, Multnomah Athletic Club, W.C.T.U., Library Reading Club, V.F.W., Masons, National Association for the Advancement of Colored People? Before choosing your subject, learn if sizable proportions of your audience will be members of particular special interest groups.

G. Knowledge of and attitude toward your potential subject: Since this element of audience analysis has already been indirectly covered and will be examined more definitively in Part III of this chapter, it is sufficient to say here that you should pick a subject within the range of your audience's interest and understanding. If it is ethically possible, your subject should be one which you can develop in accord with their basic attitudes. When it becomes necessary to take a stand contrary to the opinions of the audience, the speaker's task becomes much more difficult. Of course, the speaker must at all times remain *ethically consistent* with his convictions. One should never sacrifice intellectual integrity in order to please an audience.

H. Knowledge of and attitude toward you: One of the most important factors limiting audience response is the original attitude of the listeners toward the speaker. What is your audience's opinion of you? Do your hearers admire, respect, dislike, or distrust you? Are they indifferent toward you? Have they heard of you? Will they come to the meeting to hear your speech or something else on the program? If you are regarded as an expert in a particular field, you will be in a favorable position when speaking in that area; however, you may suffer a loss in prestige when discussing subjects other than your specialty. If you are considered a comic, it will be difficult to persuade your audience to take you seriously. If you are an "authority" brought in from out of the city or out of the state, you may enjoy somewhat higher status than would a local "authority." It is sometimes easier to impress strangers than our friends. As the Bible puts it, a prophet is not without honor save in his own country. If you are a last-minute substitute, you will probably experience a diminution of prestige in the eyes of the audience. Your auditors will be more receptive if they know that you have been selected in advance of the occasion, and if you have received considerable publicity. A wise speaker will consider carefully the impression a potential audience has of him before selecting the specific response he hopes to win.

PART. II. THE SECOND STEP IS TO ANALYZE THE OCCASION FOR THE SPEECH AND YOURSELF AS THE SPEAKER

Just as there are rules to guide us in our choice of wearing apparel for the social occasion, there are guides to help the speaker select a subject which meets satisfactorily the demands of the speech occasion.

FIND OUT THESE THREE CHARACTERISTICS OF THE OCCASION

A. What is the basic nature of the meeting?   Many times the purpose of the gathering will determine your subject for you. Why is the meeting being held? Is it a regular assembly of some particular organization, such as the weekly luncheon of the Kiwanis Club? If so, perhaps you were asked to talk because you are the principal of the local high school, or because you are the chairman of the mayor's committee for civic improvement. Even if told you could "speak on anything," you were probably invited because your current activities or your background appeared interesting. You will be expected to choose your subject accordingly.

Is the occasion to be a special assemblage devoted to a specific purpose? If so, that purpose will largely determine your choice of subject. Is the meeting a farewell celebration for one of the boys at the office, a ceremony at the opening of a new department store, a political barbecue, or a "kick-off" luncheon for the March of Dimes? Is it a stag party given a bridegroom-to-be? Is it a commencement program at a high school or university? Is it the annual stockholders' conference of your corporation? Is it a ceremony commemorating the birthday of Franklin D. Roosevelt? On any occasion having a specific purpose, your subject must conform to the object or intent of the meeting.

Sometimes the location of the gathering will help to limit your selection of subject and speech content. Where will the meeting be held? What will be the nature of the physical surroundings, the acoustics, the ventilation, the lighting, and the physical comfort of the audience? Notice how any of the following settings would severely restrict the choice of subject matter: the basement of a church; the large auditorium of a university; a fraternity social room; around a campfire in the woods; Madison Square Garden; a local baseball park; a cemetery; a union hiring hall.

What will be the mood of the occasion? Your subject must be in tune with the psychological state of the auditors. Will the people come expecting an evening of hearty laughter? Will there be playful heckling from the audience? Will the atmosphere be formal and somewhat stilted? Will there be open or cloaked resentment? Boredom and apathy? The degree of impressiveness also will help to determine the mood of the occasion and the speaker's prestige. The weekly meeting of a lodge would not afford the same receptive mental state on the part of the listeners as would a formal banquet celebrating the fiftieth anniversary of that organization's founding. The basic mood or psychological set of the audience limits its attention span and partly determines its patterns of thought and behavior.

B. What else will constitute the program? Your selection of the response you wish to win will in part depend upon what precedes and follows your address.

Will you be the only speaker? If there are others, what will be their subjects and what will be the basic mood of their talks? Imagine your consternation if a preceding speaker should talk on your topic, leaving you without a speech? A light, humorous subject will be inappropriate if the other speeches are serious attempts to grapple with some pressing problem. Ordinarily, you and the other speakers will be expected to present a unified program.

Is your talk an incidental item on the program, or is it one of the main features? Usually the major address is the last speech on the program. If your contribution is supposed to be a minor part of the proceedings, endeavor to supplement rather than to compete with the main address. Avoid the blunder made by a certain professor at a major state university shortly after Pearl Harbor. A special convocation had been called to hear the university's distinguished president analyze the effect of the war crisis upon students, faculty, the university, and the nation. Following the presidential address, the professor who served as chairman was supposed to make the usual complimentary remarks and to close the meeting gracefully. Instead, he delivered an impromptu twenty-minute oration about the sacrifices ahead. Under the circumstances such a speech was most ill-advised; it appeared that he was trying to steal the spotlight from the principal speaker.

Will non-speaking events, such as musical numbers, sports exhibitions, contests, or games appear on the program? If so, what may be their influence upon the psychological set of the audience? For instance, you cannot expect a significant intellectual response if your speech is sandwiched between the halves of an exciting football game, or between a magician's act and a minstrel show routine at a social smoker.

C. How much time is allotted to you? Many inexperienced speakers select subjects which cannot be treated adequately in the time at their disposal. In such a case, the speaker either handles his subject superficially or exceeds his time limit. To overstep time boundaries is discourteous to other speakers and to the audience. If given a time limit, it is your duty to narrow the subject to a specific phase which can be handled adequately within those limitations.

Do not use a blunderbuss, scatter-gun approach. Avoid broad themes like Russia, the national debt, war, prejudice, crime, or the history of the South. Most of these subjects would require at least a book for full discussion. Instead of speaking on poverty, limit the scope of your talk to, let us say, the slum clearance project in your own community of Toledo. Recently one of the authors heard a speaker endeavor to describe all of the nefarious practices in business and the professions in twenty minutes. How mistaken the speaker was to think that in such a short time he could present adequately the illegitimate procedures sometimes followed in the repairing of watches, autos, radios, and television sets, as well as the improprieties found in the canning industry, the drug business, and the professions of osteopathy, medicine, dentistry, and law! Almost any one of these topics would be more than ample for a full-length address. The speaker would have been much more effective if, for example, he had selected the fairly circumscribed problem of unnecessary surgical operations. Such a topic adequately developed might have made a genuine contribution.

It is entirely possible to select a subject which is well adapted to the audience and to the speech occasion, but which is not a suitable topic for YOU *as the speaker.*

A GOOD SUBJECT WILL FIT YOU IN THESE THREE WAYS

A. It will be within your field of interest: Effective speaking requires an animated, dynamic presentation. To be enthusiastic is difficult if your subject is not of fundamental interest *to you.* You will be much less subject to stage fright if you are "full" of your subject and eager to communicate your ideas to your listeners. A subject that is dull and uninteresting to you will usually result in a speech that is dull and uninteresting to the audience.

B. It will be within your range of experience: As we have already seen, the probable reason for your being invited to speak is that you possess knowledge and opinions derived from personal or vicarious experience that might be of value to your listeners. Ordinarily, a businessman is expected to talk about business, a union leader about labor and management, a preacher about morality, a civic leader about a local project with which he is affiliated, and a sports announcer about athletics. Always pick a subject about which you are already at least partially informed. Furthermore, it should be a subject on which you can get additional information. Even if it is a subject with which you have had long experience, probably you will need to secure new illustrations, interesting analogies, and the like to make your talk more persuasive.

Do not make the mistake committed by many students in public speaking classes—that of picking a topic at random and going to the library to read up on it. If you do, your reading will probably give you mental indigestion, your ideas are likely to become muddled, and you will be much more inclined to forget during delivery. When you look out from the platform into a field of faces, you will need to be thoroughly versed in your material to avoid awkward breaks in the flow of language.

You will also have more prestige when speaking on a subject with which the audience knows you are familiar. A shop foreman will enjoy higher status when speaking on problems associated with his occupation than on almost any other subject. The audience knows that he knows what he is talking about. Sometimes the ability to say "I was there" or "In my twenty years at Blenders Tube Company" will be worth a notebookful of statistics.

C. It will be suited to your personality: The word "personality" is used here in a very general sense. We mean merely that your topic should fit the conception the audience has of your physical, mental, and moral qualities. Some time ago one of the members of a golf club spoke to that organization in the advocacy of some local charity. Ordinarily this man is a very effective speaker. However, on this particular occasion he got little response. A person sitting in the back row summarized the situation well in these words: "It's probably a worthy cause, but I can't get very enthusiastic about it with ——— sponsoring it." The speaker was notoriously "tight" with his money. Every time contributions had been collected in the past, he had been among the last to contribute and usually had made a minimum donation. The club members did not like to have such an individual urge them to contribute generously. The speech just did not fit the speaker.

Perhaps some specific examples may help clarify this point. A portly gentleman who obviously needs exercise probably will be ineffective if he urges others to take up physical conditioning. A preacher who smokes and drinks is likely to have little influence in persuading others they should not indulge. An unmarried man will usually have difficulty in persuading other unmarried men that they should marry and settle down. A nonentity in the business world will find few persons willing to learn from him how to be a financial success. Many of us teachers of public address have at times had the uneasy feeling that students in our classes were reflecting: "It sounds good. But if these techniques work, why isn't he a better speaker?"

Part III. The Third Step Is to Select the Specific Speech Purpose

When the skilled archer draws back his bow and sights along the shaft of his arrow, he does not aim merely for the large straw-stuffed circular target. He aims for the bull's-eye. He has narrowed his sights from a generalized target to a specific, restricted goal. Every field agent of the Federal Bureau of Investigation spends one full day each month on the firing range, practicing with a variety of weapons. His target is a silhouette of a man. Not a plain silhouette, however, but one on which various zones are carefully indicated. His score, and to a certain extent his salary, depends upon the percentage of hits in the vital zones.

The speaker has located his *general target* when he determines which of the three general speech purposes will best fit his subject and audience: (1) to inform; (2) to entertain; (3) to persuade. The final step in selecting the speech subject is to narrow the general purpose to the *specific target,* the bull's-eye for the talk, which is the *Specific Speech Purpose.* The Specific Speech Purpose is a specific, concise, definite statement of what the speaker wishes to accomplish in his speech. It should be a goal which the speaker can *reasonably hope* to achieve in delivering his address to his *particular audience.* Let us look now at each of the general speech purposes to see how the Specific Speech Purpose is evolved for each type.

A. Do you want to inform your audience?   The primary purpose of the speech to inform is to give knowledge, to make things clear, and to bring understanding. In this type of speech you are not concerned essentially with changing mental attitudes. You do not argue, harangue, persuade, or overwhelm opposition. Your main concern is to present worth-while information clearly and interestingly, to widen mental horizons, and to bring the unknown or misunderstood into the realm of correct interpretation.

There are several main classifications of informative speaking.

1. Lectures.   One month after the atomic bomb was dropped on Hiroshima, Dr. Reuben Gustavson (then Vice-President of the University of Chicago and more recently Chancellor of the University

of Nebraska) spoke to the Executives' Club of Chicago on the
"Story Behind the Atomic Bomb." His audience, like the rest of
America, had been confused about the nature and significance of
the bomb. Professor Gustavson's address was a lecture which attempted to interpret complex scientific information in terms understandable to his lay audience. A second example of the lecture form
of speech is a talk by a political science expert explaining to the City
Club the underlying factors in the hostility to the United States on
the part of President Perón of Argentina. Another example is a
scientist telling the vistors assembled in the Palomar lecture hall
about the contributions to astronomy made by that institution's 200-
inch telescope.

2. Reports.   When an official of a corporation presents the results
of a sales campaign to a board of directors' meeting, he is giving
a report. When the local commander returns from the national
V.F.W. convention, he is expected to report at the next meeting on
the activities of the convention. The student after reading an assigned reference stands in front of the class and makes a book
report. The police sergeant who is selected to attend a special three
weeks' course in modern methods of criminology in Washington will
probably deliver an oral report to the personnel of the police force
upon his return.

3. Directions.   Men who served in the army during World War II,
or during the Korean "police action," realize what an important role
oral directions played when they formed in queues to take their
physical examinations, when they were bundled off in trains to
camp, after they were at boot camp, when they were aboard a
troop transport, when they were engaged in actual combat, and
when they returned to American bases for their service termination.
Casey Stengel is using informative speech when he assembles his
Yankees around the slide pits during baseball spring training and
describes the various methods of sliding into bases. Some other
examples of speeches giving directions are: an expert at cooking
school explaining how to make an apple pan dowdy; a forest ranger
telling his crew how to plant seedlings; a foreman of a plant explaining to his subordinates the operation of some new machinery; a
supervisor at Macy's Department Store informing a corps of new
sales girls how to perform their duties.

If you pick a subject upon which the audience is as well informed as you, one which is too technical or too "deep" for your audience, or one which is too broad for the time available, you have *not* selected a speech purpose which you can reasonably expect to achieve with your talk. If experience did not indicate otherwise, it would seem to be too elementary to state that the speaker must have a more specific purpose than the general purpose—to inform. Let us look at some examples of the Specific Speech Purpose for the speech to inform.

To have my audience understand how to file federal income tax returns

To have my audience understand the significance to the Civil War of the Battle of Antietam

To have my audience understand how to play canasta

To have my audience understand the Blue Cross plan for health insurance

To have my audience understand the functions of the quarterback in the split-T formation

To have my audience understand how steel is made by the Bessemer process

To have my audience understand the basic difficulties inherent in making a hydrogen bomb

To inform my audience on the present status of Russia's naval power

To inform my audience about the proposed style changes in women's clothes for next year

To inform my audience about the method used by the packing industry to grade beef

To inform my audience on the political career of Huey P. Long

To explain to my audience the difference between the Packard crankshaft and the conventional crankshaft

To describe to my audience how diamonds are cut

To show my audience five simple dance steps

Notice that each of these Specific Speech Purposes represents a specific, limited target rather than a generalized goal. To summarize the speech to inform: remember you are a salesman only in the sense of "selling" yourself as the speaker and "selling" the information you are to present. Your primary purpose is not to change minds, entertain, or arouse your listeners to action. Instead, your task is to give intellectual understanding.

B. Do you wish to entertain your listeners? Many times the major intent of the speaker is to get his audience to *enjoy* his address, rather than to present new information or to persuade his listeners to carry out a particular course of action. The best known speech for entertainment is the after-dinner speech, although some after-dinner addresses are designed to inform or persuade. Other speeches to entertain are sometimes presented at special meetings for recreation sponsored by various clubs and organizations, and at social gatherings of various types such as smokers, fun nights, and parties. It is easy to see that the speech to entertain may be directed at a wide range of possible responses. For several decades Admiral Richard Byrd thrilled juveniles and adults with his stories of adventure in the Arctic and Antarctic regions. A Harvard archeologist might entertain his listeners by telling them how he and his party defied Egyptian superstitions and explored King Tut's tomb. A famous Giant slugger might entertain a boys' club in Sioux City, Iowa, by telling how his ninth-inning home run won the World Series. A Detroit jeweler might amuse a Thursday evening "fun fest" meeting of the Junior Chamber of Commerce by describing some of his unusual customers. A woman, just returned from traversing the new 2,000-mile Mexican highway from the American border at Juarez to Guatemala, might tell some of her experiences to a local meeting of the A.A.U.W.

Information, of course, may be an important element in the speech to entertain, but the giving of information is not the chief purpose. The speech to entertain is designed primarily to serve as a pleasant diversion.

Let us look at some examples of the Specific Speech Purpose for the speech to entertain.

To entertain my audience by describing the antics of the American Legion members at the recent national convention in New York

To entertain my audience with a narration of my boat trip down the Amazon

To entertain my audience by demonstrating some sleight-of-hand card tricks

To amuse my audience by describing some of my professors at the University

To amuse my audience by telling some jokes I heard at last week's Advertising Club meeting

To amuse my audience with a description of the most unforgettable person I ever met

To thrill my audience by describing a rocket visit to the moon in the year 1970

C. Do you want to persuade your audience? Speeches to persuade fall into three types: those which *convince*; those which *stimulate* or *impress*; and those which *arouse action*.

First, let us see how the general purposes to convince and to stimulate may be applied to controversial issues.

A careful study of the following diagram is the starting point for an understanding of how to get people to think, feel, or act as you desire. Whenever you present a controversial issue, the mental attitude of everyone in the audience toward your argument will fall somewhere on this diagram.

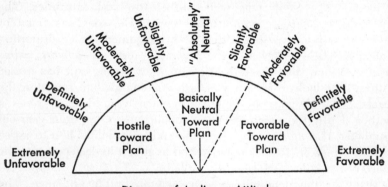

Diagram of Audience Attitudes
Toward Controversial Issues

An audience already in agreement with you cannot be convinced. The word "convince" means to change the mind-set of an individual or individuals in relation to some point of view. If a person agrees with you that Field Marshal Bernard Montgomery was a better strategist than Field Marshal Erwin Rommel, could you convince him on the matter? If your employer agrees that you should have a $10 a week raise, would you debate the point? You would have a job of conviction on your hands, however, if the boss states flatly that you are already being well paid.

As a result of your analysis of the potential audience, you have acquired some understanding of the knowledge of your listeners

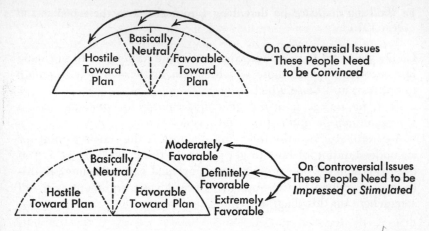

concerning the subject as well as their probable attitudes. The favorable audience is sympathetic toward the speaker's point of view and is relatively noncritical of his arguments and supporting materials. The speaker tells the favorable audience *what it wants to hear.* When someone tells you your new spring suit has a nice pattern and looks good on you, are you inclined to question the speaker? Didn't you buy the suit because you liked it? Does a mother doubt the neighbor who exclaims over her four-year-old daughter? The *moderately* favorable audience would like to agree with the speaker. It does not demand as much logical proof as the neutral or hostile audience, but probably will refuse to be swayed as easily as the definitely or extremely favorable audience. The *definitely* favorable audience is eager to believe, but is more analytical than the *extremely* favorable one, which is almost completely noncritical. The *extremely* favorable audience, such as the prewar Nazi throng, will approve almost any statement the speaker makes, so long as he continues in the appropriate vein. The basic task of the speaker in addressing a favorable group is to impress or stimulate it to a greater appreciation, a stronger conviction, a deeper devotion, a more active dislike, and so forth.

The basically neutral audience has a more open mind than either the favorable or hostile audience. While not as easily affected by emotional appeals as the favorable audience, it will not be emotionally hostile to the speaker's case. When speaking to a basically neutral audience upon a controversial issue, the speaker's purpose is to *convince* his listeners that they should abandon their position of indecision, doubt, or neutrality, and accept his views.

The hostile audience *does not want to believe*; it is emotionally conditioned against the speaker's arguments. Like the vacuum cleaner salesman, the speaker will have to get his foot in the door before he can present his wares. As we will see in Chapter 7, there are certain techniques which the speaker can utilize to create a more favorable attitude toward himself and toward his speech. (Probably by this time you see the advantage of selecting a viewpoint to which the audience is not actively opposed.) The purpose of a speech to a hostile audience is, of course, to persuade the auditors to accept the speaker's ideas. It is a speech to convince.

The following speech situations are designed to illustrate the differences between speeches to convince and those to stimulate. Remember that on controversial issues the basic opinion of the audience determines the type of speech purpose. The audience favorable to the speaker's program does not need to be convinced; it needs to be impressed or stimulated to a stronger agreement. In other words, it needs to have its attitudes reinforced. In the completely successful speech to convince, the neutral or hostile audience is persuaded that its views are wrong and that the speaker's ideas are right. (It should be pointed out, however, that a complete change of position from one of genuine hostility to one of complete affirmation is unlikely. Habits of thought possessed by an individual for perhaps twenty or thirty years will usually not be erased by a twenty-minute speech. When speaking to a definitely hostile audience, the speech is worth while if it weakens or softens opposition.)

Speech situation No. 1. If Walter Reuther should address a major convention of the C.I.O. on the "evils" of the Taft-Hartley law, he would face an *extremely favorable* audience. Most of the delegates probably believe that the Taft-Hartley law is indeed a "slave-labor bill" and should be repealed. Reuther's Specific Speech Purpose in speaking to this group might be to *stimulate* his audience to a greater opposition to the Taft-Hartley law, or perhaps to *impress* more deeply upon his audience how unjust to American labor the Taft-Hartley law is.

On the other hand, if Reuther were invited to express his views before a meeting of the National Association of Manufacturers, he would be confronted with a very different situation. Instead of an audience emotionally conditioned in his favor, he would find a group opposed to him and to his ideas. The members of the N.A.M. believe the Taft-Hartley law is fair, even generous to labor. Fearing the power of unions and resenting the diminution of their prerogatives, they do not want to believe what Reuther will tell them. In this case his Specific Speech Purpose might be to *convince* his audience that the Taft-Hartley law is unfair to American labor.

Speech situation No. 2.   If Hartley, or some other conservative Republican, were the speaker in each case instead of Reuther, the situations would be completely reversed. At the union meeting Hartley would have the almost hopeless task of persuading an *extremely unfavorable* audience. In the other speech situation, the N.A.M. members, since they already agree with him, would be relatively noncritical of his ideas.

Speech situation No. 3.   If a university dean at a meeting of the campus interfraternity council defends fraternities against a local move to oust them from the campus, he will be talking to a very favorable audience. These fraternity leaders believe thoroughly in fraternities. The dean's job is relatively simple. He and his listeners want the same thing—there is no conflict. His task is to provide illustrations, opinions, and the like which they can use to rationalize their own ideas. They are eager to believe that fraternities are democratic organizations, performing genuine services to the campus. The dean's Specific Speech Purpose might be to *impress* upon his audience the genuine contribution which fraternities make to a college campus.

Should the dean address a group of independents militantly opposed to fraternities, he would need to soften or remove their opposition. If some of the listeners had been rejected by fraternities for one reason or another, the dean might find them extremely critical of his logic and his speech materials. His Specific Speech Purpose in this situation might be to *convince* his audience that fraternities perform a vital service to the college community.

Speech situation No. 4.   If the aroused citizens of a suburb call a meeting to protest the building of an airport in their subdivision, any proponent of the plan would face an audience which wants the opposite of what he desires. His Specific Speech Purpose might be to *convince* his audience that it would be beneficial to have an airport constructed in the suburb. If he were followed to the rostrum by an opponent of the plan, the second speaker would be addressing a favorable audience. His Specific Speech Purpose might be to *impress* his audience with the disadvantages of having an airport constructed in the suburb.

An accurate understanding of the general purposes to convince and to stimulate requires consideration of three additional points.

(1) For the sake of simplicity we have discussed audiences which fall completely within the range of being favorable, neutral, or opposed to the policies of the speaker. *Many audiences are not so easily categorized.* Frequently some individuals present will be deeply prejudiced in favor of your views, others less favorably predisposed, some more or less hostile, and a large proportion essentially neutral. In such a case aim chiefly at the neutral group. Your purpose will be to convince rather than to stimulate. Attempt to conciliate the hostile wing, but unless it constitutes a significant element, concentrate instead on the neutral group.

(2) In the preceding discussions of the speech to convince we have been concerned solely with long-range influence. To achieve permanent influence, the objections of the neutral or hostile auditors must be removed by logical means. They must be shown by closely knit reasoning that your idea is superior. On the other hand, short-range or immediate influence sometimes may be secured by stimulating a neutral or hostile audience with humor, vivid illustrations, personal charm, and so on, to the extent that temporarily it "forgets" its objections. But an audience so persuaded soon "remembers" its objections and reverts to its original pattern of thinking. It has not been convinced, merely diverted. Thus the salesman who knows that he should spend the afternoon making calls may be persuaded by a friend to attend a baseball game. His enjoyment of the game may be ruined, however, by feelings of guilt—he is shirking his job and letting his family down. Many a silver-tongued politician has charmed his audience at the hustings only to find that such persuasion failed to last until election day.

(3) When talking on a *noncontroversial* subject for the purpose of arousing enthusiasm or interest, the speech to stimulate may be

directed at the neutral or lethargic group as well as to the favorable. In fact, the speech to interest is usually concerned with arousing the indifferent or the unimpressed. Specific Speech Purposes for such talks might be to *stimulate* the audience to a greater appreciation of the importance of railroads in modern America; to *stimulate* listeners to become interested in ceramics; to *impress* the audience with the role played by the barbed wire fence in the winning of the West; to *impress* upon the audience the potential influence of television upon education.

The type of material and the method of organization for speeches to convince and to stimulate will be discussed in the following six chapters. It is sufficient here to understand the basic concepts, in order to arrive at your Specific Speech Purpose.

(*Now let us look at the third type of persuasive speech, the speech to actuate,* or in simpler terms, the speech designed to produce direct, observable action on the part of the audience. Speeches to convince and to impress or stimulate are concerned only with producing intellectual agreement or emotional feeling—no immediate action is expected. The speech to actuate aims at more than intellectual agreement—the audience must become so thoroughly sold on the proposition that it will actually *do, buy, vote, sign, rent, enroll, depart, enlist,* and so forth.)

A careful selection of the Specific Speech Purpose is vitally important in the speech to actuate. The specific action the speaker requests must be activity which he can reasonably expect from his listeners. For example, a real estate salesman should attempt to sell property within the client's price range. A wise speaker will not endeavor to persuade an average audience to attempt to climb Mount Annapurna in the Himalayas. A more effective purpose would be to inform or to entertain the audience by telling about how Maurice Herzog conquered this second highest mountain ever climbed by man. Do not ask the members of your audience to do something which they cannot or will not do. If your purpose is to

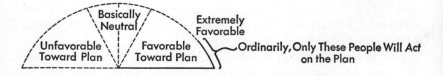

produce action, the activity requested must be within the capacities of the listeners.

If the audience is initially opposed to his plan, the speaker, for enduring results, must first convince it that his course is the best one for it to adopt, and then stimulate it to become *extremely favorable* to the proposal. Ordinarily only people who are extremely favorable will act. On the diagram below this means that the speaker has moved the audience from the left side all the distance to the right side.

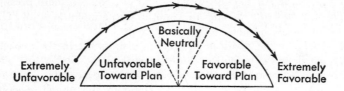

If his audience is neutral, his chances of moving it to action will be better than if it is initially opposed. If the group is favorably disposed, the speaker's task is much easier. Think of the master diagram as being a hill with a sharp ascent at the beginning which gradually tapers off at the crest. At first the hill falls away gradually, then more steeply. If circumstances forced you to push a stalled auto, where would you want the car to be located in relation to this hill? Wouldn't it be easier to push the vehicle on the relatively level ground at the top of the hill than to try to move it up the side?

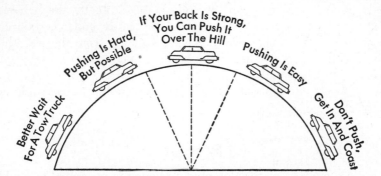

Pushing an Automobile Is Like Winning an Audience.
If Consistent with Ethics, Go in the Direction of Least Resistance

Wouldn't it be still more satisfactory if the motor stopped when going downhill? Pushing an automobile is like winning an audience; if ethically possible, go in the direction of the least resistance.

Here are some examples of the Specific Speech Purpose for the speech to actuate:

1. *To persuade my audience* to sign a petition denouncing Major Hogan
2. *To persuade my audience* to contribute to the Community Chest
3. *To persuade my listeners* to join the Y.M.C.A. physical fitness program
4. *To persuade my listeners* to vote for Fred Neal for club president
5. *To persuade the Senate* to confirm the appointment of Thomas Howell as the new Secretary of State
6. *To persuade the Board of Regents* to dismiss the football coach
7. *To persuade the union* to call off the strike
8. *To persuade the committee* to veto the tax proposal
9. *To persuade my congregation* to come to the prayer meeting on Wednesday evening
10. *To persuade the town council* to buy a new truck for the fire department

In order that these speeches may accomplish their purposes, more than intellectual agreement is necessary—action must result! It might be argued that a speaker always wants his listeners to do something as a result of his speech, even if only to incorporate certain ideas into their normal pattern of thinking. If a speaker convinces an audience that the United States was wrong to fight the Mexican War, he has probably influenced indirectly the behavior patterns of his hearers. Some time in the future under certain circumstances his listeners may behave differently from the way they would if they had not heard the speech. Such action is vague, ill-defined, and eventual rather than direct. On the other hand, the speech to actuate aims at direct, relatively prompt, observable activity.

SUMMARY

A close analysis of the potential audience is necessary to enable the speaker to select a speech purpose which he has a reasonable chance of accomplishing with that audience. The most important factors the speaker needs to consider about his audience are the range of ages represented; the number of people present; the educational and the occupational backgrounds of the listeners; the special interest groups represented; the knowledge and attitude of the audience toward him as the speaker and toward his potential subject. In addition to being well suited to the hearers, the subject should be skillfully adjusted to the purpose of the meeting, to the other events on the program, and to the time limitations of the speech. Also, the subject should be within the speaker's field of interest, within his range of experience, real or vicarious, and suitable to his personality. The speaker has located the general target of his speech when he selects the general speech purpose most appropriate for his topic and the audience: to inform, to entertain, or to persuade. The persuasive speech may be designed to convince, to stimulate or impress, or to actuate. The final step in selecting the speech subject is to narrow the general purpose to the specific target, or bull's-eye of the speech, which is the Specific Speech Purpose. The Specific Speech Purpose is the specific, limited goal which the speaker can reasonably expect to achieve in presenting his speech to a particular audience.

EXERCISES AND ASSIGNMENTS

1. On pages 106–109 there are listed over one hundred possible speech subjects representing a wide variety of fields of interest and of types of general and specific speech purposes. Select a representative list of twenty of these topics, and prepare for class discussion a brief analysis of the characteristics of the audiences and occasions for which the individual topics would be appropriate. Which of the topics would be suitable for your class?

2. Become better acquainted with the syndicated public opinion polls. Sometimes the polls record the reactions of different age groups to various social and political questions. At times they indicate differences in beliefs of persons of different levels of education and of different types of employment. In each case try to reason why these people believe as they do.

3. Analyze your own thinking to discover biases and prejudgments. If you are "neutral" toward some social, political, religious, or moral issue which possesses significance for you, is it because you have no attitude toward it? Or is it because a conflict between attitudes of relatively equal intensity has left you undecided?

4. Can analyzing an audience before a speech ever insure complete success in choosing a Specific Speech Purpose? In developing the content of a speech? Why, or why not?

5. Some psychologists say that education tends to reduce the differences in thinking and in attitudes between the sexes. Do you agree? If true, does this concept have meaning for the speaker?

6. Is it logically sound for an audience to permit the reputation of a speaker (for learning, character, accuracy of judgment, and so on) to influence its willingness to accept the speaker's message?

7. Can the speaker who is a partisan ever be completely objective in his thinking?

8. Can you define explicitly the words "will to believe"? Could this drive operate upon the speaker as well as upon the audience? What is the connection between the "will to believe" and the demagogue? The statesman?

9. In the speech to inform, if the audience fails to retain the main ideas, despite the fact that the speaker has presented information in a logical manner, has the talk been ineffective? Why, or why not?

10. Use the following form as a basis for an analysis of some public speaking situation off the campus, such as a Rotary luncheon, a church service, a political rally, a P.T.A. meeting.

Specific Speech Purpose:
    I. Identify in one sentence the purpose of the speech
    II. Was the purpose evident to the listeners?
    III. Was the purpose one which the speaker could reasonably hope to achieve with his audience?

Audience Analysis:
    I. Identify the audience (example: parents and teachers of the Roosevelt Junior High School P.T.A.)
    II. Age (general age groups represented and the dominant group[s])
    III. Sex
    IV. Size
    V. Educational backgrounds
    VI. Occupations
    VII. Special interest groups represented
    VIII. Audience's knowledge of and attitude toward the subject
    IX. Audience's knowledge of and attitude toward the speaker

X. How well did the speaker select his Specific Speech Purpose and adjust his speech materials in terms of the needs of his audience?

Occasion Analysis:

I. Identify the occasion (example: the monthly meeting of the Roosevelt Junior High School P.T.A.; location, the school auditorium; date, March 19, 1954)
II. Purpose of the meeting
III. Physical circumstances prevailing
IV. Mood of the occasion
V. Other events on the program
VI. Amount of time available to the speaker
VII. Did the speaker adjust effectively his Specific Speech Purpose and his speech content to meet the demands of the occasion?

Speaker Analysis:

I. Was the speaker vitally interested in his subject?
II. Was he eager to communicate his message to the audience?
III. Was he obviously well informed on the topic?
IV. Did the speech seem to be well suited to the speaker's "personality"?

11. Before your next talk in class, use the form given in number 10 to analyze yourself and your subject in terms of the classroom audience and occasion.

CHAPTER 3

Gathering the Speech Materials

Digging is usually a difficult and time-consuming job. Ask the gardener or the plowman. Nevertheless, before food can be eaten the ground must be turned, the seed must be planted, and the food sometimes taken from the soil; before water will flow, a ditch must be dug; before engines can turn, coal or oil for fuel must be extracted from the ground; before the blueprint becomes a house, the foundation upon which the house is to rest must be imbedded and the construction materials secured. Similarly, before a Specific Speech Purpose becomes a speech, we must search for those ideas and materials with which to build the speech.

Unless he wishes his home to collapse, the builder provides a stable foundation for the superstructure. Likewise, the successful speaker makes certain that his speech is founded upon an abundance of pertinent ideas; otherwise, his superstructure of words will crumble for lack of a firm foundation of ideas.

Accomplished speakers spare neither energy nor effort in persistently searching for their ideas. Woodrow Wilson had been a college professor for a number of years before he made his first public pronouncements on educational philosophy; he had studied politics and international relations most of his life prior to beginning the task of persuading the world to accept the League of Nations. Listeners who marveled at Daniel Webster's profound grasp of national affairs in the Webster-Hayne debate were reminded that the famous orator for years had spent most of his waking hours grappling with the very ideas he expounded so effectively in the Senate. The thorough understanding of America upon which Edmund Burke based his Taxation and Conciliation speeches was the result of persevering close-range study of the Colonies. Albert J. Beveridge's maiden speech in the Senate on the subject of the Philippines was successful partially because he had spent six months in the Orient methodically gathering material. The effective speaking of Harry S. Truman on his campaign tour in 1948, a trip which many are convinced turned the tide in his favor, was aided by a carefully prepared notebook of salient facts about the audiences, towns, regions, and cultural groups he would encounter.

When established and successful speakers almost without exception recognize the importance of painstaking preparation, you can scarcely afford to slight research in your preparation without inviting failure.

Before beginning your quest for materials, it is necessary to know what to look for and how to find it. What are these materials? They consist of facts, opinions, observations, examples, and statistics which concern your subject. How are they to be found? There are four steps in your search for materials upon which to build your speech.

THE FIRST STEP IN GATHERING MATERIALS IS TO THINK

A veteran who decided to talk on the geography of a section of the South Seas delivered a speech taken almost verbatim from *National Geographic* magazine. Although he had spent three service years in this area, it did not occur to him to make use of such experience in preparing his speech. The values of higher education are sometimes expounded in a student speech without a single reference to the speaker's personal opinions or experiences on the subject. These are examples of speakers who neglected to *think,* the first step in finding materials.

In thinking about a subject, your initial move should be to ask yourself what you already know. What experiences have you had which relate to your topic? Will your daily use of the Fleet Street bus strengthen your evaluation of the City Transit System? What have you learned from a term on the church board that will help you to explain parliamentary procedure to your audience? Have your occasional experiences as a baby-sitter furnished you with additional ideas for a speech on child care? In writing this book, we are attempting to interpret the principles of effective speaking in the light of our particular experiences, backgrounds, and training. Similarly, you should personalize your speeches by incorporating into them pertinent data learned from experience.

What of value can be culled from books you have read or courses you have completed? A lecture in Economics 201 may have crystallized your thinking on government controls sufficiently to provide a basis for further research on a speech advocating federal rent control. The development of a speech on the strengths and weaknesses of the United Nations may begin with basic premises derived from a recent reading of Emory Reeves' *Anatomy of Peace.*

The influence of environment may also be used to advantage in securing speech materials. Were you born and reared in the city, or was your childhood spent in a rural environment? What is your attitude toward organized religion? Are your parents Republicans? Do you belong to a union? What jobs have you held? These and similar environmental influences can be of unique value to you in speech preparation. The full value of experiences, former study, background, and training can be realized only if you *think.*

After probing your mind sufficiently to discover what you already know about your subject, try to pin down the nature of the materials you will still need to uncover. Although preliminary thinking may not provide a complete answer, it will undoubtedly reveal gaps in your knowledge, salient questions to which you have no answers, and problems which cannot be resolved at this stage. Reflective thinking of this nature will give purpose and direction to the remaining steps in your preparation.

Upon completing your initial thinking and moving to the next step, do not make the mistake of believing that such thinking is unnecessary to the remainder of your research. Critical evaluation of the materials you discover is essential. An informative talk will be meaningful only if you choose and discard materials with care. In preparing for a persuasive speech, constantly ask yourself, "What is the problem? Which course of action will be wisest?"

While it must be emphasized that the speaker must not slight or omit the *thinking* step, two other pitfalls should be avoided. Do not rely *exclusively* upon what you already know, unless you are a recognized expert on the subject at hand. Even authorities regularly augment their information and understanding with the wisdom of others. Also, try not to be dogmatic about your initial ideas. Make them tentative, holding final judgment until preparation is more complete.

THE SECOND STEP IN GATHERING MATERIALS IS TO OBSERVE

The old maxim, "a picture is worth a thousand words," applies in one sense to the speaker in search of materials. We refer here not to the photograph or sketch which you may use as a visual aid in your speech, but to the continuous flow of pictures registered upon the retina of the eye—the things we see. Although the reading of "a thousand words" is of great importance to your preparation (we shall subsequently consider reading as a step in finding materials), these visual "pictures" should not be neglected.

Careful observation of phenomena related to your subject can be invaluable to you in speech preparation. However, we must make a distinction between "seeing" and "observing." All of us with eyes are able to see, a function we exercise most of the time our eyes are open; however, we do not at all times *observe*. The "see-er" retains only a few visual memories. The "observer," on the other hand, retains, sorts, interprets, and evaluates his visual impressions, so that they may be of future use.

What are the characteristics of the good observer? Effective observation is *directed, complete, accurate,* and *objective. Directed* observation has a focal point, a purpose or a goal. If your desire to describe the advantages of a ranch-style house leads you to examine some of these homes, confine yourself to pertinent observations. Leave landscaping, building locations, prices of lots, personalities involved, and so on for another day—unless you have plenty of spare time.

Observation should be as *complete* as time and availability will permit. If you wish to persuade your listeners to visit Cape Cod, you will augment the information found in travel literature with observations made on your recent drive up the Cape. If this trip was taken in one day, probably you saw nothing beyond what appears in travel literature, if that much. The area offers much of interest to the observer who is able to proceed more leisurely, who is willing to leave the beaten path, and who will include in his observation terrain, customs, architecture, points of historical interest, unusual places to eat, types of people, standards of living, and the like. Allow enough time and use it wisely, if your observation is to be comprehensive.

Most of us are not *accurate* in our observations. Court records abound with the testimony of witnesses later proved unbelievably inaccurate. Most of us have heard amazing contradictions in the respective stories of neighbors describing a recent automobile accident at a near intersection. Chance observations of this kind, which are unexpected and startling, may be understandably inaccurate. Planned and directed observation, however, should be considerably more accurate. It should reveal what exists, neither more nor less.

Observation is *objective* if we do not let our prejudices and emotions color our interpretation of what we see. Attempt to evaluate fairly and honestly what you observe, rather than distorting it to fit a predetermined idea of what you *thought* you would witness. A prejudiced person moving from one part of the country to another observes only those phenomena which tend to confirm his preconceived point of view; he conveniently "closes his eyes" to the rest. His evaluation of his "home town" is probably equally colored by bias.

Observation will aid in preparing for almost any speech subject. It is of particular value in preparing the speech to *inform*. Travelogues, demonstration or "process" speeches, and expository speeches in general usually require a considerable amount of description. Description is usually more effective when it has been aided by observation. Examples of poor driving habits gleaned from extended observation may be more colorful and vivid than those borrowed from a magazine article. Observing a precision drill by the Cleveland Mounted Police Patrol will usually be of greater value than depending upon the testimony of others who have seen it. One of the principal ingredients of the speech to *entertain* is humor. Humor is where you find it. To some, that means a joke book exclusively. Wiser speakers have learned that the exaggerated situations, distortions, incongruities, and surprises of which humor is compounded are easily discovered by one sensitively attuned to his everyday environment. In a speech to *persuade* your audience to contribute to the Cerebral Palsy Fund, personal contact with those who would benefit from donations will provide vivid descriptive material; a tour of a rehabilitation center will reveal the treatment made possible by fund contributions. Such observations have a further value: first-hand visual contact of this type will aid in motivating the sincere, enthusiastic delivery so important to the success of the persuasive speech.

THE THIRD STEP IN GATHERING MATERIALS IS TO COMMUNICATE WITH OTHERS

After searching your mind and carefully observing your environment for speech materials, the next step is to *communicate with others.* Often the prospective speaker is unaware of the wealth of information, experience, and wisdom to be derived from others. The college student moves in a cosmopolitan atmosphere. His classmates may come from vastly different environments and may have had widely varied experiences. Large institutions attract students from all the states and a number of foreign countries. College faculties are replete with specialists in almost every conceivable area of human wisdom and achievement. The business world and the government services also rely heavily upon professional counsel. In this age of specialization, almost everyone is an expert on something. You will be neglecting a particularly fertile source of information for your speeches if you fail to take advantage of human contacts.

Make use of these three methods for securing information from others: (1) conversation and discussion, (2) interviews, and (3) letters.

A. Conversation and discussion. Participation in discussion groups and in informal conversations is an excellent way to add to your general education. While much of the content of the average "bull-session" is trivial, you have probably taken part in a number of thoughtful, worth-while conversations. Such discussions will be of greater significance to you if you subtly direct them toward your interests. You can then test your ideas openly and absorb new points of view.

Attend as many forums and discussion groups as possible, particularly when they deal with subjects which interest you and which may furnish information and ideas for a speech you are preparing. For maximum benefit, participate as well as listen, when the opportunity is presented.

B. Interviews. If an authority on your subject is available, by all means try to arrange an interview with him. Because an interview is limited in purpose and subject matter, it is usually a more efficient and economical method of securing information than informal conversation. A student who dabbled in local politics was aided immeasurably in his preparation for a speech on "how to campaign" by interviewing a faculty member who at the time was running for the United States Senate. Another student investigating the public speaking practices of the local Community Chest for a speech spent a day at Chest headquarters interviewing officials who directed the speaking campaign.

Here are some principles to guide you in obtaining a satisfactory interview: (1) *Do some preparation on the subject before the interview.* You will be wasting your time and that of your interviewee unless your preliminary research is sufficient to enable you to make the best use of your time. He will have neither the time nor the inclination to "start from scratch." (2) *Plan your interview.* Frame a series of specific, pertinent questions which can be answered briefly. Do not expect the person you interview to expound for a half hour on the general problem at hand. However, if the interviewee is greatly interested in your problem, he may discourse eagerly and at length without being questioned. If such is the case, ask the questions you have planned when opportunities occur. Your plans must be flexible. (3) *Conduct yourself with alertness, poise, friendliness, and respect.* Remember that your expert has agreed to give you his time, possibly at some personal sacrifice. He deserves to be treated with respect and consideration. Do not use him as a sounding board for your own theories on the problem. He has probably heard them before. Listen alertly for his points of view. Although you may disagree with him, do so silently. It may be necessary for you to write down specific information, but it is wise to minimize notetaking. If necessary, your notes may be expanded after the interview is concluded. (4) *Be brief.* The man you interview is probably busier than he appears. It is inconsiderate to impose upon him.

Another medium for securing information and ideas is the telephone. Libraries, information bureaus, and public relations offices are usually willing to respond to a phone call with the factual information at their command. A telephone interview may be arranged if a personal meeting is impossible. The principles previously outlined for good interviewing should apply when using the telephone.

If you are to derive maximum information and understanding from your conversations, discussions, and interviews, you will strive to become a good *listener*. We are likely to take for granted the process of listening. Obviously, we are forced to insulate our minds from much of the noise and talk that enters our ears. However, by carefully choosing what to listen to and by listening skillfully, the speaker in search of material will profit immeasurably. How can you become a better listener? We suggest these principles: (1) The good listener *concentrates*. Resist strongly the temptation to let your mind wander. Minimize distractions. If the speaker is worth hearing, he deserves your complete attention. (2) The good listener is *open-minded*. Many of us listen eagerly to ideas which reinforce our own opinions. When opposing views are aired we are prone to concentrate on answering the speaker rather than on listening to his arguments. You will always profit by listening carefully to arguments and attitudes different from your own—you might even be persuaded to change your mind! At least, you will be better prepared to expound your own point of view. If a speaker is worth hearing, he deserves open-minded consideration. (3) The good listener is *critical* and *evaluative*. Your listening will be more meaningful if you sharpen and use your critical and evaluative faculties. Is the speaker defining his terms? Is he proving his point? Is his evidence sufficient? Is his reasoning valid? Is he omitting or purposely ignoring an important consideration? In most listening situations, ask yourself such questions; they will increase mental activity and promote greater retention of what you hear. If a speech is followed by a question period, or if you are participating in a conversation or discussion, you will have the opportunity to voice many of these queries. (4) The good listener *remembers*. Retaining what you hear can be facilitated by employing the first three principles— concentrating, listening with an open mind, and using your critical faculties. Taking notes will also help. Keep a note pad and pencil with you at all times to record facts, figures, and other pertinent material for future reference. Jonathan Edwards, the foremost preacher of the Colonial period, carried quill and ink when horseback riding and pinned his notes to his clothes to make certain of his remembering them. If inconvenient to jot down ideas at the moment you hear them, do so at your first opportunity.

C. Letters. When individuals or information services cannot be contacted either personally or by telephone, a letter will often bring the needed information. Talking with others about your subject will frequently uncover the names and addresses of authorities, bureaus, and information services to be contacted by letter.

What principles should be followed in preparing and sending a business letter? Although it is beyond the scope of this book to consider in any detail the writing of a business letter, we offer these suggestions: (1) Think before you write, and organize your thoughts. (2) Be specific. Do not ramble or stray from the point. (3) Be brief. Write what is necessary and no more. (4) Be businesslike, but try to personalize your letter. Shun the chatty style of the personal letter, but also avoid the formality of the old-fashioned business letter. (5) Enclose a stamped, self-addressed envelope. (6) Allow a reasonable length of time for reply. You cannot expect your correspondent to answer your letter the moment it arrives. It is advisable to allow at least a week, exclusive of travel time each way, for your answer.

THE FOURTH STEP IN GATHERING MATERIALS IS TO READ

Reading is probably the easiest method of discovering speech materials. An unbelievably large amount of newly printed matter is added each year to the astronomical quantities of books, magazines, pamphlets, documents, and newspapers already filed away for your use. Speakers a few centuries ago were not so prolifically blessed with printed sources of information. How shall you go about the problem of finding written sources, deciding what to read, reading it effectively, and retaining something of what you have read?

Before considering some answers to these questions, a word of caution and a bit of advice. You may be strongly tempted to try what appears to be an easy short-cut in your search for materials. This short-cut, some speakers have found, makes it possible to omit all the thinking, observing, and conversing and most of the reading advised in this chapter. The magic formula they propose? Find a magazine article which you can parrot to your audience! For a number of reasons, this method of preparation should be shunned. First, if you summarize an article from one of the widely read monthly digests or popular magazines, you will be understandably embarrassed when you discover that many of your listeners have also read it. The embarrassment will be more excruciating if someone points out pertinent omissions, or questions your interpretation of the author. Second, it is unfair to your listeners to ask them to waste their time and attention on something that has become almost common knowledge. Third, it does not represent you at your full capacity. Each speech you give should be, in its totality, a personal creation. It should carry the stamp of your judgment, evaluation, and interpretation. Although the author of a magazine article on your subject may be more of an authority than you, his work should only *contribute* to your speech, along with the other sources suggested. If you hope for success as a speaker, avoid the magazine or newspaper story short-cut; it is likely to be a short-cut to failure.

A. What to read and where to find it. Most of you see at least one daily paper, and the majority of you read several magazines each month. You are in constant contact with books during college years, and see reviews of others you plan to read. In addition to the newspapers, magazines, and assorted books which you regularly see, take advantage of the most common repository of reading material, the library.

While nearly everyone knows the library exists, too few make sufficient use of its facilities, either through insufficient interest or through ignorance of how to use its services. Do not depend entirely upon the librarians to find your materials. While most librarians are unusually cooperative and helpful, it is inconsiderate to overwork them. Much that is in the library may be easily discovered without help, if you become better acquainted with its services.

1. *Standard references.* Your first stop in the library might be at the open shelves, where you will find encyclopedias for use in the room only. They contain comprehensive and expert treatments of almost any subject. Try the *Encyclopedia Britannica*, the *Encylopedia Americana*, or the *New International Encyclopedia*. The *Encyclopedia of Religion and Ethics* and similar specialized works may also yield materials you want. Such yearbooks as *Americana Annual* and *Statesman's Yearbook* should give the latest information on your subject. The *Dictionary of American Biography* is a helpful general biographical source.

2. Books. You may need help in discovering books which pertain to your subject. The *United States Catalog* and the *Cumulative Book Index* provide a record of almost every book published in the United States. They are fully indexed to permit finding books by looking under authors, titles, or subjects. You will also find specialized guides to books published in particular fields.

3. Magazines. Of particular value to the speech student are such magazines as *Time, Newsweek, United States News and World Report, Atlantic, Harper's, Current Events,* and *Fortune.* Regular reading of several of these magazines is important to your general education. Magazine articles pertinent to your speech subject may be found in the *Readers' Guide to Periodical Literature.* This well-known index, found in the general reading room of the library, will lead you to materials in approximately one hundred periodicals.

4. Newspapers. Students sometimes forget that newspapers may be used in research as well as in keeping abreast of daily happenings. Your library probably will have files of various newspapers extending back for many years. The *New York Times* is perhaps your outstanding newspaper source. An excellent index to the paper, which most libraries possess, will direct you to pertinent stories, editorials and columnists. Another responsible newspaper well worth your attention is the *Christian Science Monitor.*

5. Documents and pamphlets. Authoritative material printed by the various government bureaus and departments is on file in most libraries. The *Congressional Record,* containing a complete account of debates in Congress, is probably the best source for the text of a Congressional speech.

Thousands of private organizations publish bulletins, pamphlets, and brochures, many of which are free. Ask your librarian for aid in discovering those which may be of help.

B. How to read effectively. Some students believe the sole measure of effective reading is an impressive bibliography of sources consulted and a staggering number of pages read. Quantity and variety in reading are important; more significant, however, are the quality and relevance of the ideas and information derived.

If you would improve your reading efficiency, practice these four principles: (1) *Choose the most pertinent materials.* You will not have the time to read indiscriminately; therefore, develop the ability to scan. This will allow you to examine a number of articles and books rapidly. The most promising should be given closer attention. (2) *Approach each source with an open mind.* Do not slight an article or book which appears to disagree with your thinking, particularly in early reading. A good background for your subject is attained by examining all points of view. (3) *Adjust your reading habits to your material.* General background material should be read with the purpose of acquiring broad understanding. Specific facts in such reading may not be as important as basic theories, principles, and conclusions. Read general material rapidly, particularly if it is clearly organized. If your purpose is to acquire facts, statistics, or quotable testimony, read slowly to examine their validity and usefulness to your purpose. (4) *Read critically.* Some students worship the printed word. If it has been published, they believe that it must be true. Be skeptical in your reading; beware of any axe an author has to grind. Test his reasoning, examine his evidence, question his sources. Evaluate carefully his conclusions, not only for their validity, but for their relevance to your purpose. In short, do not be gullible.

C. How to retain what you read. As you read, try to remember ideas, points of view, and attitudes, rather than facts and figures. It is better not to depend upon memory if you wish to retain specific details. A quotation which seems unforgettable may elude you ten minutes later. It is advisable, therefore, to take notes.

Notes should be taken on cards of uniform size, for the same reason that playing cards are identical in size and shape—materials also need to be shuffled. Quotations and statistics should be recorded accurately, along with the exact source. Include author, title, publisher, date of publication, and page number. Entitle each card at the top with the division or topic under which your material falls. Record only one fact or idea on each card.

SUMMARY

When you have decided on your Specific Speech Purpose, the next move will be to find the materials with which to build your speech. They may be found by taking four steps: (1) *Think.* Probe your mind for experiences, readings, attitudes, and points of view pertinent to your subject. Discover what you already know and what you will need to find out. (2) *Observe.* Examine your environment for materials. You will uncover much of value if your observation is directed, complete, accurate, and objective. (3) *Communicate with others.* This will enable you to use their ideas, attitudes, and information. You may discover material in conversations, discussions, and interviews, and by writing letters. Oral communication will be more meaningful if you are a good listener. (4) *Read.* Become acquainted with the facilities of your library. Read discriminatingly and open-mindedly for new ideas and viewpoints, yet critically, lest you become gullible. Retain what you read by attempting to remember general concepts and by recording specific information on note cards.

EXERCISES AND ASSIGNMENTS

1. Read carefully the text of a speech from *Vital Speeches* (published biweekly by the City News Publishing Company, 33 W. 42 St., New York 18, N. Y.), Harold Harding's *Age of Danger* (New York: Random House, 1952), or A. Craig Baird's *Representative American Speeches* (New York: H. W. Wilson Company, annually since 1937). What evidence of the sources of the speaker's materials appears in the text? Did he use (1) personal experience, (2) observation, (3) ideas gleaned from consulting others, (4) printed sources? Prepare a written report of the speaker's presentation as evidenced from reading the speech.

2. Upon choosing the subject for your next classroom speech, prepare an oral report consisting of (1) an outline of what you already know about the subject, (2) information you will need to discover in the course of your preparation, (3) projects in observation which might be of value, (4) persons you might interview for ideas and information, and pertinent questions you might ask, and (5) a preliminary bibliography, including references from the card catalog and the periodical index, pertinent documents, and newspaper stories. Ask your classmates for their

experiences, observations, and ideas relative to the topic, and their suggestions of persons to interview and written sources to consult.

3. Arrange to interview a well-known speaker in your community on his methods of gathering materials. Among your questions might be: (1) How much do you depend upon your background and personal experiences in your speech preparation? (2) Has observation been of particular value? In what instances? (3) Do you frequently consult others personally or by letter for information and ideas? (4) Do you keep a file of quotations, jokes, epigrams, and illustrations for possible use in future speeches? (This is a rewarding long-term project for the beginning speaker.) (5) Does your preparation for a particular speech usually include some specific reading, or do you rely predominantly upon the general reading you have done and the knowledge you already possess? Report to the class the results of this interview.

4. Listen carefully to the speech of a classmate for evidence of the sources of his ideas. Does his speech draw upon a variety of sources? What are they? Either write a report or be prepared to evaluate his preparation orally.

5. Arrange and conduct an interview with an authority on a topic you intend to use for a speech. Report to the class on the material you gathered, what difficulties you encountered, how your interview might have been improved, and so on.

6. Station yourself for fifteen minutes at a busy intersection, the corner lunchroom, the college administration building, or some other spot which bustles with activity. Another member of the class should station himself at approximately the same vantage point. Without consulting one another or collaborating in any way, each should observe what goes on and prepare to report on that observation to the class. You may check one another as to the completeness, accuracy, and objectivity of observation. If your reports are at variance, attempt to discover why, with the aid of the class.

7. Choose a speech to be given in the community or to be broadcast (radio or TV) for a class project in listening. Make every attempt to be a good listener. Present to the class a critical report on the content and delivery. Compare your report with others for accuracy, completeness, and objectivity.

CHAPTER 4

Making the Outline

One of the major news stories of early 1950 was the grounding of the mammoth battleship, the "U.S.S. Missouri," upon a shoal in Chesapeake Bay. Only after two weeks of humiliating failure could the straining tugs and the grinding winches pull the "Mo's" broad bottom out of the tenacious mud. The resulting naval court of inquiry found that the responsibility for the accident rested mainly with the "Missouri's" captain, who had misjudged his course in one of the world's safest and best-charted channels. The case of the "Missouri" illustrates the principle that in order to arrive at one's destination one must map out and adhere to a satisfactory course. The speaker's job of plotting the course of his address in order to achieve the desired audience response is probably as complex as the task confronting the navigator of a vessel. Even the most careful speaker has sometimes realized at the close of his address that somehow his speech has "gone aground"—that he could have been much more persuasive had he arranged his material in a different manner. Almost all great orators of the past and present have found that for maximum effectiveness one must be diligent in planning speeches. The inexperienced speaker must be extremely careful to chart the speech so that the destination, the Specific Speech Purpose, can be achieved.

We have already seen that the first major concern in preparing the speech is selection of the Specific Speech Purpose. In Chapter 3 we discussed standard procedures in gathering appropriate speech materials. Now we will devote our attention to methods of organizing our material in such a way that we will be able to win the desired response from our listeners. The American Automobile Association distributes millions of maps and booklets on accommodations annually. Why? Because no intelligent motorist would embark on an extended trip without knowledge of where he is going and how he intends to get there. No contractor would attempt to construct a house without an architect's blueprint as a guide. The map is to the tourist and the blueprint is to the contractor what the speech outline is to the public speaker. The outline helps the speaker to arrange his ideas in the most effectively logical and psychological order, to test the merit of supporting details, to gauge more accurately the length of the speech, and to insure that the address has unity, coherence, and emphasis.

Almost every speaker makes some sort of outline on paper, because that is the most practical method of organizing one's thinking. *When the outline has been completed in final form, it is the essence of the speech itself.* The outline has much the same relationship to a speech that the skeleton of beams and girders has to a building, or that the framework of ribs and keel has to a ship. The outline is not a manuscript, a verbatim copy of what the speaker will say to his audience; rather it is an abbreviated charting of the course of the address. By means of careful planning, the speaker selects the main points he wishes to present and supports these major heads by appropriate subheadings. All of the points of the outline must be relevant to the accomplishment of the Specific Speech Purpose.

TEN RULES FOR THE LOGICAL PARTITIONING OF MATERIALS

A. The primary function of an outline is to show *thought relationships.* *Such relationships can be indicated only by means of some standard system of symbols and indentations, as is here illustrated.*

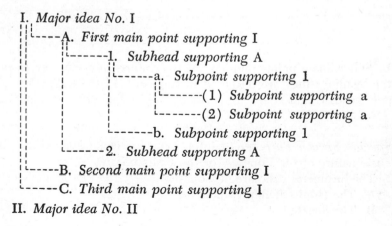

I. *Major idea No.* I
    A. *First main point supporting* I
        1. *Subhead supporting* A
           a. *Subpoint supporting* 1
               (1) *Subpoint supporting* a
               (2) *Subpoint supporting* a
           b. *Subpoint supporting* 1
        2. *Subhead supporting* A
    B. *Second main point supporting* I
    C. *Third main point supporting* I
II. *Major idea No.* II

Points being used to support other headings are called *subordinate heads,* and are always indented to the right and placed below the heading so supported. This results in the staircase effect below.

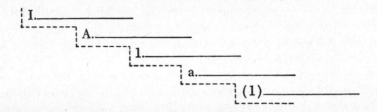

Points possessing approximately the same value, which are independent of each other, and which are logically subordinate to some other point, are called *coordinate points.* If this definition seems confusing, think of how the legs of a table answer the requirements for coordinate points. Note that each leg is of approximately the same value, each leg is basically independent of the other legs, and each leg bears a similar subordinate relationship to the top of the table. Coordinate heads are placed in a perpendicular order.

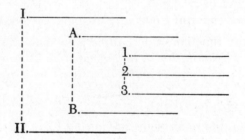

B. Subordinate points must logically reinforce, develop, or clarify the headings they are designed to support. In the following outline, heads *C* and *D* are *not* correctly used as subordinate points.

WRONG

Specific Speech Purpose: to inform my audience concerning the basic nature of the Congress of the United States
I. The bicameral structure of Congress
  A. The House of Representatives
  B. The Senate

C. *The powers of Congress*
D. *Congressional procedure*

RIGHT

Specific Speech Purpose: to inform my audience concerning the basic nature of the Congress of the United States
 I. The bicameral structure of Congress
   A. The House of Representatives
   B. The Senate
 II. The powers of Congress
 III. Congressional procedure

C. Coordinate points should not overlap. As we found in the definition of coordinate points under Rule A, such heads must be mutually exclusive—they are independent headings. In the outline below notice that main heads *II* and *IV* overlap. In this particular case, heading *IV* should be eliminated.

WRONG

Specific Speech Purpose: to convince my audience that professional wrestling should be prohibited
 I. Professional wrestling is controlled by a low-class element
 II. Professional wrestling is too dangerous to the participants
 III. Professional wrestling matches are exhibitions rather than contests
 IV. Professional wrestling is too rough

The following outline has badly overlapping main heads. Point *III* is obviously a part of I, and point *V* overlaps headings I, II, and IV.

WRONG

Specific Speech Purpose: to entertain my audience by describing my experiences during a recent visit to New York City
 I. I went sightseeing
 II. I attended several ball games
 III. I saw New York City from the top of the Empire State building
 IV. I went to several night clubs
 V. My cousin Tom took me to several interesting places
   A. He took me to the Yankee-Red Sox game of August 20

B. He took me to the Stork Club
C. He took me to see the Statue of Liberty

RIGHT

Specific Speech Purpose: to entertain my audience by describing my experiences during a recent visit to New York City

I. I went sightseeing
   A. I saw New York City from the top of the Empire State Building
   B. I visited the Statue of Liberty
   C.⎫
   D.⎬ (Other places visited)
   E.⎭
II. I attended several ball games
   A. I went to the Yankee-Red Sox game of August 20
   B.⎫
   C.⎭ (Other games attended)
III. I visited various night clubs
   A. I had dinner at the Stork Club
   B.⎫
   C.⎬ (Other night clubs visited)
   D.⎭

D. Be certain that your organization covers the subject adequately. Do not leave out necessary points. For instance, if the speaker failed to discuss the muscles of the thigh under III of the outline on page 74, the audience would receive an inadequate analysis of the muscles of the lower extremity. Ask yourself the question: "Am I leaving out of my outline points which are necessary to accomplish my Specific Speech Purpose?"

E. Usually every division should have two or more heads. The supporting points under a heading ordinarily represent a division of that heading—and, as everyone knows, when something is divided, it is split into two or more parts. However, outlining is not always a matter of divisions. Sometimes a speaker may wish to explain or to prove an assertion by means of a single supporting illustration, fact, or reason. If someone should offer you a personal check in payment for your used car, and if upon inquiry you were told by a bank official that the man had no account at the bank, would not this single piece of evidence be sufficient to convince you to reject this bogus check? In such a case there is nothing logically or psychologically wrong with having only one subhead. Usually, though, it is wise to use more than one subpoint when amplifying a heading.

F. Use parallel phrasing for coordinate heads. Do this to make memorization of the outline easier for you, to make comprehension easier and quicker for your audience, and to serve as a check on logical relationships. Compare the effectiveness of the following two outlines.

WRONG

I. It is economical to buy Blue Boy cleaner
II. Little work involved
III. No harm done to hands
IV. Does an effective job

RIGHT

I. Blue Boy cleaner is economical
II. Blue Boy cleaner is easy to apply
III. Blue Boy cleaner is gentle on the hands
IV. Blue Boy cleaner is effective

G. Avoid compound headings. A head indicates a *single* idea, not multiple ideas. If you wish to present several ideas, logic demands that you select a heading for each point.

WRONG

Specific Speech Purpose: to convince my audience that the atomic bomb should not be used against the Communists in Korea
  I. *Our use of the bomb would be a crime against humanity and would alienate friendly nations*
  II. *Our use of the bomb would be a blow to our military prestige and might cause Russia to attack us*
  III. Our use of the bomb would be poor military strategy

RIGHT

Specific Speech Purpose: to convince my audience that the atomic bomb should not be used against the Communists in Korea
  I. Our use of the bomb would be a crime against humanity

II. Our use of the bomb would be offensive to friendly nations
III. Our use of the bomb would be interpreted by other nations as a confession of military weakness
IV. Our use of the bomb would be an excuse for Russia to attack us
V. Our use of the bomb would be unprofitable from a military standpoint

H. Until the novice acquires considerable experience, he should write out each heading in the form of a complete sentence. The preceding outline is an example of Full Content outlining. However, the skilled speaker may use the Key Word method of phrasing his points. The headings in a Key Word outline contain only essential words—not complete sentences (see outline on muscle groups, pages 73, 74). Most authorities agree that the Full Content manner of outlining offers the beginning speaker a better check on his thought relationships than does the Key Word method. An effective compromise might be to write out major heads in full, definite, declarative sentences, and to use the "key words" in phrasing the subpoints.

I. Standard speech organization consists of three major sections: Introduction, Discussion, and Conclusion. As we shall find in Chapter 7, the Introduction has two main heads: the *Favorable Attention Step* and the *Clarification Step,* which prepares the audience for the ensuing Discussion or major part of the speech. The main heads of the Discussion are organized according to one of the six patterns discussed in Chapter 5: *Time, Space, Topical, Cause and Effect, Problem-Solution,* and *Proposition of "Fact."* Almost all Conclusions (Chapter 8) should contain a *Summary Step.* If the speech is designed to produce action on the part of the audience, an *Action Step* should also be included in the Conclusion.

J. An outline of the Discussion should have between two and five main heads. It is obvious there cannot be merely one main head, since this would be a restatement of the speech purpose and no division at all. On the other hand, excessive main heads make it difficult for the listener to retain the arguments presented, and frequently indicate muddled thinking on the part of the speaker. Even if the speech lasts for more than an hour, the number of main heads should rarely exceed five. The next example shows a confusing array of main points.

WRONG

Specific Speech Purpose: to inform my audience concerning the basic muscle groups of the human body
I. The muscles of the neck
II. The muscles of facial expression
III. The muscles of the thoracic wall
IV. The muscles of the abdominal wall
V. The muscles of the pelvic floor
VI. The diaphragm
VII. The deep muscles of the back
VIII. The muscles of the thigh
IX. The muscles of the groin
X. The muscles of the buttock
XI. The muscles of the calf
XII. The muscles of the foot
XIII. The muscles of the upper arm
XIV. The muscles of the forearm
XV. The muscles in the region of the shoulder
XVI. The muscles of the hand

Notice how the following arrangement facilitates easy understanding.

RIGHT

Specific Speech Purpose: to inform my audience concerning the basic muscle groups of the human body
I. The muscles of the axial skeleton
   A. The muscles of facial expression
   B. The muscles of the neck
   C. The muscles of the thoracic wall
   D. The muscles of the abdominal wall
   E. The deep muscles of the back
   F. The muscles of the pelvic floor
   G. The diaphragm
II. The muscles of the upper extremity
   A. The muscles of the hand
   B. The muscles of the forearm
   C. The muscles of the upper arm
   D. The muscles in the region of the shoulder

III. The muscles of the lower extremity
   A. The muscles of the foot
   B. The muscles of the calf
   C. The muscles of the thigh
   D. The muscles of the buttock
   E. The muscles of the groin

Summary

THE SPEECH OUTLINE IS DESIGNED TO SERVE AS AN AID TO THE SPEAKER. THE OUTLINE IS NOT THE "END" ITSELF, BUT A MEANS TO THE END—THE PRESENTATION OF AN EFFECTIVE SPEECH. We have endeavored to present in this chapter the important rules for the logical partitioning of materials. Learn these guides thoroughly before studying the next four chapters, which treat in detail the Discussion, the Introduction, the Conclusion, and the methods for supporting main headings. Here restated are the ten rules.

1. Use a standard system of symbols and indentations.
2. Subordinate points must logically reinforce, develop, or clarify the headings they are designed to support.
3. Coordinate points should not overlap.
4. Be certain that your organization covers the subject adequately.
5. Usually every division should have two or more headings.
6. Use parallel phrasing for coordinate points.
7. Avoid compound headings.
8. Write out each main head in the form of a complete sentence.
9. Standard speech organization consists of three major sections: Introduction, Discussion, and Conclusion.
10. An outline of the Discussion should have between two and five main headings.

Exercises and Assignments

1. Outline any chapter in this book. Compare your outline with that of the authors. (As you have noticed, each of the four main divisions of this text is preceded by a sectional outline.)

2. Check the outlines preceding each section of this book. Have the authors invariably followed each of the ten rules for outlining? In any case where some rule has been disregarded, can you discover the purpose of the authors in so doing?

3. Attempt to take lecture notes in your various classes in outline form. A well-organized lecture should be easy to outline. Be especially alert to catch guideposts given by the professor, such as: "The second cause is . . .," "Now let's look at certain economic implications . . .," or "Perhaps of most importance . . ."

4. An excellent method of reviewing for a test is to reorganize class notes in the form of an outline. Outlining will help make clear formerly obscure thought relationships and will help memorization.

5. Outline a speech from *Vital Speeches* magazine, or from a collection of speeches such as Harding's *Age of Danger,* or Baird's *Representative American Speeches.*

6. List all the violations of good outlining found in the following example. Recast the outline in proper form.

Specific Speech Purpose: to acquaint my audience with *Literary America,* an anthology by David Scherman and Rosemarie Redlich
   I. The authors
  II. The book contains 170 superb photographs
 III. The book contains many well-loved passages
 IV. Rosemarie Redlich is actually Mrs. Scherman
   V. Mr. Scherman, a professional photographer, took all the pictures
 VI. One striking page contains a section of James Whitcomb Riley's "Old Swimmin' Hole" and a picture of a group of children swimming in a pond
 VII. Children will be stimulated to enjoy great works of American literature
VIII. An ideal volume as a bedside book

7. Rearrange the following main and subheads in proper outline form.
Specific Speech Purpose: to inform my audience about the Fulbright Program under Public Law 584
   I. Objectives of the program
     A. Offers broadening experiences for American scholars and specialists
  II. Description of the awards
     A. Maintenance allowance
     B. Levels of awards
     C. Duration of awards
 III. Eligibility requirements
 IV. Book and incidental allowances
   V. Application procedure
     A. Must be a citizen

    B. Must be in good health
    C. Liability of grantee to tax
    D. Must have a Ph.D. for a research grant and at least three
       years teaching experience for a teaching award
  VI. Selection of grantees
    A. How to obtain application forms
    B. When to apply
    C. Principal criteria for selection
    D. Stages in the selection process
 VII. Plan promotes international understanding

8. Place the following heads in their appropriate coordinate and subordinate relationships.

defensive strength	reserve strength
fielding	managerial strength
double-play combination	coaches
offensive power	catching
pitching	manager
home-run power	utility outfielders
skilled base running	utility infielders

CHAPTER 5

Organizing the Discussion

The need for good organization in the Discussion is readily seen when we realize that it usually occupies approximately 80 to 85 per cent of the total speech, whereas the Introduction averages about 10 per cent and the Conclusion about 5 per cent. Initial and final impressions which the audience receives from the speaker and his speech are important; the main purpose of the address, however, is accomplished in the Discussion. Most modern speech teachers agree with the ancient Roman orator and statesman, Cicero, in suggesting that the speaker prepare the Discussion before the Introduction or Conclusion.

PART I. SELECTING THE MAIN HEADS

Chapter 4 explained that the organization of the Discussion consists of main heads and subheads which are arranged to the best logical and psychological advantage. The most effective selection and disposition of major points depend upon the nature of the material and upon the audience's knowledge of and attitude toward the subject. As you remember from Chapter 2, always keep the listener foremost in your mind. Constantly ask yourself: "How can I organize and develop my thoughts so they will be best suited to my particular audience?" Not infrequently, the inexperienced speaker throws his ideas together with little attention to the most effective presentation of available evidence. What would happen if a cook should dump the ingredients for an angel food cake into a pan with no semblance of orderly sequence? Would the cake come out of the oven a delicious pastry or a wad of ill-textured dough?

As a result of thinking, observing, communicating, and reading (Chapter 3), you have gathered considerable information on your subject. At this point such material is analogous to a pile of boards in a cabinet-maker's shop: the carpenter must select the pieces to be used and must plan their arrangement before constructing an article of furniture. Out of the materials you have amassed and out of the thinking you have done must come an organizational structure which will enable your speech to accomplish the Specific Speech Purpose. Part I of this chapter is concerned with your first major task in organizing the Discussion—finding the main heads. As you recall, main headings are first-degree coordinate points. Coordinate points must always be selected before attempting to find their subordinate points. This means that all of the primary heads must be determined before supporting materials are grouped under any particular main head. (Close attention will be given in Chapter 6 to the methods of supporting main points.)

Two Important Steps in Selecting Main Heads

A. The first step in choosing the main heads of the Discussion is to jot down (during or after the process of gathering the materials for the speech) the different points you might want to present in your talk. Although the experienced speaker can frequently do this in his mind, the beginner needs to write these ideas on paper. Such a list might number forty or more separate items. For the sake of convenience let us call this group of potential points the *Analysis List*. Perhaps you remember when you received your first jigsaw puzzle how you spread out all the pieces on the living room table. Your task was then to fit the separate pieces together to complete the intended picture. In a sense, your Analysis List represents possible "pieces" of your outline; select the appropriate "pieces" and fit them together in their appropriate positions.

B. The second step in selecting the main heads of the Discussion is to evolve from the Analysis List a group of from two to five main headings, under which can be arranged pertinent supporting points. In the following example we shall see that the main heads which you select may not be worded *as such* in your Analysis List and that several points in the Analysis List may be consolidated under a more general topic not present in the original list. When planning Chapter 7, "Developing the Introduction," we composed a mental Analysis List something like the following.

1. The Introduction should secure audience attention
2. Humor is a good attention step
3. The Introduction should clarify the purpose of the speech
4. Tell an interesting story about yourself
5. Tell an imaginary story
6. Tell an interesting experience that happened to someone else
7. Do not use stale humor
8. Do not poke embarrassing fun at any persons or minority groups
9. Give necessary definitions
10. Use a striking quotation
11. Use a striking question
12. Do not antagonize
13. Do not be long-winded
14. Avoid off-color humor
15. Make humor brief
16. Do not let humor get away from you
17. Use only relevant humor
18. Use other types of humor besides stories, puns, and anecdotes
19. State the main heads or arguments of the Discussion
20. Give necessary background materials
21. Bring the audience up to date on the subject
22. Refer to the significance of the subject
23. Mention common relationships, beliefs, interests, and feelings
24. Refer to the speech occasion or purpose of the meeting
25. State the POINT of the speech
26. Use a pithy statement
27. Compliment the audience
28. Do not use irrelevant material
29. Do not apologize

All of these topics are connected with the speech Introduction, just as the pieces of a jigsaw puzzle are parts of a picture. As listed above, however, this Analysis List presents a conglomeration of ideas, without apparent purpose or unity. A speech, essay, or even a brick wall, for that matter, must have coherence. The cohesive force, the mortar of the speech, is the logical arrangement binding the main heads and the subheads. In the following outline the twenty-nine points have been arranged under three main topics. Notice that the first two major heads are drawn from the original Analysis List (with the phrasing altered somewhat in conformance with rules No. 6 and No. 8 [Chapter 4] for the logical partitioning of materials). The third represents a consolidation of several of the original points. In parentheses following each heading we have recorded the number of that entry in the preceding Analysis List.

I. The Favorable Attention Step secures the interest of the audience by means of: (1)
   A. Reference to the significance of the subject (22)
   B. Humor (2)
      1. Do not poke embarrassing fun at any persons or minority groups present in the audience (8)
      2. Do not use stale humor (7)
      3. Avoid off-color humor (14)
      4. Be brief (15)
      5. Be careful that the use of humor does not make it difficult or impossible to secure a serious hearing from the audience (16)
      6. Use only relevant humor (17)
      7. Use other types of humor besides stories, puns, and anecdotes (18)
   C. Illustrative story—(*evolved from* 4, 5, *and* 6)
      1. True experience (*evolved from* 4 *and* 6)
         a. Your own experience (4)
         b. Someone else's experience (6)
      2. Hypothetical experience (5)
   D. Stimulating quotation (10)
   E. Mention of common relationships, beliefs, interests, and feelings (23)
   F. Stimulating question (11)
   G. Pithy statement (26)
   H. Reference to the speech occasion or purpose of the meeting (24)
   I. Complimentary remarks (27)
II. The Clarification Step prepares the audience for the Discussion by: (3)
   A. Stating the POINT of the speech (25)
   B. Stating the main heads or arguments of the Discussion (19)

C. Providing necessary background explanations (*evolved from* 9, 20, *and* 21)
   1. Definitions (9)
   2. Historical explanations (21)
   3. General background information (20)
III. The four most common sins of the Introduction are: (*evolved from* 12, 13, 28, *and* 29)
   A. To apologize (29)
   B. To be long-winded (13)
   C. To antagonize or offend (12)
   D. To use irrelevant material (28)

1. *In selecting the main heads of the Discussion you will need a thorough understanding of the six basic organizational patterns or thought sequences discussed in Parts II and III of this chapter.* In every Analysis List one or more logical themes or sequences are potentially present. If correctly arranged according to one of these patterns, main heads will be bound by strong ties of logical association. The simple patterns analyzed in Part II include those designated as Time, Space, and Topical. Part III presents the more advanced patterns: Problem-Solution, Cause and Effect, and Proposition of "Fact." Examine carefully your Analysis List to determine which one of the six patterns seems to fit your material best. Then on the basis of what you will have learned about that particular pattern from the remainder of this chapter, you will have relatively little difficulty in determining the major divisions of the Discussion.

It should be noted that some overlapping exists among the various patterns. A temporal sequence might also represent a spatial arrangement: A discussion of the direct shock waves following a Hiroshima-type atomic bomb blast might use a combined Time and Space Pattern—in three seconds after explosion direct shock waves have traveled 2,500 feet and produced complete blast destruction, in another second the shock waves have traveled an additional 1,500 feet and left severe damage, and so forth. The Topical Pattern causes beginning students some difficulty because of the sweeping character of its definition: "The Topical Pattern refers to a division of the Discussion into its natural or conventional topics or parts." One of the authors sometimes calls it the "catch-all pattern" because, in a limited sense, almost any organization may be labeled "Topical."

However, despite these and other overlappings, there is sufficient dissimilarity among the types for us to categorize them into the six separate patterns.

2. *Your Specific Speech Purpose frequently suggests a particular disposition of the main heads of the Discussion.* As we have already learned, the Specific Speech Purpose should be established before you attempt to organize the speech. Now let us see how the purpose of your talk may help determine the pattern used for the main heads.

a. THE SPEECH TO INFORM. Chapter 2 states that the speech to inform is concerned with the giving of directions, reports, or lectures. When your purpose is to explain how to do something, the primary heads can almost always be disposed according to a time sequence. Look over your Analysis List and pick out the major divisions of time inherent in the directions you are to give, then array under each major head the proper subordinate points. Usually a lecture or a report can be organized by means of a Time, Space, or Topical Pattern. See first if your Analysis List fits conveniently into a time order. If not, ascertain whether geographical divisions are logically present. If neither pattern seems appropriate, your main points probably will fall into certain natural or convenient divisions, i.e., the Topical Pattern. Seek out the natural topics (as was done in the example on pages 79, 80, and 81), establish them as first-degree coordinates, and group under them suitable subordinate ideas. As you gain experience, you may wish under certain circumstances to use one of the more advanced patterns given in Part III.

b. THE SPEECH TO ENTERTAIN. Although the Time Pattern is frequently feasible, possibly the Topical Pattern is the method most often used in organizing the speech to entertain.

c. THE SPEECH TO PERSUADE. Invariably the Discussion of the speech to persuade may be organized according to either the Problem-Solution or the Proposition of "Fact" pattern. In either case the main heads are largely selected for you by the pattern itself. If you wish to persuade your listeners to accept a new program or course of action, utilize the Problem-Solution sequence. (Here is an example of the Specific Speech Purpose advocating a new policy: To convince your audience that the United States should adopt a program of universal military training.) A speaker who proposes the adoption of a policy usually must explain the exigencies of the present situation (the Problem) that demand the adoption of the speaker's plan (the Solution). Under these two first-degree heads are several of second-degree. When using this pattern all you need to do is to array suitable supporting materials under the recommended primary and secondary heads.

When your purpose is to persuade the audience to accept as true a particular statement or point of view (such as convincing your audience that Russia plans war against the United States), your main heads will usually fall into the Proposition of "Fact" pattern. In Part III of this chapter you will learn how to establish the validity of your assertion by organizing the Discussion under two main heads: (1) standards of judgment and (2) matching of the evidence against the standards. In addition to the Problem-Solution and the Proposition of "Fact" patterns, sometimes Topical and Cause-and-Effect plans can be used effectively in organizing the persuasive speech.

PART II. SIMPLE PATTERNS OF ORGANIZATION

A. Time Pattern. A chronological order according to time or, in other words, a temporal sequence of events is frequently the most effective method of organizing the speech to inform. The Time Pattern is the natural plan for a speech describing a "process" or giving directions of the "how-to-do-it" variety—you are explaining an operation which in "real life" is based upon a time order. If describing the Bessemer process, you would start with the raw ore and trace its transformation into steel. This, of course, is a step-by-step process. If you were teaching a group of home owners how to lay a cement floor, you would probably use the Time Pattern. One has to follow a definite temporal sequence when laying a concrete floor: the natural first step must come first, followed by the second step, then the third, and so on. Obviously, concrete could not be poured before the ground is leveled, before the supporting wire network has been inserted into the wooden frame, or before the frame is constructed. In giving preliminary instructions to a group of draftees just arrived for induction examinations, a sergeant will need to follow a Time Pattern. These men have to be told: (1) to take off their clothes; (2) to put their clothes in a canvas bag; (3) to check their valuables and their canvas bag; (4) to wait in a certain area for their names to be called; (5) when summoned, to fall into line in a designated place; (6) to keep in order as the line goes through the various stages of the physical examination. By arranging his directions in accordance with the chronological sequence of events, the sergeant will give his charges a clear conception of what is expected of them.

Let us look at three outlines illustrating how the Time Pattern is used to organize the main heads of the Discussion. In the first example the speaker's Specific Speech Purpose is to inform the audience concerning the developmental history of the U.S.A.F. B-47, the Boeing stratojet bomber.

I. The beginnings of Boeing's research on the B-47 in 1943
   (Here the speaker would discuss the initial difficulties in getting the research program under way.)
II. Boeing's early testing program for the B-47, 1944 to 1947
   (The speaker would tell of the various stages in the testing program from the first wind tunnel tests, through the "flutter tests," to the actual delivery of a full-scale model of the B-47 to the Air Force, Dec., 1947.)
III. The further testing program by the Air Force in conjunction with Boeing, Dec., 1947, to Aug., 1950
   (The speaker would describe the most important elements of this phase of the testing program. Probably he would include here a mention of the transcontinental non-stop flight made by a B-47 from Moses Lake, Washington, to Andrews Field, Maryland, in less than four hours.)
IV. The first "finished" B-47 delivered to the Air Force in August, 1950
   (The audience would expect the speaker to describe some of the outstanding features of this craft which make it superior to its predecessors, thus showing the results of the seven years of exhaustive research and tests.)

The Specific Speech Purpose for the second example using the Time Pattern is: to inform the audience about the construction of a glass brick bookcase. Since the importance of such a subject may not be obvious in these days of international conflict, let us plan the Introduction as well as the Discussion.

INTRODUCTION:

I. *Favorable Attention Step:*

(In order to stimulate interest in his speech, the speaker might point out the savings which could be realized by making a bookcase out of selected boards and glass bricks. He could show pictures to prove how fashionable such bookcases are. He could point out how the case could be increased or decreased in size and how easily it could be dismantled for shipping or for moving to another location. He could explain that all books need the protection afforded by cases such as the glass brick case.)

II. *Clarification Step:*

(Here the speaker might state the POINT: that he is going to show how easily and cheaply the case can be constructed. He might also list the main steps in constructing the case to prepare the listeners more adequately for the Discussion.)

DISCUSSION:

I. The first step in constructing a glass brick bookcase is to select the materials
II. The second step is to prepare the boards for finishing
III. The third step is to varnish the boards
IV. The fourth step is to put the boards and bricks together as the finished bookcase

The following Time Pattern might be used to develop a talk on the history of French trade unions since the liberation of France:

I. The first period: 1944–1946
  A. A period of social reforms by the government
  B. A period of rapid revival of unions
  C. A period of rapid assumption of control of many unions by the Communists
II. The second period: 1946–1948
  A. First there was latent civil war in the trade unions
  B. Then there was open warfare
III. The third period: 1948–1954
  A. Stabilization has taken place among the unions
  B. The French worker has experienced increasing frustration

B. Space Pattern. The main heads of speeches to inform are sometimes disposed according to a spatial or geographical sequence. We all are familiar with "space patterns" in our lives. The purchase price of tickets to athletic events is dependent upon the geographical location of the seats—the closer to the center of activity, the higher the price. For example, at some major league parks, box seats are $2.50; grandstand seats, $1.50; and bleacher seats, $1.00. In addition to their national organization, the Speech Association of America, the professional speech teachers of the United States have the following geographical or regional organizations: Eastern, Southern, Central States, and Western. Most of the major college football teams are grouped in conferences basically geographical in nature, such as the Big Ten, the Ivy League, the Southern, Southeastern, Southwestern, and Pacific Coast Conferences.

A woman directing her husband in the rearrangement of furniture is using a "space pattern": "Put the davenport over against the west wall; the lamp and the overstuffed chair go in the corner; place the piano along the east wall; try the coffee table in front of the sofa." An architect explaining to his clients the floor arrangements of a new warehouse will use a spatial sequence: "The first floor will look like this," he might say as he spreads out the blueprints, "with the right wing . . . the left wing . . . the central storage area . . . The second floor will contain . . . The third floor will have . . ." In a speech to inform an audience about the distribution of authorized Hudson dealers, the main headings of the Discussion might be:

I. Distribution of Hudson dealers in the Eastern states
   A. In the Northeastern states
   B. In the Southeastern states
II. Distribution of Hudson dealers in the Central states
   A. In the North Central states
   B. In the South Central states
III. Distribution of Hudson dealers in the Western states
   A. In the Northwestern states
   B. In the Southwestern states

If discussing the atmosphere surrounding the earth, one might use this spatial arrangement:

I. Troposphere
II. Tropopause
III. Stratosphere
IV. Stratopause
V. Ionosphere

The speaker must actually use a *sequence* when applying the Space Pattern. Such an arrangement of primary points might start with the northernmost geographical entity and move in sequence to the most southern, or from the first floor upwards to the top floor, or from the bark of a tree to the heart wood, or from the right flank of a battle line through the middle to the left flank, or from near to far, or from front to back.

C. Topical Pattern.   As one would judge from its title, the Topical Pattern refers to a division of the Discussion into topics or parts. Very frequently the subject matter divides itself automatically and naturally into certain heads.

The flexibility of the Topical Pattern can readily be seen by the following examples:

(1) If attempting to prove that coal strikes are harmful to all concerned, you might use these main heads:
  I. Coal strikes are harmful to the miners
 II. Coal strikes are harmful to the mine owners
III. Coal strikes are harmful to the general public

(2) If your purpose is to tell a Little Theatre group how to produce a play, your Topical Pattern will be something like the following. (Were it not for the fact that main head IV, "Building the Set," may occur at the same time as II and III, the outline would be temporal as well as topical.)
  I. Choosing the play
 II. Selecting the cast
III. Rehearsing the play
 IV. Building the set
  V. Presenting the play

(3) The natural divisions of a speech advertising a vacation retreat on the southern shores of France might result in these main topics:
  I. The desirability of the climate
 II. The beautiful scenery
III. The hospitality of the people
 IV. The pleasant hotel and cottage accommodations
  V. The economy of such a visit

(4) Eulogies of great men frequently follow a Topical Pattern, as is shown in the following:

I. The extent of Churchill's influence during his political career
II. The personal source of Churchill's influence
III. Churchill's probable place in history

(5) A lecture to a group of the Daughters of the Confederacy on the major battles of the Civil War might assign a primary head for each battle. If you selected the five most important conflicts, your main topics might be:

I. The Battle of Bull Run
II. The Siege of Vicksburg
III. The Battle of Gettysburg
IV. The Battle of Antietam
V. The Siege of Richmond

(6) A jeweler lecturing on diamonds might arrange the first-degree points in this fashion:

I. Occurrence of diamonds
II. Production of diamonds
III. Preparation of diamonds
IV. Uses of diamonds

(7) In attempting to sell the trustees of a corporation on a program of management training, a public-relations specialist might use this topical arrangement:

I. A program for top management
II. A program for middle management: department managers
III. A program for lower management: supervisors and pre-supervisors

(8) A lawyer might follow this pattern when speaking to a group of businessmen about recent judicial decisions affecting the field of marketing:

I. Regulation of monopoly
II. Regulation of product characteristics
III. Regulation of price competition
IV. Regulation of channels of distribution
V. Regulation of unfair competition

(9) The following topical headings could be used in a speech on recent trends in advertising:

I. Recent trends in newspaper advertising
II. Recent trends in direct-mail advertising
III. Recent trends in radio advertising
IV. Recent trends in television advertising
V. Recent trends in magazine advertising

We have established that the Topical Pattern is the natural division of a subject into its component topics or parts. Now let us examine certain requirements for placing the main heads in the most effective logical and psychological order.

Ordinarily, you should arrange your major headings so that the strongest, most interesting topics are placed first and last, with the weakest, least interesting ones in between. Psychologists tell us that if a series of numbers is presented to an audience, the first and last numerals mentioned will be remembered more often than any others. Hence, begin and close your case with your most compelling arguments. By means of your preliminary analysis, you know which of your topics will be most important and interesting to your listeners. If at a meeting of union men you are delivering a speech (see page 87) designed to show that coal strikes are harmful, you would arrange the main heads in this manner:

I. Coal strikes are harmful to the miners
II. Coal strikes are harmful to the mine owners
III. Coal strikes are harmful to the general public

Being union men, the listeners will be more concerned about the miners than the mine owners and, since they are a part of the general public, will be vitally interested in this topic. Probably least important and least interesting to this audience are the harmful results to the mine owners. Therefore, the discussion about the owners should be placed in the middle between the more "interesting" heads.

When speaking on a technical or involved subject, proceed from the simplest topic to the most complex. Think how unsuccessful a university course in statistics would be if the professor began the semester with difficult problems of standard deviation, distribution curves, and complicated formulas that the class should normally encounter only near the end of the term. The accepted procedure in specialized courses like statistics is to begin with material which the students should have mastered prior to enrolling. Then, as the students gradually build up new understanding, they are able to strike out into more difficult fields. A golf professional instructing beginners in approved methods of gripping a club will not begin with a description of those grips designed to cause deliberate hooking or slicing. It is true that tournament golfers are able to curve the ball around obstacles by varying the hand grip on the club. However, pupils will become confused if exposed to the more difficult grips before understanding thoroughly the normal, standard manner. A dance instructor teaches a class of beginners how to walk in time to music, then how to follow simple steps to rhythm, before introducing the complicated routines of the conga or the rumba. An engineer instructing a class in the various uses of the slide rule might arrange his "topics" in the following simple-to-complex sequence:

I. Using the slide rule for multiplication
II. Using the slide rule for division
III. Using the slide rule to secure roots
IV. Using the slide rule to secure logarithms
V. Using the slide rule to find the functions of angles

When using the Topical Pattern, arrange the main heads in an order of understandability from simple to complex. Thus you will enable the audience to acquire necessary background information as the speech progresses. You should take every precaution to insure that your material remains within the comprehension of your listeners.

PART III. MORE ADVANCED PATTERNS OF ORGANIZATION

A. Problem-Solution Pattern. Every day we are confronted with problem-solving situations. We must determine what to buy at the grocery store for Sunday dinner, which tie to select to go with a new gabardine suit, how to get our office force to work more efficiently, what to do about the couple next door who have noisy, late parties, how best to invest the $5,000 Uncle Harry left in his will, and so forth.

As a public speaker you may wish to inform an audience about a problem and how that problem is being solved. A weather bureau official might show how modern methods of storm detection and protection have minimized the destructiveness of hurricanes. The personnel manager of a large industrial concern might tell a meeting of the board of directors about a problem in labor relations encountered recently in the plant and how his department handled the situation successfully. Much of the teaching at the advanced military schools, such as the National War College, is based upon the problem-solution method: i.e., here is a problem of logistics and this is a way the problem could be solved; here is a problem of strategy and here are some possible answers. In general, the application of the Problem-Solution Pattern for the speech to inform is similar to the methodology we will discuss in the following pages for the persuasive speech.

A talk advocating the adoption of a particular policy or course of action is using problem-solution. Here are some sample Specific Speech Purposes which are well adapted to the Problem-Solution Pattern for organizing the Discussion.

To convince my audience that: (1) reciprocal trade agreements should be curtailed by the federal government; (2) Los Angeles should be granted a major league franchise; (3) a $7,000,000 parking garage should be constructed in the downtown area; (4) the disobedient prisoners in cell block number five should be placed in solitary confinement; (5) a loan of $25,000,000 should be granted by our bank to the Zeno Corporation for the construction of a new factory; (6) the Atlantic and Pacific Tea Company should be broken up into several autonomous corporations; (7) a program of compulsory military training should be adopted in the United States. (For additional examples see exercise 7, pages 107, 108.)

The basic format of the Problem-Solution Pattern: In using this method the customary procedure is to present the problem and then offer the solution. The main heads of this basic format may be arranged as follows:

I. *Problem Step*
  A. Importance of the problem
    (As we will see in Chapter 7, this heading probably should be placed in the Introduction as a part of the *Favorable Attention Step*)
  B. Nature of the problem
    1. Aspect no. 1

    2. Aspect no. 2
    3. Aspect no. 3
    4. Aspect no. 4
  C. Cause or causes of the problem

II. *Solution Step*
  A. Explanation of the plan
  B. The plan will work
    1. The plan will solve the problem
      a. Plan will solve aspect no. 1 of the problem
      b. Plan will solve aspect no. 2 of the problem
      c. Plan will solve aspect no. 3 of the problem
      d. Plan will solve aspect no. 4 of the problem
    2. The plan can be put into operation
  C. The plan is the best solution available
  D. The plan will not create additional severe problems

By following this simple outline which will fit almost any problem-solving talk, you may be assured of presenting a well-organized address. The basic format is a broad highway, well marked and mapped. *As you gain experience, you may wish to omit certain heads, or to rearrange them to fit the exigencies of a particular address or speech situation.*

Now, we will take up in detail each of the main heads of the basic format. First let us examine main head A of the "Problem Step": "Importance of the problem." As indicated in the outline on page 91, this heading probably belongs in the Introduction as part of the Favorable Attention Step. However, for emphasis and completeness let us mention this vital element as a part of the Problem Step. Before they will give close attention, the listeners must recognize that the problem possesses significant import to their lives. Problems of genuine importance may not be so recognized by the audience, unless the significance is set forth by the speaker. (For a more complete discussion refer to pages 164–166.)

The second major heading B under the "Problem Step" is "Nature of the problem." Before an undesirable situation or condition can be remedied, a clear understanding of the nature or character of the problem must be present. As the famed inventor Charles F. Kettering once said, "A problem well stated is a problem half solved." You must present a felt need which should be satisfied, a situation which should be improved, a genuine and serious problem which should be solved. Before an audience will accept a new policy it must be convinced that the present situation or the *status quo* is unsatisfactory. If no need for change exists, why should a new policy or program be instituted? In order for a health commissioner to persuade the city council to prohibit bathing at the municipal beaches, he would have to prove that the water was polluted and unsafe for swimming.

We recommend that the beginning speaker handle this main head, "Nature of the problem," by dividing the problem into its major aspects or phases. (See the diagram on pages 91, 92.) When the speaker in his address comes to main head *B*, "The plan will work," of the "Solution Step," he will show how his plan will solve each of these phases. In a speech advocating the adoption of socialized medicine, the problem might be divided into these parts:

Main head *B, Nature of the problem,* under the *Problem Step*
1. The general health of the nation is unsatisfactory
2. People of meager income cannot afford adequate medical attention
3. Certain areas of the country have a disproportionately small share of the available medical facilities
4. Medical research is not progressing rapidly enough

In an attempt to persuade the managerial staff of his club to hire a rookie named Greenfield, a baseball scout might use the following sequence:

Main head *B, Nature of the problem,* under the *Problem Step*
1. The Green Sox need greater infield reserve strength
2. The Green Sox need pinch-hitting power
3. The Green Sox need better team morale

By glancing ahead to page 95, the reader will find an explanation of the method which may be used to answer these parts of the problem.

Main head *C* under the "Problem Step": "Cause or causes of the problem," is not always important in the analysis of a problem. Also, the causes of a problem may be obvious, therefore needing no explanation. If you should go to a doctor with a broken arm, it would not be necessary for him to learn what caused the break in order to set the arm. If you were urging that federal funds be appropriated to relieve slum conditions in your city, you would need to present clearly the picture of the existing conditions, but not necessarily what caused those conditions.

However, at times the validity of a solution will depend upon how accurately you have analyzed the cause of the difficulty. We have seen that a doctor does not need to know the cause of a simple fracture of the ulna in order to set the bone. However, to carry the analogy a little further, should you complain to a physician about pains in the stomach and in the lumbar region of the back, it is exceedingly important that he diagnose the cause of your symptoms accurately. If he determined mistakenly that you were suffering from gallstones, the resulting operation would not solve your difficulty. Your aches would continue until the real cause of the trouble was found, thereby permitting correct therapy. Similarly, if speaking to a school board about a delinquent child, you will have to be accurate in your diagnosis of the reasons which motivate the boy's abortive behavior. In this case an incorrect determination of the cause might result in an unsatisfactory solution. Perhaps you believe the child's unorthodox conduct is produced by unfavorable home influence. Therefore, in your judgment the best solution is to take him from his parents and lodge him in the city's home for unwanted and wayward children. However, your plan will not solve this problem if the real cause lies in a severe hearing loss. Because the child cannot understand directions and class instruction he believes he is dull and inferior to other children—hence his becoming a disciplinary problem. Not infrequently, the speaker must prove that he has diagnosed carefully and accurately the cause of the problem.

Now that we have analyzed the parts of the "Problem Step," let us examine the different divisions of the "Solution Step." Main head A is naturally an "Explanation of the plan" or program which you advance as the solution. After presenting the various aspects of the "Problem Step," you will need to explain the policy or course of action you are advocating as the answer to the problem. Clarity of exposition is exceedingly important here. The audience must understand the nature of the plan you are proposing. Sometimes a single sentence of explanation will suffice. If you were urging the Civil Service board to fire a policeman, your "Explanation of the plan" (which, of course, would follow your presentation of the "Problem Step") would probably consist of a simple declaration: "Gentlemen, in view of the proven charges against this man, the only course of action is to fire him immediately." However, if you were advocating the establishment of a permanent United Nations police force, you would have to explain carefully the nature of this force: the number and types of troops, how the members would be selected, and how this force would be financed.

The second main head *B* in the "Solution Step" is to demonstrate that "The plan will work." You must prove that your course of action will solve the problem and can be put into effect. Frequently students seem offended when fellow classmates refuse to accept a solution upon an assertion that it will solve a certain problem. Unless you are an individual of tremendous prestige, the audience will not be jarred from its customary pattern of thinking and behaving by an unsupported claim that the *status quo* could be improved if your plan were adopted. In many cases, proposed plans would solve existing problems *if* they could be put into effect. Such "solutions" are not solutions at all; it would be impossible to get them into operation. We have heard asserted that the best way to stop cheating in universities is for everyone to be honest. If all students were honest, there would certainly be no cheating. But how do we get this plan of universal honesty into practical execution? A speaker suggesting that a $7,000,000 garage be constructed in the downtown area to solve the parking problem, must *prove* that his plan will actually work. He must marshal evidence to show that such a building would reduce appreciably existing parking difficulties. Indeed, he must go further: he must prove that the construction could be financed, that a proper site could be secured, and that materials would be available.

Previously we suggested that the inexperienced speaker handle the heading, "Nature of the problem," by breaking the problem into its major parts. When this procedure is adopted, the speaker must show under the appropriate main head, "The plan will work," that his program will solve each of these phases and that the plan can be put into effect. For the purpose of clarity we will repeat the subheads (listed on page 93) of the speech advocating socialized medicine, then will illustrate how the speaker could develop the main head, "The plan will work."

Main head *B, Nature of the problem,* under the *Problem Step*
 1. The general health of the nation is unsatisfactory

2. People of meager income cannot afford adequate medical attention

3. Certain areas of the country have a disproportionately small share of the available medical facilities

4. Medical research is not progressing rapidly enough

Main head *B*, *The plan will work*, under the *Solution Step*
1. The plan will solve the problem
   a. Socialized medicine will improve the general health of the nation
   b. Socialized medicine will provide adequate medical attention to people of all income groups
   c. Socialized medicine will provide a fair geographical distribution of the available medical facilities
   d. Socialized medicine will stimulate medical research
2. The plan can be put into effect
   (The speaker could state here that the plan can be financed, that the public wants it, that the doctors and nurses will cooperate with the plan, and that sufficient facilities can be provided to make the plan work)

On page 93, we discussed the "Nature of the problem," for a talk suggesting the purchase of a rookie named Greenfield. We will repeat those main heads and then give the arrangement of the heading, *The plan will work.*

Main head *B*, *Nature of the problem*, under the *Problem Step*
1. The Green Sox need greater infield reserve strength
2. The Green Sox need pinch-hitting power
3. The Green Sox need better team morale

Main head *B*, *The plan will work* under the *Solution Step*
1. The plan will solve the problem
   a. Tom Greenfield would make an excellent utility infielder for the Sox
   b. Greenfield would greatly strengthen the Sox's pinch-hitting power
   c. Greenfield is a great team man, a booster of morale
2. The plan can be put into effect
   (The speaker could show that the club which owned the rookie's contract would release him for a nominal sum, that the Green Sox club could easily afford to buy the contract, and that the

player was eager to join the Sox and could arrive for active duty
within two days)

The reader will realize that the two preceding outlines are not
intended to represent complete outlines. We have included them for
the purpose of illustrating the methodology in proving that "the
plan will work." We have omitted other heads of the "Problem Step"
and the "Solution Step" present in the basic format.

Main head C of the "Solution Step" is to show that the plan proposed is "The best available solution." When the audience is aware
of several possible solutions to a problem, the speaker needs to
demonstrate that his plan is the most satisfactory one. The technique of accomplishing this purpose is called the method of residues.
When a chemist pours a fluid into a test tube and filters off the
liquid, the solid material remaining is the residuum or residue.
When using this method the speaker will show why other possible
policies are unsatisfactory, eliminating them as "answers." He should
then demonstrate how his plan is superior to the other programs. In
addressing the Senate Banking and Currency Committee during
August of 1950, an advocate of the Bernard Baruch proposal (total
mobilization of the nation's economy) might have used the method
of residues in this way. After presenting the problem and the nature
of the Baruch plan as the solution, he might have taken up Taft's
"hands-off" program and shown that it would be completely inadequate; he might then have shown how President Truman's program
of partial mobilization would be a "dangerous invitation to inflation." If successful in convincing the Senators that no mobilization
at all would be infeasible, and that partial mobilization would be
dangerous, they would have had no alternative but to accept the
Baruch plan of total mobilization.

Perhaps a word of caution should be interjected here. Under
certain circumstances it may be psychologically weak for the speaker
to introduce counter proposals in order to show their weaknesses.
Unless your plan is obviously stronger than the other propositions,
you probably should not use the method of residues. If your listeners
are not likely to think of other possible solutions, or if they are
emotionally conditioned in favor of another policy, it is usually wiser
not to bring up alternatives. A cardinal rule for the speaker who
would be persuasive is, whenever possible, to keep the attention of

the audience focused upon the benefits and services offered by his plan.

The final main head *D* under the "Solution Step" is to prove that "The plan will not create additional serious problems." Your remedy for an unsatisfactory condition might solve the problem, and might be the best available solution, but even then might not be suitable. In solving the existing problem your solution might create additional difficulties as bad as or worse than the initial ones. A politician advocating the adoption of federal aid to education must prove that such a program would not result in thought control in the schools. Many persons feel that should the federal government supply funds it would establish mandatory standards and controls exerting insidious pressure upon teachers and administrators. Such a consequence would be a much more disastrous situation than that now presented by inadequate financing.

Following World War II and prior to the Korean "police action," speakers for military preparedness had little difficulty in convincing Congress that Russia constitutes a menace to our national security and that increasing expenditures for defense would give us additional security. However, military conservatives reasoned that the tremendous appropriations necessitated by a seventy-group air force, for example, would result in dislocating the delicate balance of our economy, which in turn might lead to uncontrollable inflation. Since such inflation would be "worse" than the original problem of semi-preparedness, Congress did not heed the warning voices.

The authors recommend that you learn thoroughly the Basic Format of the Problem-Solution Pattern. Once this is accomplished, you may adjust the basic procedure to meet needs imposed by time limitations or by the type of material available. In the following outline of a speech (addressed to an audience of middle-aged businessmen) using the Problem-Solution Pattern, observe that the problem does not lend itself to a division into major phases. Nor is it necessary for the speaker to show under the heading, "The plan will work," that the recommended course of action can be put into effect. In this case it is obvious that the listener can, if he wishes, put the solution into operation.

Specific Speech Purpose: To persuade my audience to enroll for the Y.M.C.A. physical-fitness program.

INTRODUCTION:

I. *Favorable Attention Step:*
(The speaker could use any of the nine methods which will be discussed in Chapter 7. Probably he would refer to the significance of the subject by showing the direct relationship of physical fitness upon health, life span, business success, appearance, and personality.)

II. *Clarification Step:*
(The speaker could use any or all of the three methods analyzed in Chapter 7. In this particular speech a brief statement of the POINT should be sufficient.)

DISCUSSION:

I. *Problem Step:*
A. Nature of the problem
(Show that most persons in or nearing middle age need physical reconditioning.)
B. Cause of the problem
(Give logical reasons why people lose their physical fitness as they near middle age: overeating, too little exercise, and absorption in business and family affairs.)

II. *Solution Step:*

A. Explanation of the plan:
(Explain the nature of the Y.M.C.A. program for reconditioning middle-aged men—what is done during the classes, how long each session lasts, how many times a week the class meets, how many weeks the course extends, how much it costs, and who directs the group.)
B. The plan will work:
(Prove that the course will improve one's physical condition. Use examples of men who have benefited by the course, offer testimonials of satisfied ex-students, and give statistical evidence that the average student loses weight.)
C. The plan is the best solution:
(Convince the audience that the Y.M.C.A. program is superior to other methods of physical reconditioning because it is more economical, more fun, more effective, and safer.)
D. The plan will not create additional severe problems:
(Show that the Y.M.C.A. program will not interfere with one's normal routine. The classes do not take much time, and do not enervate because of overexercising or because of rigid dieting. There is no embarrassment connected with the course because

everyone in the class is attending in order to improve himself physically.)

CONCLUSION:

I. *Summary Step:*
   (Summarize briefly the most important points presented in the Discussion.)

II. *Action Step:*
   (Make a direct plea that after the meeting the listeners call the Y.M.C.A. physical education director, Dr. Dorsi, at Mulberry 25367, and enroll for the physical fitness program.)

Notice that references to the "Importance of the problem," were inserted as a part of the Favorable Attention Step of the Introduction. For the sake of completeness the Conclusion was also included. A full discussion of the organization of the Conclusion will appear in Chapter 8.

An abbreviated method of using the Problem-Solution Pattern: In this method the speaker is concerned only with presenting the major phases of the problem and with showing how his plan will solve them. The chief advantage of the *Abbreviated Problem-Solution Pattern* is that it is much easier to use for a short speech (under ten minutes) than is the Basic Format. However, the Basic Format is more complete and, in general, is more persuasive.

THE ABBREVIATED PATTERN

I. First argument
   A. Aspect No. 1 of the problem
   B. The plan will solve aspect No. 1 of the problem
II. Second argument
   A. Aspect No. 2 of the problem
   B. The plan will solve aspect No. 2 of the problem
III. Third argument
   A. Aspect No. 3 of the problem
   B. The plan will solve aspect No. 3 of the problem
IV. Fourth argument
   A. Aspect No. 4 of the problem
   B. The plan will solve aspect No. 4 of the problem

APPLICATION OF PATTERN

I. First argument
   A. The general health of the nation is unsatisfactory
   B. Socialized medicine will improve the general health of the nation

II. Second argument
A. People of meager income cannot afford adequate medical attention
B. Socialized medicine will provide adequate medical attention to people of all income groups
III. Third argument
A. Certain areas of the country have a disproportionately small share of the available medical facilities
B. Socialized medicine will provide a fair geographical distribution of the available medical facilities
IV. Fourth argument
A. Medical research is not progressing rapidly enough
B. Socialized medicine will stimulate medical research

B. Cause-and-Effect Pattern. Occasionally the most effective method of arranging the main heads of the Discussion is to use a causal relationship. Such a pattern may proceed from the *cause* to the *effect* (result), or from the *effect* to the *cause*. The speaker needs to make absolutely certain that the incidents, events, and factors which he offers as having produced a particular result actually have exerted a causal influence—thus avoiding the fallacy of *false cause*. The speaker must also avoid committing the familiar fallacy *post hoc ergo propter hoc* (after this, therefore because of this). We must not assume that merely because one thing follows another in time, the preceding happening causes the latter. The fact that your employer detected an error in your sales report this morning is not the *result* of your having seen a black cat last night, although black cats are supposed to cause bad luck. Science has completely repudiated the theory of prenatal influence. Yet recently in a conversation with one of the authors, a middle-aged woman violently condemned a mutual acquaintance for having caused his son to be born maimed and paralyzed. She was identifying illogically a causal connection with a time sequence. She reasoned that the child was born defective because several months earlier the expectant mother had been startled when her husband prankishly tossed a live turtle into her lap. Admittedly, this is an extreme example; however, the *post hoc* fallacy appears frequently when the Cause-and-Effect Pattern is used. Also, the speaker must avoid the fallacy of *false simplicity*. Do not oversimplify the cause by ignoring elements which have exerted significant influence in producing the given phenomenon or effect. It is fallacious to argue that since the desire for religious self-determination was important in causing the Pilgrims to seek homes in the American wilderness, it was the sole factor.

A historian reading a paper to a group of scholars on the subject of the important Colonial religious revival of 1739 to 1745 (called the Great Awakening) might use this causal relationship:

THE CAUSE

I. The basic predisposing causes of the revival:
(Under this head he would discuss the basic theological, economic, social, and political factors which over an extended time span motivated the revival.)
II. The immediate, precipitating causes of the revival:
(Here the speaker would analyze the events which gave immediate rise to the revival, such as Jonathan Edwards' revival at Northampton, Massachusetts, and the arrival of the famed English evangelist, George Whitefield.)

THE EFFECT

III. The nature of the Great Awakening.
IV. The influence of the Great Awakening upon American history.

A Southerner discussing in some northern city the race problem of the South might use the Cause-and-Effect Pattern. Many critics have no sympathy for and little understanding of the attitude of the Southern whites toward the Negroes. By explaining the causes as well as the nature of the present situation, the speaker might be able to offer his hearers a new insight into the problem.

I. Causes for present race relations in the South:
(Under this heading the speaker would attempt an adequate interpretation of what has happened in the past to produce a type of race problem peculiar to the South.)
II. The nature of present race relations in the South:
(Here the speaker would describe the race situation as it exists today in the South. The present conditions are, of course, the effect or result of the causes discussed under the preceding main head.)

Sometimes it is more effective to discuss the effect before analyzing the cause. This would be true in the following example in which the speaker's purpose is to persuade the listeners that they should drive carefully.

I. Automobile accidents have horrible results.
   (To prove this point the speaker could offer statistics on the yearly toll of lives and maimings as a consequence of auto accidents. He would probably describe in some detail several disastrous wrecks. He might discuss other results of accidents such as lawsuits, inability to continue one's occupation, and expenses of hospital treatment.)
II. The causes of automobile accidents are well known.
   (The speaker would show the major causes of wrecks, such as carelessness, driving after drinking, mechanical failure, and speeding.)

C. Proposition of "Fact" Pattern. Note that the word "fact" is enclosed by quotation marks. Such "facts" are not scientifically demonstrable. They cannot be put in a test tube for analysis, nor laid upon a scale for weighing, nor inserted in a maze for experimentation. Instead, they are debatable, subjective points of view which can be proved true or accurate only by logical argument; they are not amenable to measurement by the yardsticks of science.

A *Proposition of "Fact"* attempts to prove that a particular thesis, opinion, belief, view, or proposition is a "fact," i.e., is true, valid, accurate, or workable. Here are some Specific Speech Purposes which can be organized according to the *Proposition of "Fact" Pattern*: To convince an audience that (1) Stan Musial is the best hitter in modern baseball; (2) Chiang Kai-shek's government is corrupt; (3) Al Capp's drawings of Daisy Mae are indecent; (4) "pop" quizzes are unfair; (5) the legal profession is overcrowded; (6) T. S. Eliot's *Notes Toward the Definition of Culture* is unsatisfactory reading; (7) the sales tax discriminates against the low-income group. (For additional examples see exercise 9, page 108.)

Notice that none of the preceding speech purposes advocate the adoption of a policy or a course of action. We are concerned here with propositions of "fact," not with propositions of policy which are inherent in the Problem-Solution Pattern. (The reader is referred to pages 107 and 108 for a list of speech purposes for the Problem-Solution Pattern.)

Two basic steps are involved in the organization of the Proposition of "Fact" Pattern. First, the speaker must determine the yardsticks, standards of measurement, or criteria which are accurate gauges of whether or not the proposition is a "fact." Second, he must

match the proposition against the standards. If the proposition
meets the criteria, it is a "fact"; if it does not, it is not a "fact." As
an example of how this procedure works, we will assume that you
have applied at a large construction firm for the position of structural engineer to be stationed in South America. The personnel
director pulls from his files a manila folder containing the carefully
prepared requirements the successful candidate must possess. Here
are some of the possible queries the director might ask: Are you a
graduate of a recognized engineering school? Was your grade average "B" or better? Can you speak Spanish? Have you had a minimum of five years' experience as a structural engineer? Can you
provide suitable references? If you can answer "yes" to each of these
questions, you will be an acceptable candidate. You will have proved
your proposition of "fact": "I am qualified for the position of structural engineer with this firm."

Here is a schematic outline of the Discussion of a speech using
the Proposition of "Fact" Pattern.

    I. Criterion No. 1
      A. State the criterion
      B. Show how the proposition meets this criterion
   II. Criterion No. 2
      A. State the criterion
      B. Show how the proposition meets this criterion
 III. Criterion No. 3
      A. State the criterion
      B. Show how the proposition meets this criterion

Although the novice should use the pattern above, the experienced
speaker might find it unnecessary to state each criterion as such,
especially if the audience is cognizant of the appropriate yardsticks
or criteria. The skilled speaker might omit all of the main heads
labeled *A* in the following example.

Specific Speech Purpose: To convince the school board that John
Housener would make a fine head basketball coach at Central High
School

    I. Criterion No. 1
      A. A high-school basketball coach should be a good moral example
      B. Housener is a fine moral example for high-school athletes

II. Criterion No. 2
  A. A coach should have a sound knowledge of basketball science
  B. Housener possesses exceptional knowledge of basketball know-how
III. Criterion No. 3
  A. The position demands a man of successful experience
  B. Housener has a brilliant record as a high-school coach
IV. Criterion No. 4
  A. A coach should be skilled in public relations
  B. Housener has a genial personality which enables him to get along well with students and townspeople alike

In preparing the preceding outline, the speaker determined what qualifications the head basketball coach at Central High School should have; then he proved that his candidate, Housener, possessed the requirements. He has built a strong case. He has shown that his candidate is a fine moral example for his students to emulate, that he is a fine court strategist with an impressive record, and that he has the type of personality to bring out the best qualities of his players and to keep pleasant relations with parents and adults of the community.

SUMMARY

Most speakers organize the Discussion of the speech before the Introduction or Conclusion. The two steps in selecting the main heads of the Discussion are: (1) Compiling an Analysis List and (2) Evolving from this list the two to five major divisions. The main heads, being coordinate points, must be selected before supporting materials are placed under any particular head. Select primary heads according to one of the six basic patterns. Although the speech to inform may be organized according to any of these methods, Topical and Time Patterns are most frequently used. Topical and Time Patterns also are the standard ways of developing the speech to entertain. Speeches to persuade invariably can be planned according to a Problem-Solution or a Proposition of "Fact" Pattern. Topical and Cause-and-Effect sequences may also be used to develop the persuasive speech. With a little practice, the inexperienced speaker can become adept at the use of all of these basic methods of organization.

1. Prepare a three-minute speech involving a personal experience. Notice that because in "real life" one happening chronologically follows another, such a talk almost inevitably follows a Time Pattern.

2. Prepare a three-minute speech in which you state agreement or disagreement with a newspaper headline. Give two to five reasons for your stand. You are now using a Topical Pattern.

3. In a three-minute talk attempt to persuade the class to enroll for a particular course. Describe the nature of the course and the benefits students would derive from the course.

4. Make a five-minute "how-to-do-it" talk or a "process" talk in which you select two to five main steps or stages as your main heads. This is a Time Pattern. Possible topics:
   (1) How to fell a tree
   (2) How to draw a contour map
   (3) How to make ceramics
   (4) How to make slip covers
   (5) How to convert an attic into a play room
   (6) How to conduct a business meeting
   (7) How to make a time and motion study
   (8) How to conduct a marketing survey
   (9) How to organize a political club
   (10) How to clean a gun
   (11) How to finger paint
   (12) How to quit smoking
   (13) How to make a hooked rug
   (14) How a book is prepared (from its inception until it reaches the bookstore)
   (15) How plywood is made
   (16) How the wounded are evacuated from the front lines
   (17) How false teeth are made
   (18) How meat is koshered
   (19) How a feature article is prepared for *Time* magazine.
   (20) How a case is handled by the United States Supreme Court

5. Deliver a five-minute talk based upon a Spatial Pattern. Possible topics:
   (1) The physical characteristics of an atomic submarine
   (2) A ram jet engine

(3) The layout of a formal garden
(4) A window display
(5) Your college campus
(6) The renovated White House
(7) A famous golf course
(8) A dude ranch
(9) A fishing reel
(10) A jai alai court
(11) A stained glass window in a church
(12) Kezar Stadium or Soldier Field
(13) The Abraham Lincoln Memorial in Washington, D.C.
(14) The basic design of the Pentagon Building
(15) A gun turret on a battleship

6. Deliver a five-minute speech using a Topical Pattern. Possible subjects:
(1) Standard offensive and defensive football formations
(2) Contributions to society of the Kiwanis Clubs
(3) The objectives of F.E.P.C.
(4) Openings in industry for college graduates
(5) The business cycle
(6) Being a good listener
(7) Ways in which card sharks cheat
(8) Vitamins for health
(9) Methods by which manufacturing can be stimulated in New England
(10) Evils of the share-crop system
(11) Advantages of proper training for our policemen
(12) New methods for treatment of the insane
(13) Safety in the home
(14) Types of fallacies used by politicians
(15) Interesting customs of the Chinese

7. Prepare a seven- to ten-minute speech using each of the steps of the basic Problem-Solution Pattern. In giving this speech to a "real" audience, would it be more effective to omit certain of these main heads? Why? Appropriate topics:
(1) Fee-splitting among physicians should be made a federal offense
(2) All hidden taxes should be abolished in favor of heavier income taxes
(3) America should adopt a policy of free trade
(4) Jail sentences should be mandatory for all those convicted of drunken driving

(5) Women should be given equal legal rights and responsibilities with men

(6) Big cities should be given fair representation in state legislatures

(7) Universities should adopt a grading system based upon two marks: passing or failing

(8) Fraternities and sororities should be abolished in high schools

(9) All candidates for the Presidency should be compelled to take a rigid health examination

(10) Hazing at universities should be abolished

(11) Congress should adopt the Hoover Commission suggestions for the reorganization of our legislative system

(12) The present electoral system in voting for President and Vice-President should be abolished in favor of a system of direct popular vote

(13) Labor unions should be compelled by law to make public annual financial reports of receipts and expenditures

(14) A program of sex education should be instituted in our public schools

(15) A fifty-dollar deductible health insurance program should be adopted by the federal government

8. Using the same basic material as in exercise 7, deliver a five-minute speech based on the short pattern of Problem-Solution.

9. Prepare a seven- to ten-minute speech using the standard Proposition of "Fact" Pattern. Sample topics:

(1) The Old Guard dominates the Republican Party

(2) Big city machines control the Democratic Party

(3) Ben Hogan is the greatest star in the history of golf

(4) Reducing pills are harmful

(5) The administration of President Truman blundered into the Korean War

(6) Joseph Martin is an isolationist (or an internationalist)

(7) College football is too commercialized

(8) Government employment offers unusual opportunities for young lawyers

(9) Milk is a splendid health food

(10) The local transit system is inefficient (or efficient)

(11) Socialism in England has been a failure (or a success)

(12) German nationalism constitutes a potential threat to peace

(13) Turnpikes help rather than hurt local merchants

(14) Reciprocal trade agreements promote international good will

(15) The only way to avoid World War III is for America to keep strong

10. Prepare a five-minute speech using the Cause-and-Effect Pattern. Some possible subjects:
  (1) Corruption in our state government
  (2) The financial condition of our fraternity (or of our business)
  (3) Spirit at our university (or at our factory)
  (4) Vice in our nation's capital
  (5) Waste in the armed services
  (6) Unnecessary medical operations
  (7) Excessive smoking
  (8) Our antiquated executive system
  (9) Teachers' pay
  (10) Reno—the nation's divorce mill
  (11) The New South
  (12) The present crisis in the U.N.
  (13) The new titans of industry—labor leaders
  (14) The French economy of today
  (15) The present balance of power between the East and the West

11. In examining the previous lists of topics, did you notice that many topics could be organized according to more than one type of pattern? Make a list of these subjects with other possible plans for their organization.

CHAPTER 6

Discovering and Using
The Supporting Materials

Chapter 5 discussed the selecting and the arranging of the main heads of the Discussion. In this chapter our concern is to learn to develop these points in accord with the knowledge, interests, and attitudes of the audience, the particular needs of the occasion, and the logical demands of the subject. Main headings by themselves present only a sparse framework of the major pattern or sequence of thought. They are mere statements or assertions without the necessary supporting materials to make them clear, vivid, and persuasive.

PART I. FORMS OF SUPPORT

Just as the builder has certain materials which he uses to construct a house, so a public speaker has definite materials which can be utilized to develop the main heads of the speech. Instead of plaster, lumber, and mortar, the speaker uses illustrations, statistics, comparison, testimony, restatement, explanation, deductive and causal reasoning, and visual aids. The typical manner of using the forms of support is to state the heading under consideration, present the supporting material, and then show how that evidence has helped develop the point. This is called the *didactic* method. Occasionally the speaker may wish to present the supporting material first, and then to point out the argument or heading it amplifies. Such a method of *implication* should be used sparingly by the beginning speaker. Whichever type of presentation is used, each item of support must develop, amplify, or clarify its immediately superior heading. Furthermore, to have the desired effect it must be well adapted to the intellectual and emotional needs of the listeners. In the following sections we will discuss the strengths and weaknesses of each form of support, point out certain overlappings, and offer some rules for the effective use of each type.

ILLUSTRATION OR EXAMPLE

From the earliest days of man's history, the story-teller has commanded rapt attention. An illustrative narrative vividly presented has high entertainment value. Everyone enjoys hearing a story. Anyone who has read the New Testament knows that Christ resorted almost exclusively to the narrative as his teaching methodology because of its persuasiveness and its interest-provoking qualities. Aristotle urged his students to use at least one example to support every important point. James A. Winans, one of the patriarchs of modern speech teaching, called the example "the very life of the speech." Alben Barkley suggests that the beginning speaker become skilled in the use of illustrations. Perhaps of all the forms of support the example is the most adaptable and the most effective.

What is an illustration? It is the narration of a happening or incident which brings into clearer focus the point under consideration. The chief power of the illustration is that it tells a story vividly, thereby making possible a combined appeal to both the intellect and the emotions. The three types of illustration are the detailed factual, the undeveloped factual, and the hypothetical.

A. The detailed factual illustration

1. *Nature and purpose of the detailed factual illustration.* This type of example is an extended narration of a true occurrence or event. It tells the story of how something happened. The use of dialogue and of detail concerning the motives, appearance, and behavior of the persons involved, the locality, weather, smells, sounds, action, and the like enable the speaker to paint a graphic word picture that carries the audience along as the story unfolds. The detailed factual illustration offers persuasive evidence. In order to prove that state boxing commissions should retire fighters who risk permanent injury, you might relate the true story of a particular fighter: because he persisted in fighting even after it grew obvious that he was absorbing terrific and repeated batterings he became "punch drunk." If told convincingly and supplemented by additional

evidence, your example should exert an impelling effect. The detailed true illustration also promotes interest and clarity. To explain the neighborliness of the man who just moved in next door, you might mention how he came over to help you cut grass one morning and even brought some clippers to trim the hedge. By telling the story you should have vividly clarified your statement that the man is a good neighbor. Notice how the following excerpt from a student's speech, delivered after the close of World War II, made his point vivid, clear, and persuasive.[1]

Statement of the Main Head

Everyone thinks of war in dramatic terms of horrible loss of life, the thousands of wounded and disabled, and the wasteful economic destruction. Any of these is certainly a sufficient reason to convince us that we never again can afford to engage in war. But let us not forget this other group of war casualties, the ordinary guys who came back—who present an additional, powerful reason for resolving that we must not have another international holocaust. No, the war is not over for them, either. Because of them, also, we dare not afford another war.

Illustration No. I

Those of us who may be forgetting should consider the case of John, a good friend of mine who was with the Marines in Iwo Jima. Fact of the matter is, John got the top of his head blown off by a Jap mortar shell. And the platinum plate in his skull will always give him headaches. John's a university student now, and last semester he flunked every subject. Not that John isn't intelligent. But the VA doctors are worried about his nervousness. They tell him it interferes with his concentration. When John talks about the war, he gets just a little too excited. He tries to pass it off glibly, by bragging about how many notches he had in his rifle stock. But privately, he'll tell you he killed only one Jap while he was overseas—killed that Jap by beating him over the head with the butt-end of a carbine. And as he tells you about it, he's still a little horrified at what he did; a little terrified at the mental picture he

---

[1] George W. McBurney, "The Road Back," *Winning Orations, Northern Oratorical League Contests, 1945–1950,* Minneapolis, copyright 1951 by The Northwestern Press, pp. 158–161.

gets of that Jap lying there in Iwo's volcanic cinders with his skull split open. Four years later, John is still haunted by a murder committed in the name of "peace in our time." Four years later, he's still traveling the road back and vainly searching for peace of mind.

John has a lot in common with the 1,700 veterans who left the University of Minnesota last year. About half of them withdrew either because of "academic reasons" or because of a rather ambiguous thing known to psychologists as "personality maladjustment." Per-

Application of Illustration to Main Head

haps many of them couldn't concentrate either. When you spend from two to five years learning the gentle arts of murder and destruction, "personality maladjustment" isn't such an unusual ailment. Or, as Erich Remarque said another day, after another war: "Do you think that four years' killing can be wiped off the brain with the flabby word 'Peace' as with a wet sponge?"

Dare we forget that we cannot afford another war?

Then there's the case of Fred, one of my Dad's business associates. For three solid years, Fred was stationed on one of those nameless South Pacific islands, building an air strip which was never used. Nothing heroic about that. But when Fred finally got home, his lovely wife, Alice, just couldn't understand him. And his little boy

Illustration No. II

seemed to be afraid of him, which could probably be explained by Fred's personality when drunk. Fred finally divorced Alice and married a washed-out blonde he'd met in a local tavern. He says he's happy now. But his look belies his speech. Yes, Fred and Alice and their families have made their sacrifices in the name of "peace in our time." But their mental peace was lost on the road back.

Fred's story helps explain why the divorce rate in the United States nearly doubled between 1945 and 1948.

Application of Illustration to Main Head

Of course, all broken hearts and broken homes cannot be traced directly to armed service experiences. But as sociologist Grace Overton has written: "No other major human activity disintegrates families like war."

Dare we forget that we cannot afford another war?

And then there's the story of "Moose," a fraternity brother of mine who's a college football player. Five

Illustration No. III

Application of Illustration to Main Head

Illustration No. IV

years ago, Moose was a gunner in a B-17. He saw some rough action in Italy, but he'd much rather tell you about his army social life than his combat experiences. He was a punk kid then, a year out of high school. But before long he could drink his whole squadron right under the table. And he'll tell you about the time in Italy when the C.O. brought three truckloads of women into the squadron billeting area. The chaplain protested "through channels," but by the time any action was taken, the women had been there three days. And the C.O. simply said, "The boys are having a good time."

Moose is a "reconverted civilian" now. No combat fatigue for him. Of course, he drinks a little too much and about the only thing which interests him concerning women is sex. Moose made his little contribution to "peace in our time." But his road back to mental peace still stretches far into the future.

Ah, well, so Moose does drink a little. What's unusual about that? Well, the VA treated 20,000 veterans for alcoholism during the three years immediately following the war. Twenty thousand of the nation's finest— more than the population of an average-sized American city—a total loss to themselves and society because they're suffering from various stages of delirium tremens. And this 20,000 doesn't include the countless thousands like Moose who either have an "occasional drink" or who should be treated for alcoholism, but aren't.

Dare we forget that we cannot afford another war?

And finally, let's take the case of George. George went overseas early in 1945 as an infantry replacement. He got the Purple Heart and the Combat Infantryman's Badge, was recommended for the Bronze Star, and came home a family hero. But he'll never forget the shock of seeing his best friend crushed to death by a sixty-ton tank; or watching a battle-crazed GI fire on an American patrol; or helping subdue a drunken kid from California who went half insane when he discovered he'd shot a German woman he'd mistaken for a soldier. When he first came home from Europe, George's family weren't quite sure what had happened to him. His mother told him he "looked hard, talked hard, and was tough and crude." But today I guess I'm back to normal.

John, Fred, Moose, and I didn't win the war. We weren't heroes. In GI terminology, we were expendable. By comparison with the sacrifices of thousands of others, our contribution to "peace in our time" was ridiculously insignificant. But each of us has had difficulty in travel-

Application of Illustrations to Main Head

ing the road back. And some of us still have far to travel before we can have individual peace.

Although we can never forget the loss of human life and the material destruction which World War II vented upon humanity and civilization, we are forgetting the spiritual and emotional upheaval which it caused. We have been so engrossed in the obvious tragedies that we have missed the subtle ones. Is mental paralysis any less serious than physical disability? Is not a broken home more of a tragedy than a bomb-wrecked house? Is a drunkard any less of a liability to himself and society than a veteran with a leg gone?

The physical and economic costs of the war belong to the past. The spiritual and emotional costs belong to the present and future. The fourteen-million veteran-survivors of World War II will soon be the generation which leads the nation. Then they will no longer be expendable. In terms of the future, we dare not forget that we cannot afford another war.

2. Rules for the effective use of the detailed factual illustration: (1) The illustration must be relevant. Resist the temptation to use an example merely because it is a "good story." Because of the interest-getting qualities of the illustration, listeners will remember first the example and then the point it amplifies. A strained relationship between the illustration and its major head will inevitably produce confusion and misunderstanding. (2) Make clear to the audience the relationship of the example to the heading it supports. Recall that the preceding excerpt from a student's speech on the cost of war made a direct application of each illustration to the speaker's argument. (3) Use sufficient detail to be clear and vivid, but avoid obscuring the point with unnecessary particulars. (4) Develop the example in a plausible manner. In order to stimulate formation of the desired picture in the minds of the listeners, details must be presented in the proper order. A discussion of a skirmish in the Korean campaign should include early in the narration an explanation of the topography. Otherwise, the auditors will be uncertain as to the nature of the terrain. Once they have mentally placed the scene in a river valley or in rice-paddy country, confusion will result if you say, "Oh, I forgot to mention that these men were fighting in mountainous country with cliffs sometimes as sheer as elevator shafts." (5) Use a sufficient number and variety of illustrations. A general audience will usually include various economic, social, and intellectual levels and a correspondingly wide range of interests, attitudes, and experiences. One example may be insufficient to support an important point, since it may not be equally interesting or meaningful to all of the listeners. Therefore, when necessary, use several illustrations drawn from the major fields of interest represented in the audience. The utilization of several examples to support a particular head adds psychological strength by giving the impression of presenting a considerable mass of evidence. It offers logical strength by offering a more comprehensive coverage. (6) Occasionally it may be necessary to defend your examples as being fair representatives of the great mass of evidence rather than exceptions. (7) Use the Factors of Interest (discussed in Part III of this chapter) to develop the example. If deficient in vivid imagery, much of its power will be lost. (8) The details used to develop the example should be accurate. For example, if you use an illustration from the shop because some of the listeners are foremen, you must demonstrate an accurate grasp of information. Otherwise, not only your example, but your entire speech may be discredited.

B. The undeveloped factual illustration

1. *Nature and purpose of the undeveloped factual illustration:* This type of example is undetailed, condensed, and true-to-fact. Consisting of only essential elements, it is much shorter than the typical full-length illustration. Of course, a maximum word length cannot be assigned to the brief example. The basic point for the beginning speaker to remember is that some factual illustrations might be as long as ten or fifteen minutes, while others might be less than ten seconds.

The short illustration has several important values. Since the abbreviated example requires less time than the detailed one, a greater number of condensed illustrations can be presented within a given period. Thus the speaker is enabled to present a more adequate coverage and to appeal to additional fields of interest. The following excerpt from a student's speech demonstrates that by careful word choice two short illustrations may constitute a persuasive appeal although consuming no more time than a single extended example.

Statement of Main Head   How many of you have seen a person dying of cancer? Unfortunately, I have. Several years ago a friend of my father's was stricken with this disease. I visited him in the hospital. The man I remembered as *Short Illustration* a handsome, active, lively man had become emaciated and lifeless, a living cadaver who waited passively for death. I also had another occasion to visit a cancer victim. She had been a pianist, a woman whose life had been devoted to music. But at the peak of her career she too was stricken. I shall never forget the smell of *Short Illustration* medicine that hung heavy in that sickroom, nor those sunken, haunted, discolored eyes that peered from over protruding cheekbones as she gazed at her fleshless hands and murmured, "If I could only play just once more."

Application of Short Illustrations to Main Head   These were my only experiences with cancer and for that I say, "Thank God." I can think of nothing more appalling than actually watching your own body slowly waste away while enduring incessant agonies, a condition from which death is the only relief.

James H. Halsey, President of the University of Bridgeport, in his address on "Higher Education's Appalling Responsibilities"[2] shows that it is possible to compress much supporting evidence into a short space of time by means of the abbreviated example.

Statement of Main Head   These are days of crises and on every hand we see numerous evidences of attempts to curb freedom of thought and freedom of expression. Throughout the country we hear charges of "Communism" and "subversive" hurled at people who might disagree with the prevailing trend of thought. Responsible citizens have become victims of smear tactics, character assassins, and

[2] *Vital Speeches*, November 1, 1951.

guilt by association. People are becoming fearful and timid. Social scientists have to be careful in their research work or in announcing their findings, and well-qualified citizens hesitate to risk their reputations in government service.

Short Illustration

Dr. Robert M. Hutchins, former chancellor of the University of Chicago, says that even he, who has certainly never tried to be a conformist, has been so intimidated of the guilt by association charges, that he refuses to join any organization, even one whose sole objective is merely to preserve and perpetuate Mother's Day in America.

Short Illustration

No doubt all of you recall the incident in Madison, Wisconsin, last Fourth of July, when American citizens were afraid to say they believed in the Declaration of Independence or the Bill of Rights. One hundred and twelve people were asked to sign a petition that contained nothing except quotations from these two immortal documents, and one hundred and eleven refused to sign the paper. Most refused because they were afraid it was some kind of subversive document and thought that if they signed it they would be called Communists.

Application to Main Head

In a democracy it is essential that all public issues be fully and objectively discussed. If the truth is to be established, all ideas, opinions, and facts, even those which some of us personally may disagree with, must be given full and open expression. Furthermore, these discussions must be kept on an impersonal plane, free from prejudice, self-interest, and vindictiveness.

The usefulness of the undetailed illustration for making a swift but vivid historical survey is shown in the following passage from President Truman's address on the first anniversary of the opening of the Korean hostilities.[3]

Statement of Main Head

At the same time [we tried to settle postwar problems with the Soviet Union] we made it clear to all the world that we would not engage in appeasement. When the Soviet Union began its campaign of undermining and destroying other free nations we did not sit idly by.

[3] *Vital Speeches*, July 15, 1951.

We came to the aid of Greece and Turkey when they stood in danger of being taken over by Communist aggression in 1947. As a result these countries today are free and strong and independent.

We came to the aid of the peoples of France and Italy in their struggle against the political onslaught of communism. In each of these countries communism has been defeated in two free elections since 1947. There is no longer any danger that they will vote themselves into the hands of the Soviet Union.

Series of Short Examples

We came to the aid of the brave people of Berlin when the Kremlin tried to take them over. We and our allies kept Berlin alive by the airlift and it is still free today.

We came to the aid of China when it was threatened by Communist civil war. We put billions of dollars worth of arms and supplies into China to aid the Chinese Nationalist Government. We gave them more help than we gave Greece or Turkey or Berlin or Italy. . . .

We are continuing to give aid to the Chinese Nationalists on Formosa, and that aid will be effective if they are willing to do their part.

Full-Length Illustration In Actual Speech Text

On June 25, 1950, one year ago today, the Communist rulers resorted to an outright war. They sent Communist armies on a mission of conquest against a small and peaceful country. . . .

There was only one thing to do in that situation—and we did it. . . . Today, after more than a million Communist casualties—after the destruction of one Communist army after another—the forces of aggression have been thrown back on their heels. . . .

We've been fighting this conflict in Korea to prevent a third world war. So far we have succeeded. We have blocked aggression. And we have kept the conflict from spreading. . . .

Application of Illustrations to Main Head

Never before in history have we taken such measures to keep the peace. . . . We have shown that we will fight to resist aggression. . . . Never before has an aggressor been confronted with such a series of positive measures to keep the peace. Never before in history have there been such deterrents to the outbreak of a world war.

2. *Rules for the use of the undeveloped factual illustration:* With certain additions, suggestions for the effective presentation of the short example are the same as those for the detailed illustration. (1) Select only the details which will give the essential elements of the illustration. Avoid all misleading or unnecessary data. (2) Rarely use an abbreviated example in isolation. Its brevity does not permit the developing of a complete word picture; therefore it does not exert as strong an appeal to the intellect or emotions as would an extended illustration. A more persuasive method is to present two or more short examples in the form of a series. For greater strength, such a series may be used in conjunction with some other form of support, especially the detailed example. The extended illustration would permit the speaker to make a strong appeal to the thinking and emotions of his listeners, and the short examples would give added strength through their more extensive coverage.

C. The hypothetical illustration

1. *Nature and purpose of the hypothetical illustration:* Sometimes when you are unable to secure a suitable factual example, you may wish to use an imaginary incident or happening. A hypothetical example frequently can be woven to meet the needs of your listeners better than can a true-to-fact illustration. It is a vivid method of explaining a complicated or technical process. For example, instead of describing how a theater panel board controls lighting effects, place an imaginary technician at the board to pull the appropriate switches, turn the wheels, and punch the buttons. The narration of such a fictitious situation adds human interest to an otherwise dull explanation. The hypothetical illustration is also an excellent method for predicting future events. The horrors of a third world war were strikingly portrayed in the October 27, 1951, issue of *Collier's*, which was devoted to a "Preview of the War We Do Not Want." Among the articles was one by Edward R. Murrow, depicting his "experiences" on a hypothetical A-bomb mission to Moscow. In another article Lowell Thomas reported his eye-witness account of an imagined air-borne operation to destroy the Soviet A-bomb stockpile in the Ural Mountains. Such fictitious narrations made potential happenings seem graphically real.

This passage from a student's speech uses an extended hypothetical illustration to vitalize and clarify an otherwise abstract idea.[4]

Statement of the Main Head

Civilized man, today, refuses to view sickness with superstition or treat it with magic. Science has traced the cause of bubonic plague and that of smallpox. Sanity rules in the field of medicine. As we have conquered in the realm of disease, so must we conquer the social plague of war—isolate its germ and immunize humanity against it.

But whence does the infection come? Let us go back to about 1920. We are interested in a home where there is a mother and a baby. A home in America? Possibly—or in France or Germany. The mother watches over her child as it sleeps; holds it to her breast when it wakes; soothes it when it cries; and plays with it during its gayer hours. She guards it against harm and holds out protecting and encouraging arms as it learns to take its first faltering steps. To all this the child makes a loving response. To him the world is a place of affection. Between the mother and child is the strongest bond that ever earth has known, a bond that has built the family, the tribe, the nation, the world—a bond of love. Surely the germ of war is not here.

Extended Hypothetical Illustration

The baby grows to manhood. The year is 1944. We find him on the Normandy Peninsula. The fighting has become hand-to-hand. His bayonet drips with human blood. Blood is splattered on his clothes and on his face, but that doesn't matter. All that matters is the task before him. He stumbles forward over the bodies of comrade and foe, every muscle taut, every nerve set. With hate gleaming from his eye he looks for another enemy to gore with that cold steel he thrusts to the front.

Why the contrast? What has changed the life of this individual from one of love and harmony to one of chaotic madness?

Let us return to the mother and baby and trace the life of the child from the cradle to the Normandy

[4] Adapted from a prize-winning speech by Glen S. Faxon, Oregon State College.

Peninsula. On his fourth birthday he gets a set of tin soldiers and a toy cannon. Christmas comes and he receives, on the birthday of the Prince of Peace, a miniature tank. He starts to Sunday School and on the Sabbath studies the life of the biblical hero Samson, slaying a thousand Philistines with the jawbone of an ass, or of God blessing the Israelites with victory and leading them to the slaughter of other enemies. School begins. The day starts with a pledge of allegiance denoting separation, not cooperation of mankind. National songs are sung—a French boy learns "March On, March On to Victory" and a German lad sings "Deutschland Uber Alles." He studies a nationalistic brand of history. If he lives in Russia, he learns that Russian scientists have made all of the world's important discoveries.

As an older boy he joins a youth organization. While he may learn to do a good deed each day, he is clothed with a uniform representative of his nation's military forces—khaki, the brown shirt, or the black. If he lives in a Fascist country, he is initiated into military tactics.

Is it any wonder that, when the epidemic reaches a peak in 1944, we find this boy a victim of the black death of war? From early childhood he has been inoculated with its germs—germs contracted at home, at school, Sunday School, through the movies, novels, and even the comic strips of "Steve Canyon" and "Terry and the Pirates."

Application of
Illustration
to Main Head

2. **Rules for the effective use of the hypothetical illustration:** In addition to the suggestions mentioned previously for the detailed factual illustration, there are several additional points you should consider when using the fictitious example. (1) Never present a hypothetical example as being true to fact. Such intellectual dishonesty, if discovered, will prejudice your audience against you and your speech. (2) Ordinarily, avoid using an invented example if a true one is available. (3) The hypothetical illustration must be consistent with reality. It must appear reasonable, probable, and capable of happening. Wild flights of the imagination usually make ineffective illustrations. (4) Do not use the hypothetical example for purposes of conviction. Since the audience realizes that the hypothetical did not actually happen, other forms of support, such as the

factual illustration, quotation, or statistics, are much more persuasive as logical support. The relative power of the hypothetical and the factual illustration was once vividly demonstrated in the neighborhood of one of the authors. A mother was having difficulty keeping her two sons from putting things in their ears and noses. Her recitation of hypothetical examples of possible harmful effects failed to impress the boys. But, after one of the boys was sent to the hospital with an infected ear, the mother had a compelling true example to discourage such behavior.

STATISTICS

A. **Nature and purpose of statistics:** Statistics are figures which help the speaker develop an argument. When skillfully presented, statistical evidence is persuasive proof. Unfortunately, however, it is one of the most misused forms of support. Too frequently speakers fail to consider the limited capacity of an audience to assimilate an uninterpreted, uninteresting series of numbers.

What would seem more innately dull than a recitation of figures to indicate the relative centralization of the steel industry? Yet Benjamin F. Fairless in an address [5] before the Baltimore Association of Commerce made such data stimulating and meaningful.

Statement of Main Head	And if [the government is] going to break up every industry which is as highly "concentrated" as the steel industry, *nearly half of the units in our American industrial machine will be torn apart.*
	Yes, that is the exact, indisputable fact.
	The United States Census Bureau has recently completed its latest count of more than 400 American industries, and has reported on the degree of so-called "concentration" in each. And remember, I am speaking of entire *industries*—not individual companies.
Presentation of Statistical Evidence	Now how many of these industries do you think are more highly "concentrated" than the steel industry. Three? . . . Ten? . . . Fifty?
	Well, guess again. The Census Bureau's own report on "steel works and rolling mills" shows that this industry is not anywhere near the top at all. It is in the great middle, along with the great body of all American

[5] *Vital Speeches*, June 15, 1950.

industries. In fact, it stands 174th on the list. *So there are 173 entire industries which are more highly concentrated than steel.*

Now what are some of these industries where the "concentration of power" in the hands of the "big four" is so great as to menace our national welfare and to arrest the pursuit of happiness?

You'd never guess.

There is the pretzel industry for one. Honestly, that's right. I mean it.

And there are the candle-makers, too.

Then there are straw hats and streetcars, breakfast foods and chewing tobacco, wallpaper and cigar boxes, lead pencils and pianos. Then we have women's neckwear and boys' underwear. And, oh yes—window shades and garters.

Now if every one of these—plus 159 other industries—is more highly "concentrated" than steel, and if "concentration" is really as wicked as our theorists tell us it is, I can't for the life of me understand why all these high-priced Congressional Committees are wasting their time on me.

Application of Statistics to Main Head

B. Rules for the effective use of statistics: The following suggestions should help make your statistics more meaningful and persuasive. (1) The statistic should closely support the heading it is intended to reinforce. (2) Do not use too many statistics. A speech crammed with figures usually produces confusion and apathy. (3) Avoid being overprecise. The rounding off of figures makes them easier to understand and to remember. For instance, it would be sufficiently accurate to say "nine and a half billion" rather than "$9,514,867,293.51"—there are only two numbers instead of a confusing total of twelve. Simplifying statistics to approximate accuracy is even more important when presenting several sets of figures. Of course, under certain circumstances exactness is essential. The purpose for which the statistics are being used should determine whether approximate or exact accuracy is desired. (4) Bring statistics within the sphere of the experiences and interests of the audience. Mere numbers have little value unless interpreted according to the needs of the listeners. Today, the terms "millions" and "billions" are used glibly, if not carelessly, by government planners, military experts, and the lay public. A surprising number of people, including college students, do not realize that a billion dollars is a thousand times greater than a million dollars. Sensing that such abstract figures are beyond the comprehension of most of us, Alexander Summer, President of the National Association of Real Estate Boards, explained graphically the difference between millions and billions: "A million dollars in crisp new $1,000 bills would make a pile eight inches high. But if we tried to pile up a billion dollars, we'd find that it stretched up in the sky 110 feet higher than the Washington Monument." A statement that the anniversary edition of a newspaper required 1,182,000 pounds of newsprint and 23,600 pounds of ink could be made more vivid by explaining that the newsprint would fill twenty railway box cars, and that the ink would fill ten thousand quart milk bottles, or every fountain pen south of the Mason-Dixon line. (5) A thinking audience will be more likely to accept statistics if you can attribute them to some such recognized source as the Department of Agriculture, the Nielsen ratings, or the American Automobile Association. (6) It has been stated frequently that figures do not lie, but liars do figure. We know that it is possible for self-interest to motivate the slanting of statistical evidence. In the election year of 1952 the United States Department of Commerce offered statistics to "prove" that the American people were 262 per cent more prosperous in 1952 than in 1929. As the United States Chamber of Commerce pointed out, however, the Commerce Department had lumped *federal* spending with *consumer* spending. The Chamber estimated that "real" living standards had improved only about 3 per cent a year, or a total of about 36 per cent for the twelve-year period. You may at times have to defend your statistics by demonstrating that the compiling agency is free of ulterior motives. (7) The value of most statistics, and some in particular, declines rapidly with the passage of time. For instance, it would be grossly inaccurate to use a Gallup photo quiz poll conducted in 1949 as a basis for a declaration in 1953 that 21 per cent of the American people *"are"* unable to recognize a picture of General MacArthur, and 60 per cent *"cannot"* identify Senator Taft's picture. In the interval between 1949 and 1953 President Truman dismissed the General, who received a remarkable reception upon his return to this country from Japan, conducted a series of major addresses from Washington, D. C., to Miami, and from Texas to the state of Washington, and keynoted the Republican National Convention of 1952. During those years, Mr. Taft served as "Mr. Republican" in Congress, waged a spirited campaign for the Republican presidential nomination, whistle-stopped parts of the Mid-West in support of Dwight Eisenhower, and, before his death in mid-year, became the majority leader of the Senate under the Eisenhower Administration. Probably a much higher percentage of people could correctly identify these two men in 1953 than in 1949. (8) If the statistics are a vital link in your argument, and if they have not been prepared by a source readily accepted by the audience, you may find it necessary to explain the methods used to compile and interpret the data. In this connection certain tests may be applied: Are the samples fairly selected and sufficiently numerous? Do they cover the area adequately? Have the data been accurately reported and classified? Have they been correctly interpreted with proper inferences drawn? Even the most carefully prepared figures from the most reputable sources bear careful scrutiny. As an example, the pleasant 85-degree summer temperature readings in a large Southern city, although officially recorded by the United States Weather Bureau, are sometimes inaccurate. The Weather Bureau is located high above the downtown street level on the fourteenth floor of a building. The temperature on the street two hundred feet below is occasionally ten to fifteen degrees above the official reading. (9) At times statistics may be made more persuasive by referring specifically to the source where they may be found, i.e., the *New York Times*, September 12, 1953, the *World Almanac* for 1954, the December 24, 1953, issue of *Time* magazine.

COMPARISON OR ANALOGY

The analogy is a mode of reasoning in which resemblances are noted between objects, ideas, or institutions and inferences drawn on the basis of the similarities. The two types of comparisons are the literal and the figurative.

A. The literal comparison

1. *Nature and purpose of the literal comparison:* This type of analogy compares ideas or objects of the same class, such as rivers to rivers, cities to cities, armies to armies, fighter to fighter, automobile to automobile, and disease to disease.

One function of the literal comparison is to serve as logical proof. The basis of analogical reasoning is this: if two things possess essentially comparable characteristics, a proposition which is true of one may be true of the other. Sometimes listeners may be motivated to endorse a formerly unacceptable inference concerning an idea if they are shown the resemblances between that idea and a second idea of which they approve. During the industrial disturbances of 1944, Eric Johnston attempted to persuade union leaders that labor could avoid entering the nation's "doghouse" only by "repentance and good works." [6] His evidence: Between 1921 and 1930 management moved from the "master bedroom" of American society to the "dog-house" because of a misuse of power; labor between 1933 and 1944 made a similar misuse of power; therefore, unless unions reformed, labor would follow management into disrepute.

Statement
of Main Head

But, gentlemen of labor, I'll tell you something straight. Right now you have a priority at the mourner's bench. Right now you're just where we of management were ten years ago.

What a chance we in management missed! From 1921 to 1930 we had everything all our own way. A friendly administration in Washington. Low taxes. And a friendly public. And what did we do with our power? On the economic side we gave this country a balloon boom that had to burst. On the moral side we produced men like Insull and Hopson and Musica, who undermined confidence in business.

First
Half
of
Analogy

So what did we get? Beginning with 1933, we got the biggest public beating that any group of Americans ever took. Congress socked us with a new law just about every other day. It socked us with good laws. It socked us with bad laws. It socked those of us who were criminal. It socked those of us who were decent. Who cared? The public wanted us socked, and socked we were.

Gentlemen of labor. I must accuse you of not being very original. How faithfully you have imitated us of management! From 1933 to 1942 you rode high. You were tops. A friendly administration in Washington. All

[6] *Vital Speeches*, April 1, 1944.

Second
Half
of
Analogy

sorts of favors fed to you daily from the Washington political table. Management weak and intimidated. So what did you do with your power? On the economic side you gave yourselves a labor boom, regardless of the consequences to any other element in the population. On the moral side you produced men like Browne and Bioff and Scalise who gave all labor a black eye.

You forgot the very thing we forgot:

In the architecture of American society it's just three jumps from the master bedroom to the dog-house.

Now the dog-house is yawning for *you.* The Federal Government and many of the State Governments are

Inference
or
Application
of Analogy
to the
Main Head

beginning to sock you with laws. Some of these laws may have too many teeth. Some of them may bite chunks out of good unions as well as out of bad unions. Who's going to care? If the public wants you socked, why, socked you will be.

And don't think that you can duck any of it by yelling "anti-labor" and "reactionary" and "Fascist." We didn't escape any blows coming our way by yelling "anti-business" and "bureaucrat" and "Communist." You can't stop hell with vocabulary. When the devil is after you the only recipe is repentance and good works.

So how about a few good works?

A second purpose of the literal comparison is to make ideas clearer by comparing a known or understood idea with one that is unknown or misunderstood. At the ceremony commemorating the 175th anniversary of the signing of the Declaration of Independence, President Truman used the following analogy to make more explicit the difficulties in setting up the United Nations Organization.[7]

Statement
of Main Head

There is another way in which our situation today is much like that of the Americans of 1776. Now, once more, we are engaged in launching a new idea—one that has been talked about for centuries, but never successfully put into effect. In those earlier days we were launching a new kind of national government. This time we are creating a new kind of international organization. We have joined in setting up the United Nations to prevent war and to safeguard peace and freedom.

[7] *Vital Speeches,* July 15, 1951.

Literal
Analogy

We believe in the United Nations. We believe it is based on the right ideas, as our own country is. We believe it can grow to be strong and accomplish its high purposes.

But the United Nations faces stern, determined opposition. This is an old story. The Declaration of Independence was also met by determined opposition. A spokesman for the British King called the Declaration "absurd," "visionary," and "subversive." The ideas of freedom and equality and self-government were fiercely opposed in every country by the vested interests and the reactionaries.

Today, the idea of an international organization to keep the peace is being attacked and undermined and fought by reactionary forces everywhere—and particularly by the forces of Soviet communism.

The United Nations will not succeed without a struggle, just as the Declaration of Independence did not succeed without a struggle. But the American people are not afraid. We have taken our stand beside other free men, because we have known for 175 years that free men must stand together. We have joined in the defense of freedom without hesitation and without fear, because we have known for 175 years that freedom must be defended.

2. *Rules for the effective use of the literal comparison:* (1) The analogy should be well adapted logically and psychologically to the remainder of the speech. (2) The essential elements of the two ideas or objects involved should be comparable. One of the chief weaknesses of the analogy as a means of logical proof is that the characteristics of any two ideas, objects, institutions, or relationships must necessarily vary considerably. Therefore, it is essential that the two things under comparison be alike in significant details, and that points of similarity be as numerous as possible. (3) Since it is inevitable that differences will exist between the halves of an analogy, do not attempt to conceal genuine dissimilarities. Admit them, but show that they do not affect the validity of the analogy for your purposes. Of course, if the unlikenesses do emasculate this particular comparison, avoid using it. (4) Do not direct attention to unimportant differences, for the audience may attach undue

significance to such differences. (5) The basis for comparison should be well known and accepted by the audience. To point out similarities between two unfamiliar things merely serves to connect unknowns. To present resemblances between two ideas neither of which is acceptable to the audience does not further conviction. (6) The facts upon which the analogy is based must be accurate. As in all forms of support, the data used in developing the analogy must be reliable, objective, and verifiable.

B. The figurative comparison

1. *Nature and purpose of the figurative comparison:*   The figurative analogy stresses unique relationships between objects or ideas of different classes, as a man to a mountain, a government to a ship, a countenance to a thundercloud, or charity to rain. Its chief value lies in its capacity for striking, graphic imagery. An idea frequently assumes greater clarity and significance if singular resemblances can be pointed out between that idea and a second which appears to be completely different. Usually figurative comparisons are brief and take the form of similes and metaphors. Geoffrey Crowther, editor of the *Economist*, used this unusual relationship in a broadcast over the British Broadcasting System.

Our [economic] system is stiff and rigid and unadaptable. We all know what happened to the brontosaurus because he could not adapt himself to new circumstances, and the fear that I have about the British economy is that it is getting a little into the state of the brontosaurus.

Shortly after the Korean War began, Senator Paul Douglas called attention of Congress to the menace of Russia by this figurative analogy:

The manifestation of Communist aggression in Korea during these last six montns is but the showing of the fin of the shark above water. It is but a fraction of the striking power of the man-eater which lies beneath the surface. Day before yesterday it was Czechoslovakia; yesterday it was China; today it is Korea. What will it be tomorrow?

During his campaign for the presidency in 1952, Adlai Stevenson frequently made vivid use of pithy figurative comparisons. He poked sharp wit at the Republicans by remarking: "Now as far as Republican leaders are concerned, this desire for a change is understandable. I suppose if I had been sewn up in the same underwear for twenty years I'd want a change too." In order to explain the nature of inflation, and to shift the blame from the Democrats to the Russians, he said: "The cause of inflation can, I believe, be made plain. Let's stay in the kitchen a moment. It is as though we were making bread and while we answered the phone a malicious neighbor [Russia] dumped a whole cup of yeast into the bowl. That's the inflation story. In fact, that is inflation."

In his funeral oration three generations ago at his brother's grave, Robert Ingersoll expressed a strong emotional appeal with this comparison:

Life is a narrow vale between the cold and barren peaks of two eternities. We strive in vain to look beyond the heights. We cry aloud, and the only answer is the echo of our wailing cry. From the voiceless lips of the unreplying dead there comes no word; but in the night of death hope sees a star, and listening love can hear the rustle of a wing.

Occasionally, an extended comparison may be appropriate. In 1951, when speaking to the Dallas Chapter of the Society for the Advancement of Management, Mr. Charles E. Wilson compared government control to a camel and competitive industry to a tent: [8]

The title I have chosen for my talk, as most of you know, is "The Camel's Nose Is Under the Tent." The expression comes from an old Arabian fable, and to an Arab it spells trouble and disaster. The fable of the Arab and his camel goes something like this:

One cold night, as an Arab sat in his tent, a camel gently thrust his nose under the flap and looked in.

"Master," he said, "let me put my nose in your tent, for it is cold and stormy out here."

"By all means, and welcome," said the Arab, and turned over and went to sleep. A little later he awoke and found that the camel had not only put his nose in the tent but his head and neck as well.

Extended Figurative Analogy   The camel, who had been turning his head from side to side, said, "I will take but little more room if I place my forelegs within the tent. It is difficult standing without."

[8] *Vital Speeches,* November 1, 1951.

Application
of Analogy

"You may also plant your forelegs within," said the Arab, moving a little to make room, for the tent was small. Finally the camel said, "May I not stand wholly within? I keep the tent open by standing as I do." "Yes, yes," said the Arab. "Come wholly inside. Perhaps it will be better for both of us." So the camel came forward and crowded into the tent.

The Arab with difficulty in the crowded quarters again went to sleep. The next time he woke up he was outside in the cold and the camel had the tent to himself.

Independent of how he got there, the important point is that the camel of government control now has his nose under the tent of free competitive industry and is crowding in. We will all have to watch him or he will take over the tent, and we will lose our economic freedom and with it all our other liberties. Of course, if the camel is really successful in taking over the tent, the members of the Society for the Advancement of Management had better be studying how to become government bureaucrats—not how to become more effective members of our marvelous American industrial system.

2. *Rules for the effective use of the figurative comparison:* (1) Do not use the figurative comparison for logical proof. Since the things being compared are of different classes, the bonds of association will be logically weak. The famed psychiatrist Dr. William Menninger once attempted to defend his thesis that the cure of mental illness is more important than exact diagnosis by stating: "One does not have to know the cause of a fire to put it out." The weakness of this figurative analogy as proof was revealed when one critic asked: "In the case of an oil fire wouldn't it be necessary to know that the blaze was caused by burning oil?" The questioner's point was obvious: chemicals, not cascading streams of water, should be used to put out an oil fire. Dr. Menninger's analogy was vivid but not convincing. (2) The figurative analogy should be striking, relevant, appropriate, and credible. Avoid analogies which offer only strained, incongruous relationships. (3) Usually the figurative comparison

should be brief. Unless exceptionally vivid, it should not consume more than thirty seconds.

TESTIMONY

A. **Nature and purpose of testimony:** Testimony usually takes the form of a direct quotation or a paraphrase and may be drawn from a great variety of sources: a remark by a bus driver, a telecast of a news commentator, a formal state paper by the President, a headline from the evening paper, an advertisement in the classified section, an excerpt from the *Congressional Record*, a dialogue between the attorneys for the defense and the prosecution, statements from a famous historical figure, a verse from the Bible, and so forth.

One advantage in using testimony is that it is easy to secure. The speaker may select a quotation from millions of pages of printed matter or from billions of words expressed orally. Frequently, testimony is persuasive. An audience which is unwilling to accept a program upon the speaker's personal recommendation may be rendered more receptive if shown that prominent experts or the general public endorse the plan. As William Trotter states in his *Instincts of the Herd in War and Peace,* we are more sensitive to the opinions of our fellow men than to any other single influence. Practically all of our actions and thoughts are controlled by our social consciousness. Testimony can also be striking and attention-commanding. A student vitalized the difficulties of cancer research by this quotation:

Professor Oberling said before the Cancer Institute of Paris, "Today we are sadder and wiser . . . we have the uneasy sensation of knowing both too much and too little at the same time. Too much because we offer a whole series of solutions. . . . The real cause is where all the causes meet. This point, we may be sure, is in the cell. And it is here that we know too little." He goes on to say that the doctors are like one who is asked to explain the workings of an automobile from its external appearance. "We can analyze it, tell what it is made of, what its fuel is, but we may not open the hood."

A direct quotation or a paraphrase may also serve to make an idea clear. Examples: to explain the arduous efforts needed for a young singer to qualify for the Metropolitan, cite Patrice Munsel on the subject; to interpret the seriousness of syndicated crime in the United

States, quote Senator Estes Kefauver or J. Edgar Hoover; to illustrate the difficulties of controlling the crowd at the National Open golf tourney, use statements by some of the players or attendants.

There are two major weaknesses in the use of testimony for logical proof. Such evidence does not actually *prove* that a certain plan is desirable or that a particular thing has happened. It indicates merely that the person or persons making the statement possess certain beliefs. Historians are constantly discovering that what has been traditionally taught about a happening in the past needs reinterpretation. Not infrequently a convict who has served perhaps twenty years is released because belatedly unearthed evidence has demonstrated that he has been wrongly imprisoned. Witnesses had testified against him; a jury had stated that he was guilty; a judge had pronounced sentence; society had accepted the judicial decision. However, such human judgment did not alter the true facts of the case. Nor was the course of events upset when a prominent commentator in the summer of 1941 predicted that the German armies would overrun Russia within six months.

Another weakness of testimony is that thinking listeners realize it is possible to find statements to fit almost any side of any question. Occasional revolutions were advocated as a beneficial tonic by Thomas Jefferson. Child labor was endorsed by Alexander Hamilton. America's entrance in the Mexican War was denounced as immoral by Abraham Lincoln. The Old Testament preaches the stern philosophy of an eye for an eye, while the New Testament teaches forgiveness and gentleness. Economists differ on the ability of the nation to withstand the pressures of inflation. Even eye-witness testimony to an accident is frequently contradictory.

Obviously testimony overlaps other forms of support. A direct quotation or a paraphrase may contain statistics, comparison, illustration, explanation, and causal reasoning. The identifying feature which separates testimony from most other forms of support is that the speaker accredits the statements he is making to some source other than himself.

B. Rules for the effective use of testimony: (1) Testimony must be relevant and appropriate. (2) If you have implied that you are presenting an exact quotation, be completely accurate in giving the verbatim report. Do not amend the statement in any way. (3) Avoid lifting a passage out of context in such a way that the meaning will be altered. An example of changing the meaning by leaving out modifiers would be to omit the phrase, "If Russia attacks Yugoslavia," from the statement: "If Russia attacks Yuogslavia, we will have total war." (4) Indicate to the audience when you are paraphrasing. Your word choice should faithfully reflect the intended meaning of the original quotation. (5) Avoid using the words "quote" and "end of quotation" unless it is exceedingly important that the listeners know exactly which words belong to your source. Otherwise, let a change of pitch, rate, or emphasis indicate when beginning and ending a quotation. (6) Refrain from introducing a quotation by a trite phrase such as: "I have a quotation here," or, "I will now read you a quote." Instead, say something like this: "Last week in a speech in Chicago Senator Wills stated . . . ," or, "On his twenty-first birthday Theodore Roosevelt wrote these words in his diary. . . ." (7) Keep quotations short. Use two or three different references rather than one long quotation. (8) The source of the quotation should be intellectually and emotionally acceptable to the audience. Listeners are more receptive to ideas advanced by individuals they respect and admire. If the person who has made the quotation is unfamiliar, explain why his observations are significant. Mention his title, or his background of academic, scientific, political, or life experiences that qualify him as an authority. A critical audience will reject testimony which appears to be motivated by prejudice or self-interest, will insist that the statement be based upon first-hand information, and will place reliance in only those sources possessing reputations for consistent and accurate judgments. (9) The recency of the quotation may be of considerable importance. One's thinking must undergo alterations in order to adjust to changes in environment. Avoid using an out-of-date quotation to represent the present thinking of an individual, particularly if there is reason to believe that he may have changed his mind. (10) Sometimes the manner in which the statement was made affects its validity. Was the person emotionally disturbed? Did he make the remark carelessly in an off-guard moment? Did he expect to be quoted? Was the statement carefully prepared and representative of his thinking on the subject? Was it accurately recorded by a responsible agency? (11) If speaking to critical listeners, it may be necessary to document the testimony. In such a case, specify where you read the statement. If the testimony was presented orally, explain whether you heard it personally. If second-hand, where did your informant get his information? How reliable is the intermediary?

RESTATEMENT AND REPETITION

A. **Nature and purpose of restatement and repetition:** Few members of an audience understand the nature of an idea or its significance the first time it is presented. Some amplification and reiteration is necessary to insure retention and appreciation. From a broad philosophical point of view, reiteration is employed whenever any form of support is used to develop a main head. In a more limited sense, however, reiteration consists of either restatement or repetition. Restatement says the same thing over again in a different way, while repetition utilizes identical phrasing. The difference between restatement and repetition is demonstrated in the following extracts from the student's speech quoted on pages 112–115.

Basic *Statement*	. . . But let us not forget this other group of war casualties, the ordinary guys who came back—who present an additional powerful reason for resolving that we must not have another international holocaust. . . . Because of them, also, we dare not afford another war.
Restatement	. . . John, a good friend of mine . . . is still haunted by a murder committed in the name of "peace in our time." [9] Four years later, he's still traveling the road back and vainly searching for peace of mind. . . .
Primarily *Repetition*	Dare we forget that we cannot afford another war?
Restatement	. . . Yes, Fred and Alice and their families have made their sacrifices in the name of "peace in our time." But their mental peace was lost on the road back. . . .
Repetition	Dare we forget that we cannot afford another war?
Restatement	. . . Moose made his little contribution to "peace in our time." But his road back to mental peace still stretches far into the future. . . .
Repetition	Dare we forget that we cannot afford another war?
Restatement	. . . George's . . . mother told him he "looked hard, talked hard, and was tough and crude."

[9] The phrase "peace in our time," although repeated several times, is labeled "Restatement" in the marginal notations because in each instance it is introduced in a different manner.

Restatement

. . . our contribution to "peace in our time" was ridiculously insignificant. But each of us has had difficulty in traveling the road back. And some of us still have far to travel before we can have individual peace.

Restatement

. . . We have been so engrossed in the obvious tragedies that we have missed the subtle ones. Is mental paralysis any less serious than physical disability? Is not a broken home more of a tragedy than a bomb-wrecked house? Is a drunkard any less of a liability to himself and society than a veteran with a leg gone?

Primarily
Repetition

. . . In terms of the future, we dare not forget that we cannot afford another war.

As this passage indicates, repetition may exercise a powerful persuasive appeal. However, unless skillfully used, it becomes monotonous. Restatement is less likely to grow tiresome and has the advantage of offering a fresh slant to the original idea. Almost all of the illustrative examples which are presented in this chapter demonstrate that restatement is an excellent means for interpreting supporting materials in terms of the main head. You will recall the standard method of using the forms of support: state the main head; give the supporting evidence; apply the evidence to the main head through restatement.

B. Rules for the use of restatement and repetition: (1) Do not use restatement or repetition as a substitute for logical proof. Reiteration promotes clarity and emphasis, and may exert an emotional appeal; but, since it consists of saying the same thing over again, it cannot serve the purposes of logical conviction. (2) Repeat important names, dates, and so on at least once. An unusual name might be spelled out for easier comprehension. Important ideas should be repeated at least twice. (3) Usually avoid using repetition immediately after presenting the original statement. Example: a speaker should not repeat a sentence like "The Republican Party is a party of depression, isolation and confusion" without some intervening continuity. (4) Adjust the usage of restatement and repetition to the needs of the audience and to the subject. What is appropriate in one situation might be monotonous and redundant in another. (5) Rhetorical questions are effective methods of restating an idea. In the example on page 115, the speaker used a series of three rhetorical questions to restate the essence of his illustrations of John, Fred, Moose, and himself, and to tie them to the original statement or main head. (6) We have stated before that other forms of support besides restatement and repetition may serve, under a liberal interpretation, as means of reiteration. In this passage a student uses a paraphrase and a brief quotation to repeat an idea:

Peace to the common man depends upon *universal* freedom. Lincoln said that America could not exist half free and half slave. I say to you, neither can the world! On *Life's* editorial page, of reecnt date, we read this question and answer, addressed to Americans from the "ancient beaches of Europe": "Do you suppose you can keep that idea [that all men are equal] locked up in a single country? . . . We say that free men can no longer be free *alone* . . . they must be free *together*."

(7) The efficacy of visual aids to serve as reiteration will be discussed in Part II of this chapter.

EXPLANATION

A. **Nature and purpose of explanation:** In Chapter 5, the topical arrangement of the main heads of the Discussion was termed a "catch-all" pattern. Probably explanation can be similarly characterized as the "catch-all" type of supporting material. Whatever does not seem to fit the other forms of support can usually be called explanation. Unfortunately, explanation cannot be defined more specifically than to say that it is exposition for the purpose of making an idea clear. Broadly speaking, the entire speech to inform may be considered explanation because its sole purpose is to convey information or to explain something. In the more circumscribed meaning as a form of support, explanation refers to the exposition necessary to make plain and intelligible a particular main head. In the following example, observe how Senator Brien McMahon made clear to the United States Senate his program for atomic defense.[10]

. . . Specifically, I propose that we make our best and cheapest weapon—the atomic weapon—the real backbone of our peace power.

I propose an atomic army and an atomic navy and an atomic air force—in place of the conventional defenses we now maintain. . . .

Here is what I mean by an atomic army: Fewer foot soldiers armed with rifles and more specialists equipped to fire an atomic shell wherever

[10] *Vital Speeches,* November 1, 1951.

the enemy masses his troops. Fewer mortars and more short-range guided missiles with atomic warheads. Fewer flame throwers and more radiological warfare. I have in mind air-ground teamwork, with light planes capable of hurling atomic weapons at enemy troops, supply dumps, and transportation choke points.

Here is my conception of an atomic navy: Nuclear-powered submarines almost unlimited in range; nuclear-powered aircraft carriers capable of launching planes which carry the atomic bomb on both strategic and tactical missions; ship-based atomic artillery; ship-based guided missiles with atomic warheads; atomic mines; and target-seeking torpedoes which deliver atomic explosives.

An atomic air force, for its part, will seek out and destroy, with atomic weapons, the enemy's industrial sinews of war. It will fire missiles with atomic pay loads. It will deliver the hydrogen bomb when that most terrible of weapons is achieved. Even more, it will visit atomic fury upon the very airfields and bases from which an aggressor would strike against our cities.

We must have atomic weapons to use in the heights of the sky and the depths of the sea; we must have them to use above the ground, on the ground, and below the ground. An aggressor must know that if he dares attack he will have no place to hide.

An important method of promoting understanding is through the use of definitions. The standard method of defining is to place the word or idea into its logical category, genus, or class, and then to distinguish it from other members of that class. As an example, we might define a two-platoon system "T quarterback" in this manner.

GENERAL CLASS	DIFFERENTIATING CHARACTERISTICS
Under the two-platoon system a "T" quarterback is: a football player	(1) who plays exclusively on offense
	(2) in the backfield
	(3) of a team employing the "T" formation.
	(4) He serves as the field general of the team,
	(5) calling signals from
	(6) his position directly behind the center.
	(7) He handles the ball on all except kicking plays,
	(8) either fading back to pass,
	(9) handing the ball to some other back,
	(10) or running with it.

Even this definition, which is more detailed than most dictionary explanations, would need further amplification and clarification for an audience unfamiliar with football. Notice how James H. Halsey utilizes a more extended, yet simple and concise, exposition to bring into clear focus the nature and difficulties of "communication." [11]

By communication, I mean the process whereby individuals, groups, organizations, institutions, and even nations express their opinions and make known their wants and desires. The principal means of communication which man uses involves the use of speech and writing. Unfortunately these instruments too often prove unsatisfactory, ineffective, and sometimes the actual cause of misunderstanding. Hence if we hope to eliminate the cultural lag, we must improve our system of communications.

Today our society is so complex and requires so many specialists that communication is difficult and sometimes almost impossible. This is true in spite of our mass media of communication such as newspapers, radio, and television. This situation is often described as a problem in semantics or word meaning.

The chemist cannot understand the sociologist; the business man cannot understand the professor; the soldier cannot understand the statesman; the Republican cannot understand the Democrat; and almost nobody can understand the lawyer or the psychologist or the Russians.

We have numerous troubles in communication right here on our own campus. Sometimes you students do not understand us, and we do not understand you. Sometimes the faculty does not understand the administration, and we in administration do not understand the faculty. In every instance of misunderstanding on our campus, I am positive that the principal cause is due to faulty communication.

You can imagine the problems which arise internationally and in the United Nations where so many different languages are involved and where there must be dependence on incomplete and sometimes inaccurate translations.

Then imagine the magnitude of the problem with the illiterates throughout the world. How can we explain Americanism and democracy and private enterprise and liberty to people who cannot read and write? I am told there are 70,000,000 illiterates in Latin America and probably 500,000,000 in Asia. Is it any wonder we have trouble in communicating with strangers abroad who speak different languages when sometimes we do not understand each other here in America, or Connecticut, or even in Bridgeport?

[11] *Vital Speeches,* November 1, 1951.

B. Rules for the use of explanation: (1) Explanation should be an integral part of the speech and should be carefully adjusted to the intellectual needs and interests of the audience. (2) It should be simple. Make the task of comprehension as easy as possible for the listeners. Public speaking must be instantly intelligible, because few audiences are willing to concentrate actively on understanding the meaning of the speaker. Avoid involved, abstract discussions. Use easily understood, nonambiguous, nontechnical words. As a student once said, "Spare yourself no pains to save the listener pains." (3) Keep explanations brief. Long-winded exposition is lethal to audience interest. Be concise and to the point. If considerable development is necessary, relieve the tedium of exposition by using appropriate illustrations, analogies, and testimony. (4) While it is an excellent starting-point for the clarification of an idea, exposition may need reinforcement by the use of other forms of support.

Deductive and Causal Reasoning

Although deductive and causal types of reasoning are among the most frequently used methods of development, they are also probably the most difficult to understand. (Causal reasoning is a type of induction. Other forms of induction, i.e., reasoning from statistics, specific instance, and analogy, have been discussed previously in this chapter.) The following analysis is not designed to be a definitive examination of such forms of logical thinking, for that would require a book-length dissertation. Nor do we imply that a thorough technical knowledge of deduction and causation is a *sine qua non* of effective speaking. However, we do urge the student to acquire a working understanding of the basic principles involved. Many of the materials used to support the main heads of the persuasive speech involve deductive and causal reasoning. The concepts discussed here should be of help in testing the validity of your reasoning and the clarity of your thinking.

A. Deductive reasoning: Deduction typically proceeds from a general law or accepted truth to a particular judgment. It is based upon the assumption that what is true of the whole will be true of one of the parts, or, what is true of an entire category or class will also be true of any member of that category. Thus, it follows that if all textbooks have covers, *Practical Public Speaking,* being a textbook, will have a cover. Deductive reasoning is based upon the syllogism, which contains three propositions: the major and minor premises and the conclusion. The conclusion, of course, is the product of the logical association existing between the major and minor premises. In public speaking, the entire syllogism is rarely stated in full. Usually at least one of the premises is considered sufficiently obvious that it can be omitted. Instead of using a complete syllogism, a speaker could say: *"Practical Public Speaking* will have a cover because all textbooks have covers," or *"Practical Public Speaking* is a textbook and will therefore have a cover." In the first case, the audience is expected to realize that *Practical Public Speaking* is a textbook, and in the second, to supply the proposition that all textbooks have covers. Occasionally, speakers will leave out an obvious conclusion such as: "Whichever nation has the most atomic weapons will win World War III, and we have a vast superiority in the atomic field." Such elliptic syllogisms are called enthymemes. Despite the omission of one or more propositions, the remaining premise(s) can always be expanded into a full syllogism for a better check of the logical relationships. Deduction is based upon one of three types of syllogisms: categorical, hypothetical, or disjunctive.

1. The categorical syllogism: The form of the categorical syllogism is demonstrated by the following set of symbols. (For the sake of simplicity, the following discussion is concerned only with that type of categorical syllogism which proceeds from a universal affirmative premise to a particular conclusion.)

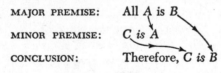

MAJOR PREMISE: All *A* is *B*

MINOR PREMISE: *C* is *A*

CONCLUSION: Therefore, *C* is *B*

In this construction, *B* is called the major term; it is always the predicate term of the conclusion. *C* is the minor term and is invariably the subject of the conclusion. *A* is called the middle term because it serves as a mediator between the other two terms, and never appears in the conclusion. "All *A* is *B*" is the major premise because it contains the major term; it is a universal, categorical assertion. "*C* is *A*" includes the minor term and is therefore known as the minor premise. This example utilizes the complete structure of the categorical syllogism.

	MIDDLE TERM	MAJOR TERM
MAJOR PREMISE:	All effective speakers	prepare their speeches
	MINOR TERM	MIDDLE TERM
MINOR PREMISE:	John Holwell	is an effective speaker
	MINOR TERM	MAJOR TERM
CONCLUSION:	Therefore, John Holwell	prepares his speeches

The enthymeme, "Of course he's a good driver. He operates a Greyhound bus," implies that the man is an excellent driver because one must be thoroughly competent to be hired by the Greyhound company. The complete syllogism would be:

	MIDDLE TERM	MAJOR TERM
MAJOR PREMISE:	All Greyhound bus operators	are good drivers
	MINOR TERM	MIDDLE TERM
MINOR PREMISE:	Mike Klop	is a Greyhound bus operator
	MINOR TERM	MAJOR TERM
CONCLUSION	Therefore, Mike Klop	is a good driver

Here are the rules for the use of the categorical syllogism: (1) The major premise must be accurate; otherwise the conclusion drawn by the syllogism may be invalid. (2) The syllogism must contain only three terms: major, minor, and middle. The meaning of these terms must remain constant. (3) The syllogism must include *only* three propositions: major premise, minor premise, and conclusion. (4) In the strict logical sense, the middle term must be distributed (used in the universal meaning of "all" or "every") in at least one of the premises. However, public speaking deals with probabilities rather than certainties. Usually, the major premise needs some sort of qualification, because true universality is exceptional rather than common. For example, instead of "all effective speakers prepare their speeches," it would be more accurate to say that "practically all effective speakers prepare their speeches if they have the opportunity." Some orators like Patrick Henry and Clarence Darrow apparently made little formal speech preparation. Then, too, almost every speaker is forced occasionally to speak impromptu.

Therefore, it is not completely true that all effective speakers always prepare their speeches. (5) Any term which is distributed in the conclusion must also be distributed in one of the premises. A universal conclusion cannot be drawn from two particular premises. (6) No valid conclusion can be drawn from a syllogism containing two negative premises. (7) If one premise is negative, the conclusion must likewise be negative. No affirmative conclusion can be drawn from a syllogism including a negative term. (8) If the conclusion is negative, one of the premises must be negative. No negative conclusion can be drawn from two affirmative premises.

2. *The hypothetical syllogism:* The major premise of the hypothetical syllogism is always characterized by an "if" or conditional clause. Such a syllogism states that if certain conditions or requirements are met, certain results will follow. The hypothetical formula is illustrated by the following symbols.

MAJOR PREMISE: If *A* is *B*, *C* is *D*

MINOR PREMISE: *A* is *B*

CONCLUSION: Therefore, *C* is *D*

Frequently in public speaking the hypothetical syllogism is abbreviated into a statement of the major premise. Examples:

If you rehearse, you will give a better speech.
If you are employed by Hollis Brothers, you have a good job.
If a strong wind begins to blow, storm warnings will be raised.
If he falls from the tightrope, he will be killed.
If you take a speech course, you will meet interesting people.

Any of these enthymemes could be expanded into a complete syllogism, as is shown in this example.

MAJOR PREMISE: If you take a speech course, you will meet interesting people
MINOR PREMISE: You will take a speech course
CONCLUSION: Therefore, you will meet interesting people

There are three criteria for testing the validity of the hypothetical syllogism. (1) The minor premise must affirm the antecedent (the "if" clause), or deny the consequent (main clause) of the major premise. (2) If the minor premise affirms the antecedent, the conclusion will automatically affirm the consequent (see the example above). (3) If the minor premise denies the consequent, the conclusion must deny the antecedent. This point is illustrated by the following formula and example:

MAJOR PREMISE: If A is B, C is D
MINOR PREMISE: C is not D
CONCLUSION: Therefore, A is not B

MAJOR PREMISE: If it rains, the game will be postponed
MINOR PREMISE: The game will not be postponed
CONCLUSION: Therefore, it will not rain

Obviously the conclusion must be suspected if the minor premise denies the antecedent or affirms the consequent. It does not necessarily follow that the game will not be postponed even though the skies are clear. Conceivably, other causes might delay the game such as a death among the players, a breakdown or wreck of the bus bringing the players to the community, or a power failure if the game is played under lights. On the other hand, it would be fallacious to reason: if the game is postponed, it will therefore rain.

3. *The disjunctive syllogism:* In the disjunctive syllogism the major premise offers alternative (either-or) possibilities. If the minor premise denies one of the alternatives, the conclusion will affirm the other. If the minor premise affirms one of the alternatives, the conclusion will deny the other.

TYPE NO. I

Formula

MAJOR PREMISE: A is either B or C
MINOR PREMISE: A is not C
CONCLUSION: Therefore, A is B

Enthymeme

The president must be at home for he is not at the office

Complete Syllogism

MAJOR PREMISE: The president is either at home or at the
office

MINOR PREMISE: The president is not at the office

CONCLUSION: Therefore, the president is at home

TYPE NO. II

Formula

MAJOR PREMISE: A is either B or C

MINOR PREMISE: A is B

CONCLUSION: Therefore, A is not C

Enthymeme

The president is at home, therefore he couldn't be at the office

Complete Syllogism

MAJOR PREMISE: The president is either at home or at the
office

MINOR PREMISE: The president is at home

CONCLUSION: Therefore, the president is not at the office

The proper use of the disjunctive syllogism depends upon the
adherence to the following rules: (1) The alternatives must be
mutually exclusive; i.e., they must not overlap. (2) The alternatives
should be exhaustive. They should cover all possibilities. It might be
fallacious to say that a man is either a Republican or a Democrat.
Perhaps he is an Independent or a Socialist. (3) The minor premise
must affirm or deny one of the alternatives. If it affirms, the conclusion must deny the second. If it denies, the conclusion must
affirm the other.

B. Causal reasoning

1. *Nature and purpose of causal reasoning:* We made an initial
acquaintance with causal reasoning in Chapter 5 in connection with
the Cause-and-Effect Pattern for arranging the main heads of the
Discussion. Here we are concerned with the effective use of causal-
ity to develop the main heads. The basic philosophy inherent in
causal reasoning is that for every happening there is a cause. Such
reasoning is an addition to the relevant facts. It involves an infer-

ence, interpretation, or judgment concerning the relationship among the facts. To illustrate: If you urge a prominent club woman to take a course in parliamentary procedure, you may imply that such a course will enable her to become a more skilled parliamentarian. When a specialist states that a patient's sinusitis is caused by a deviated septum, he is asserting a causal relationship between sinusitis (the effect) and the deviated septum (the cause). Causal reasoning may proceed from cause to effect or from effect to cause.

The cause-to-effect sequence argues from a known fact forward to an alleged result. It always involves a chronological pattern such as (1) from the more distant past to the more recent past—Neville Chamberlain's policy of appeasement was a direct cause of Britain's unpreparedness for World War II; (2) from the past to the present— the bad fall the jockey took yesterday will make him more cautious today; (3) from the present to the future—the Board's decision to expand production will create jobs for thousands of workers; (4) from the near future to the more distant future—when the Russian people learn the truth about American motives, they will revolt against their masters in the Kremlin.

The effect-to-cause pattern of thought moves from a known fact or result backward toward the past in order to determine the probable cause(s). This time order may proceed (1) from the present to the past—our present state of unpreparedness is basically the result of our demilitarization following the last war; (2) from the more recent past to the more distant past—the defense will attempt to prove that Mr. Charwell's death was due to natural causes attending old age.

2. Rules for the use of causal reasoning: The basic rules governing causal reasoning have already been discussed in Chapter 5. In addition to avoiding the errors of false cause, false simplicity, and *post hoc ergo propter hoc,* the speaker should carefully establish the authenticity of all facts involved.

PART II. VISUAL AIDS

A. Nature and purpose of visual aids: Various studies, including wartime investigations by the armed services, have indicated that most of our learning is acquired by means of the eye rather than the ear, and that we learn more quickly if both of these senses are stimulated. Therefore, whenever possible, a public speaker should help develop his main heads by the use of visual aids such as graphs, charts, maps, diagrams, pictures, blackboard drawings, scaled or full-size models, actual objects or specimens, moving picture films, and slides.

Combining appeals to the eye and to the ear promotes clarity. Descriptive words alone are sometimes inadequate to make a point clear. Any parent who has attempted to explain to children the physical appearance of jungle animals is vividly aware that one visit to a zoo would be more instructive than many thousands of words of explanation. An archaeologist speaking on the ancient civilization of the Incas and the Aztecs could make his discussion more meaningful by incorporating into his lecture large photographs, slides, or motion pictures. A horticulturist should include demonstrations in a lecture on the proper methods of grafting. Medical students cannot learn how to conduct operations unless the instruction includes practical exhibitions. One of the major advances in medical education in recent years was made in December of 1951 when the University of Kansas Medical Center inaugurated a regular schedule of "closed circuit" color-television demonstrations for its students. In the operating room a TV camera was mounted directly over the surgeon's table. By means of a throat microphone the operating surgeon explained every step. The students gathered in the school auditorium were able to watch every movement by means of several color-television receivers. A second professor, sitting in the auditorium with the students, could use a direct circuit to ask the surgeon for any necessary amplification or clarification.

Visual aids add interest to the speech. They relieve the monotony of the speaker's oral delivery and, if attractively prepared and presented, are appealing forms of support. Who wouldn't be interested in viewing a demonstration of a police dog disarming a man, a film on an erupting volcano, or a working, accurately scaled model of a new type of helicopter?

Sometimes visual aids serve as superior logical proof. According to the old saw, "seeing is believing." A detergent concern once advertised that the suds from a single box of its soap could fill the bed of a tandem truck. When challenged to prove the claim, the company called in photographers and successfully conducted the test.

The resulting picture-spread in a national magazine probably persuaded many housewives that the soap would provide an ample supply of suds for any household chore. A spot-remover salesman might prove the efficacy of his product by deliberately spilling some ink on his tie and then removing the stain through the application of the reagent. A prosecuting attorney could project on a screen the thumb print of the defendant and that found on the murder weapon. Using a pointer, he could trace the lines of the prints to prove that the whorls were identical.

B. Rules for the use of visual aids: (1) Visual material must closely support the point under consideration. (2) It should be adjusted to the interests, experiences, and mental capacities of the audience. Many displays which are suitable for a specialized audience are too technical for a more general audience. (3) Do not permit the presentation of the visual aid to consume more time than the demonstration is worth. Weigh the time needed to exhibit the material against its value to the speech. (4) Carefully plan and rehearse the use of the visual aid in advance. By knowing exactly what you are going to do and how to accomplish it, you will avoid wasting precious time during the speech. Your display should be executed with dispatch and smoothness. If you are to use slides, check beforehand on the outlets, the length of the cord, the lighting, and the position of the screen and the projector. The slides should be prearranged in the proper order and in the correct position for the carriage. Practice sketching the blackboard diagrams which you plan to use in your talk so that you can draw rapidly and accurately while maintaining oral continuity and good eye contact. Ascertain that all mechanical parts of the exhibit are in working order. See that all charts and pictures are arranged in the proper order. Insure the presence of any needed equipment such as pointer, eraser, wall hooks or chart holders, table, cloth on which to wipe hands, clamps, asbestos pads, matches, wrench, string, chalk, or pot holders. If you are using assistants, they should be thoroughly briefed on their jobs. (5) Visual material should be large enough to be seen easily by everyone in the audience. (6) Aids should be sufficiently clear to be understood almost immediately. Do not clutter a graph, drawing, diagram, slide, or map with too many details. What would be acceptable for a textbook may be too complex for public speaking.

Use several displays so as not to crowd many ideas into a single exhibit. Unnecessary details should be omitted; they make it more difficult for the audience to understand the essential points.

(7) Do not stand between the visual aid and the audience. (8) Avoid turning your back upon the listeners. For instance, when directing attention to some detail in the display, face the audience, stand either to the left or right of the visual aid, and hold the pointer in the hand nearest the display. (9) Direct your glance and your discussion to the audience rather than to the visual aid. Inexperienced speakers tend to concentrate on their display; if you lose contact with the listeners, you cannot accurately judge their reactions. Maintain almost constant eye contact even when completing a drawing, or setting up or dismantling a display. Especially avoid such obvious discourtesies as talking to the blackboard with your back turned to the audience. (10) Before the speech be sure to remove any objects which may distract attention from your visual material. (11) Labels for diagrams should be brief and sufficiently large and distinct. (12) Avoid long, awkward interruptions in oral continuity. Do not make the audience wait while you prepare a demonstration. Attention once lost is difficult to recapture. (13) Do not present your visual aid until the proper moment has arrived. If the listeners are permitted to look at the display beforehand, some of their attention will be diverted from the speech. By the time the speaker is ready to use the aid it will have lost much of its stimulating qualities. When you have completed the demonstration, put the aid out of sight: turn the charts to the wall, place a cover over the specimen, or put the model back into its case.

(14) Usually the speaker's platform is the best position from which to present visual aids. A second method is to pass such material around among members of the audience. In using the latter mode, the speaker risks losing valuable time and attention. If the material is distributed before the speech, the auditors will probably look at it before the speaker is prepared to discuss it, thus distracting attention from the talk and destroying the suspense value of the visual aid. If the material is passed out during the speech, time is consumed and some disturbance is inevitable. If the listeners receive the visual information after the talk, they will frequently throw it away without examining it. Perhaps the best procedure for passing out materials is to have assistants distribute the information during

a pause in the speech. After everyone has a copy or sample, explain the application of the visual aid to the speech, and then persuade the audience to lay aside the aid and to concentrate on the speech. It is no simple matter, however, to regain attention after an interruption of this sort. One real estate salesman recognized this difficulty in a speech to prospective home owners by saying: "And now, ladies and gentlemen, let me suggest that the ladies put their model of the Ruark home in their pocketbooks. And you men, why don't you put yours in your coat pocket? By doing this, you can be sure to take them home to admire or to give to Junior to play with. Then, there's a second reason I want you to put them away. To be perfectly candid, I can't compete with these miniature Ruark homes. If you left them out on your laps, I probably couldn't get your attention again this evening."

PART III. FACTORS OF INTEREST

As William James has said, to a new-born infant the world is a "blooming, buzzing confusion." Gradually, his environment becomes more meaningful because he learns to focus attention upon specific elements in his surroundings. He is soon able to interpret and to respond to a nursing bottle, grandma's cooing and gurgling sounds, or brother's friendly tickling. This process of concentration, or selection from a multiplicity of stimuli, becomes more important as his neuromuscular system matures. The environment, in conjunction with memories of past experiences and physical states of being, presents such a host of stimuli that the human organism lacks the ability to respond to the totality of the situation. Since we cannot respond to everything about us or within us, we must consciously or unconsciously choose that to which we will attend. An extreme example of the principle of the selection of stimuli is the "absent-minded" professor who fails to recognize students or colleagues on the campus. Although he may be unaware of crossing streets, opening doors, or hearing salutations from friends, he is not absent-minded. On the contrary, his mind may be working furiously to solve, let us say, a knotty problem in statistical analysis, or to determine why a white rat suddenly became frustrated in a psychology experiment. Through years of careful discipline he has learned how to barricade his mind against interfering stimuli.

The necessity for the selection of a given stimulus and the consequent rejection of other stimuli does not cease when an individual becomes part of an audience. In an imaginary, but fairly typical, audience, the striking brunette in the third row may repeatedly glance at her new diamond ring. Her basic interests of romance and wedding plans may conflict with her attempts to listen to the speech. The little man sitting behind her may be emotionally disturbed because of a dispute with his wife. Perhaps there is an air of hostility between him and the plump wife in the next seat. They may find their emotional problems more absorbing than the speech. The important-looking gentleman on their right may be engrossed in planning promotional schemes for his advertising firm. The burly, ruddy-faced individual near the aisle may be worried over his team's performance in Saturday's game. Whom should he start at end? Will the tackle's knee mend sufficiently for him to play? Is the team psychologically ready? What did the president of the booster's club mean this afternoon when he said, "Let's hope you win this one, John"? The woman in the back row may have difficulty in keeping her two children quiet. Probably she now feels that the speech is not worth her struggles to maintain family decorum. In short: *The speaker is in direct and constant competition with memories, needs, emotions, problems, physical states of being, and other stimuli, which attempt to crowd into the conscious minds of the listeners.*

If you are like most persons, you sometimes read a page or even an entire chapter in a textbook or trade manual before you realize that you have assimilated almost nothing. There has been little, if any, acquiring of information, because you were not attending. Other stimuli have captured your attention; the stimuli furnished by the printed symbols in the book have been too weak to cross the threshold of response. In a like manner, unless listeners give attention to a speech, they cannot receive information, be entertained or be persuaded. To be an effective speaker you must "sell" your listeners on attending to the stimuli supplied by yourself and your speech. Perhaps your most important single problem is to capture and to maintain favorable attention.

Usually psychologists consider that there are two major types of attention: voluntary (forced) and involuntary (effortless). Sometimes auditors may feel a compulsion to listen through a sense of duty, out of respect for the speaker, or to glean sufficient data to pass an examination. However, relatively few persons have the desire or the ability to force themselves to concentrate throughout even a short speech of ten minutes. Of course, as the length of the speech increases, the difficulties of maintaining interest multiply. Instead of relying upon voluntary interest, attempt to make your message so interesting that the listeners will be carried along without conscious effort on their part. Fortunately, certain techniques, sometimes called Factors of Interest, may be used to promote involuntary attention. Before incorporating any supporting material into a speech, evaluate its interest appeal in terms of elements such as these: proximity, vivid concreteness, significance, variety, and humor.

PROXIMITY

One of the bitter complaints of troops returning from Korea during the winter of 1951–1952 was that the American public seemed relatively unconcerned with a "police action" half way around the globe. Kaesong, Panmunjom, Shunsen, Pyongyang, Inje, Heartbreak Ridge, and the Iron Triangle seemed far away to most people. Although the supply of whole blood fell more than two hundred thousand pints below the armed services' standards for safety, appeals for donors brought only a sluggish response. Unlike World War II, when almost every home was directly affected, there was at this time no violent disruption of industry, economy, entertainment, or home life—except for an unfortunate minority. For those with loved ones in the fighting, the Korean War had poignant personal meaning. For them, news from the shell-pocked front involved the life, death, maiming, or capture of a son, husband, or sweetheart. But for most Americans, the conflict was too remote from their daily lives to make them realize that it was their war. As the military and civilian leaders knew, the individual citizen would give only limited support to the mobilization effort until in some way the war entailed personal obligations and sacrifices.

With certain exceptions, our lives revolve around our own interests and needs. Compelling qualities of interest are less frequently evidenced in that which is distant in time, space, interest, or feeling. The following diagram illustrates the principle of proximity. Usually the closer the speech materials come to the "bull's-eye," the greater will be their appeal to involuntary attention.

Bring your material as close as possible to the wants, experiences, and desires of your audience. Do not discuss how inflation will affect people in general; tell how it will affect your listeners. If speaking in Chicago, do not refer to a traffic accident in San Diego; your audience will be much more interested in a crash at the intersection of South Clark Street and Jackson Boulevard. An infant prodigy a thousand miles away may be less interesting than a local genius. Since it is closer to their personal needs, a middle-aged audience will be more receptive to a reference to the problem of excessive weight than will a youthful group. A meeting of union men will have little curiosity in a description of the canapes, the imported china, the fashionable dresses, or other details concerning Mrs. William Barfield's afternoon tea. The same men, however, may have a keen interest in a statement concerning the annual carpenters'-bricklayers' barbecue. Usually a class in public speaking will be more concerned about Adlai Stevenson's methods of speech preparation than those employed by Pericles. As one adult student said, "I've never heard of Pericles before. He may have been a great Grecian orator twenty-five hundred years ago, but he's only a name to me. On the other hand, I have seen Mr. Stevenson dozens of times on television."

Other examples utilizing proximity might be: mentioning someone in the audience by name; calling attention to some object in the room or on the platform; referring to something previously said by the chairman or some other speaker on the program; presenting a hypothetical illustration involving the members of the audience.

Vivid Concreteness

As is well known, the words used by a public speaker are vocal symbols capable of stirring up meanings in the minds of the listeners. Through common acceptance, such symbols have come to stand for certain objects, ideas, actions, or relationships. Communication is possible because both the audience and the speaker have attached similar meanings to the words. It is difficult, however, for many inexperienced speakers to realize that meaning cannot be bundled up like a Christmas present and given to someone else. It is insufficient for the speaker to think in terms of specific reality. He must also phrase his ideas in specific, vividly concrete language (see Chapter 12). Otherwise, his word symbols cannot stimulate the desired meanings in the minds of the auditors.

Concrete thinking on the part of the audience can be promoted by the use of imagery. Imagery, expressed through the language of the speaker, sets off in the hearer's neuromuscular system a complex pattern of neural events based upon memory of previous stimulation. Thus the listeners vicariously experience sensory impressions similar to those they would feel in the actual presence of the things being discussed.

Consider how limited would be the meaning conveyed if a speaker should say, "The two men had a conversation." The word symbol "conversation" has little imagery value. Vivid concreteness could be achieved, however, by describing the appearance of the men, how they shook hands, their physical actions such as slapping the back or gesturing, the intensity with which they spoke, and by giving snatches of dialogue. If you were telling an audience about your visit to the New Orleans waterfront, you could employ almost all of the various types of imagery. Visual imagery could be invoked by describing the physical characteristics of the ships tied up at the docks. Auditory imagery could be stimulated by telling of the boat whistles, the creaking noise of the loading cranes, the cries of the gulls, and the shouts of the longshoremen. Olfactory imagery could be utilized by mentioning the smells of the dank holds of the ships, of the stagnant water, and of the pineapples and bananas being unloaded. Motor or kinaesthetic imagery could be employed by describing the straining efforts of the men in the holds moving the cargo into a position under the hatches. Tactile imagery could be used by recounting how, in the semi-darkness, you felt your way along the rough surface of a bulkhead. Even gustatory imagery could be brought into play by mentioning the bitter taste of the strong coffee you were served aboard one of the ships.

SIGNIFICANCE

During late December of 1951 and early January of 1952, one of the worst hurricanes in a quarter of a century pounded the North Atlantic. The ferocity of the storm, its significance to the lives and economic welfare of seamen and landsmen made it front-page news. Many people noted with interest that the westward passage of the luxury liner, "Queen Mary," was delayed several days, and that among the detained passengers was Prime Minister Winston Churchill who, with his retinue of thirty-five ministers and advisers, was on his way to a Blair House conference with President Truman. One of the most thrilling sagas of man's struggle against the sea grew out of this storm. A seven-thousand-ton freighter, the "Flying Enterprise," seven days out on its Hamburg-New York crossing, was disabled by fifty-foot waves. Although her hull and deck were cracked and she was reeling helplessly, her Captain, Kurt Carlsen, refused to join the crew and passengers in abandoning ship. About a week later, the British tug "Turmoil" arrived and secured a tow line to the stricken vessel. Countless persons followed eagerly the press and radio reports of Captain Carlsen's valiant efforts to bring his ship and his million-dollar cargo of automobiles, pig iron, and coffee beans into Falmouth harbor. Finally, when less than forty-five miles from port, the steel tow line snapped, Carlsen was taken aboard the "Turmoil," and the "Enterprise" surrendered to the crashing seas. At Falmouth a crowd of 10,000, including 350 newsmen, greeted the skipper; commercial offers totaling almost $100,000 poured in; upon his return to New York, half a million people cheered his ticker tape parade up Broadway.

What made this storm and its corollary adventures so absorbing to people on both sides of the Atlantic? And what is its application to speech-making? A small gale, being much less significant, would have received little, if any, attention from the public. Since the "Queen Mary" is one of the most majestic ships afloat, we were interested in her difficulties, but had little curiosity about the scores of smaller craft which were so inconvenienced. Winston Churchill is considered by many to be the "Man of the Half-Century." Whatever happens to him is of significant interest to most of the world. The story of Captain Carlsen stimulated attention because he was fighting to save his life, his ship, and his cargo. We are almost always interested in significant struggles of man against the elements, man against himself, man against man, team against team, and army against army. Here was adventure we could experience vicariously from the safety of our armchairs. Here was action, suspense, and bravery. A sharp contrast to the impelling qualities of the Carlsen story is afforded by the experience of one of the authors. About the time Captain Carlsen was being picked out of the water by the "Turmoil," one of the authors was adrift in a skiff off the Florida coast. Night had settled and sharp swells pitched the light boat violently. However, he was in no genuine danger (although, being a landlubber, he was somewhat alarmed); lights on the shore were easily visible; the outboard motor was soon coaxed to life; and, furthermore, minor mishaps of this sort are common occurrences to fishermen. When, upon returning home, he attempted to recount his "adventure" to his wife, she yawned discreetly and said, "Tell me later, dear; Edward R. Murrow is going to talk about Captain Carlsen and the 'Flying Enterprise.'"

A speaker promotes involuntary attention when he discusses vital, significant considerations. In the following series, notice that ordinarily the items in the left column would possess much higher interest appeal than those in the right.

a prominent person . . . . an unknown individual
a vital decision . . . . an unimportant decision
a major accident . . . . a minor collision
an epoch-making discovery . . . . . . a routine high-school laboratory experiment
a great athlete . . . . a mediocre athlete
a significant social movement . . . . . a localized, ephemeral social action
a dangerous murderer sought
    in an F.B.I. dragnet . . . . a sneak thief wanted by the local sheriff for petty larceny

Of course, this does not mean that audiences will invariably be more interested in materials which concern the important rather than the less important. General significance is only one of several factors of attention. A minor topic especially rich in some other quality of interest, e.g., proximity, might be more stimulating than a nationally important consideration.

Speech materials will possess greater interest value if they involve vital motives or drives. Because of the principle of proximity, the individual members of the audience will respond more readily if the speaker appeals to their own impelling wants or desires. However, through derived interest, audiences are also attentive to the operation of basic human wants in the lives of others. *One of our most fundamental drives is the preservation of our physical well-being.* Through self-identification we may also become interested in the struggles of others to maintain their health and well-being and to save their lives, as in the case of Captain Carlsen.

We are also keenly interested in increasing our prestige and influence, and, to a lesser extent, in the efforts of others to attain respect and power. The desire for satisfactory group status, especially among young people, is one of the most impelling drives. Our manner of thinking, dress, and behavior is based largely upon our social consciousness. Most of us are also eager to acquire power and authority over others, because these in turn lead to higher personal and group esteem.

Another impelling motive, and one that seems to be increasing in strength, is our desire for economic security. Several decades ago, the basic philosophy of America seemed to be a desire for opportunity, but today (despite the election results of 1952) the popular demand is for security. We are acutely conscious of the need to protect ourselves and our families from economic hardships resulting from unemployment, sickness, injury, and old age. In these times of inflation and high taxes, everyone is concerned with increasing the value of his property, raising his salary, saving on fuel bills, and paying less for groceries.

Almost everyone possesses a deep-rooted interest in companionship, loyalty, affection, and sex. Americans are, by and large, a gregarious people. We are a nation of joiners. Much of our social and business life is conducted on a basis of friendship. We have sentimental attachments for our family, our university, our place of employment, the town's baseball club, and our country. We have feelings of loyalty, ranging from weak to intense, toward those who hold similar social, political, religious, or economic beliefs. Conversely, we experience antipathy or dislike toward those whose ideas differ from ours. References to either our friends or enemies may attract attention. Interest in sex is evidenced by even the octogenarian. Women are said to choose perfumes, clothes, and cosmetics that will enhance their attractiveness to men. Sales promotion experts realize that the sex appeal of a shapely model in, let us say, a soft-drink advertisement will attract masculine attention. The male viewer, of course, can hardly avoid noticing that the girl is holding a bottle of cola in her hand.

All of us wish to live our lives with as much personal freedom as possible. We desire relief from external restrictions for ourselves, and are interested in the efforts of others to achieve such freedom. The Thirteen Colonies fought the Revolutionary War, in part, at least, to free themselves from excessive restraints on trade and commerce imposed by England. The spirit of nationalism now agitating the Moslem countries is another manifestation of the desire for freedom from foreign domination. Through empathy we may identify ourselves with a youth who rebels against dictatorial parents. A city apartment dweller may be persuaded to buy a home in the country, if the real estate agent skillfully portrays the greater freedom from external restraints afforded by rural living. It is true, of course, that in the main we obey the customs of society and expect others to do so. However, we resent control when it impinges too sharply upon our freedom of action.

VARIETY

Any constant source of stimulation such as the ticking of a clock or the steady drone of a speaker's voice quickly loses its capacity to provoke a response. If we attempt to concentrate on the key of a typewriter, we soon find our attention wandering. Yet we can lose ourselves in an exciting quarter of basketball because basketball presents a variety of activity. Variety may be only the "spice" of life, but it is a necessity to a speaker. Monotonous sameness in speech content deadens audience interest.

Here are some specific suggestions for the application of the principles of variety in developing the main heads of a speech: (1) A pleasing balance in the forms of support helps maintain attention. Do not overdo the use of any single type of support, but weave into the talk an appealing selection of the various types. (2) When using a particular form of support in series for cumulative effect, apply the principle of variety in the choice of the amplifying materials used. For instance, the excerpt on pages 112–115 utilized four consecutive factual illustrations, yet each example brought out an idea sufficiently different from the others to maintain interest. (3) Do not appeal exclusively to a single type of imagery, but stimulate as many of the various sensations as possible. (4) Direct your materials toward a variety of the impelling motives and basic drives. (5) After you have mastered the didactic method of constructing the ideas of the speech, you might, for the sake of change, occasionally employ the method of implication. (6) Vary the typical direct style of discourse by the use of rhetorical questions. (7) The occasional insertion of conversational dialogue also helps prevent monotony. (8) Most speech materials have little suspense value; therefore, when possible, stimulate curiosity to help hold attention. For instance, when telling a story or a joke save the punch line for a climax at the end.

HUMOR

Fresh, sparkling, appropriate humor can be of value in getting and keeping attention. Listeners rarely maintain an attitude of indifference or dislike toward a speaker who can stimulate them to laughter. In using humor there are certain cautions the speaker needs to keep in mind.

Do not poke embarrassing fun at any person or minority groups present in the audience, even if it is obvious you are only "kidding." Avoid insinuating comments like stating that you saw Joe Smithers at the Golden Shores Club last week with a curvaceous blonde. The audience may roar at Smithers' discomfiture, but neither he nor Mrs. Smithers will appreciate your low-grade humor. Not long ago a speaker acutely embarrassed a dignified Circuit Court Judge by relating how the Judge once got inebriated and caught a plane to Denver instead of making his intended flight to New York. Unless you are certain your auditors will appreciate humor of this type, you will be wise to use only innocuous material.

Instead of ridiculing individuals or minorities present in the audience, poke a little fun at yourself. A witty, belittling anecdote about yourself is almost always good for a laugh and further serves to prove that you are a "regular fellow" and no "stuffed shirt." During the presidential campaign of 1948, Norman Thomas stimulated involuntary attention by occasional references to his repeated failures to secure the Presidency. Even non-Socialists could not help liking a man who was so candid and so objective.

Stale material has limited attention-getting power. Ordinarily avoid securing humor from the widely read *Reader's Digest*, standard joke books, or the recent broadcasts or telecasts of a popular comedian like Bob Hope. If your audience knows what you are going to say, your humor loses much of its punch. Try to make the humor you use as much your own as possible. When using the humor of others, change the names of the characters, alter the background of the story, use new twists and angles, and make special adaptations to fit your audience and the speaking situation.

Avoid off-color humor. Do not feel that you must be smutty in order to be funny.

Be brief. Make every word count. If necessary, write out the humorous material as you think you will give it in the speech. Rework the phrasing until you have eliminated verbiage, leaving a concise, pithy expression of what you may wish to say. The object of this written exercise is not to produce a passage for you to repeat verbatim in your speech, but rather to clarify the essential points of the story or anecdote in your own mind.

Use humor only if it possesses a direct application to the subject, audience, or occasion. Make sure the audience sees the connection.

If the general theme of your speech is serious, be careful that the use of humor does not make it difficult or impossible to regain the serious attention of the audience.

Learn to use other types of humor besides stories, puns, and anecdotes. Effective, fresh, attention-securing humor can be found in a witty turn of phrase, a clever bit of repartee with the chairman, a humorous reference to the occasion or speech situation, or an unexpected twist to an old quotation or poem.

SUMMARY

The main heads of the Discussion of the speech represent only a skeletal framework. They must be developed by means of supporting materials. The basic oral forms of support are extended and short factual illustrations, hypothetical illustrations, statistics, literal and figurative comparisons, testimony, restatement and repetition, explanation, and deductive and causal reasoning. Frequently the use of visual aids helps make the main points clear, interesting, and persuasive. Involuntary attention may be stimulated if certain factors of interest are utilized in the development: proximity, vivid concreteness, significance, variety, and humor.

EXERCISES AND ASSIGNMENTS

1. From the written text of a speech by some prominent person, pick out each form of support and each factor of interest used. What appeals to basic drives were made? Which types of imagery were employed? (As we have indicated before, excellent sources for speech texts are: A. C. Baird's *Representative American Speeches* for any year, Harold Harding's *Age of Danger*, and the magazine *Vital Speeches*.)

2. Prepare a three-minute speech constructed around two or three factual illustrations.

3. Analyze a news report by some prominent radio or television commentator to discover the forms of support and the factors of interest used.

4. Write a description of some event or happening. Use as many of the various types of imagery as possible.

5. Prepare a five-minute speech employing as many as possible of the basic drives.

6. Can any one of the factors of interest be selected as the most important? If so, which? Why? If not, why not?

7. Which of the forms of support are best suited for logical proof? Which the least suited? Why?

8. Make a careful study of one of the forms of support. Deliver in class a brief report on its strengths and weaknesses as logical proof and on its capacity to clarify and to interest.

9. Give a five-minute talk in class on the importance of and the nature of a particular factor of interest. Also, be sure to tell how a speaker could make practical use of this factor.

10. Explain to the class why a particular drive discussed in this chapter deserves to be considered a basic motivating force in our lives. Tell how it can be used in speech making. As in exercises 8 and 9, use plenty of examples to illustrate your ideas.

11. For one day keep a list of mistakes in deductive and causal reasoning you hear at school, home, and at your job.

12. Prepare a four-minute talk involving the use of some visual aid. Possible demonstration topics:
  (1) Making a pair of beach sandals from a pair of old shoes
  (2) Holding a baseball for different types of pitches
  (3) Fitting eyeglasses into their frames
  (4) Applying stage make-up
  (5) Skinning game
  (6) Landing a plane on an aircraft carrier
  (7) Making a dress
  (8) Cleaning a carburetor
  (9) Making puppets
  (10) Operating a movie camera
  (11) Removing a fossil from its place of discovery
  (12) The operation of a fire extinguisher
  (13) Different kinds of knots
  (14) Man-to-man and zone defenses in basketball
  (15) The Siege of Vicksburg
  (16) How a submarine submerges and resurfaces
  (17) Simple plumbing repairs
  (18) The insides of a television set
  (19) Some sights of Paris
  (20) The circulatory system of a human being

CHAPTER 7

Developing the Introduction

As in the business interview, the successful outcome of the public speech depends in part upon initial impressions. No effective salesman would walk into the office of a stranger, sit down at the desk, and begin to transact business. Instead, he would introduce himself and state the purpose of his call before attempting to make a sale. In ordinary circumstances the public speaker should not launch into the middle of a speech without some sort of introduction. The primary functions of the Introduction are to stimulate favorable attention and to prepare the audience for the Discussion. How long the Introduction should be depends upon the circumstances involved, as we shall see later; but the average length is about 10 per cent of the entire speech.

STIMULATE FAVORABLE ATTENTION

Through past experience with dull speakers, the American public has been conditioned to expect the worst. Therefore, you must establish yourself at the outset as an interesting, animated speaker with a worth-while message. You must sell yourself and your speech. A dull, flat, awkward beginning will severely weaken, if not completely destroy, the effectiveness of your entire address. The inexperienced speaker should begin every talk with a *Favorable Attention Step*. Let us look now at certain relatively sure methods for creating favorable audience interest.

A. Refer to the significance of the subject.   One of the most reliable methods of securing immediate attention is to show your listeners how important your topic is *to them*. Do more than point out the significance to people in general; go a step further and make clear the application to the members of the audience. (Review in Chapter

6 "Significance" and "Proximity" as Factors of Interest.) A shoe salesman does not attempt to fit all customers with a single style, size,
and color. As a public speaker you must custom-tailor your material
to fit the needs of your listeners. Demonstrate that your message
will save them money, save them time, make them more popular,
increase their earnings, reduce their auto insurance rates, improve
their appearance or their health, protect them from bodily injury,
and so on. In this way the audience will realize that you have
something meaningful to say. Examples: (1) In the opening of his
speech to the National Federation of Women's Republican Clubs,
Dr. You Chan Yang, Korean Ambassador to the United States,
stressed the significance of his subject ("Give Us Guns and Save
Your Sons"):[1]

You pay the embattled people of Korea a great honor by inviting me,
their servant, to address you here today. These are times of dreadful
mental anxiety for all of us—all of us who remain in a shrinking free
world.

Thousands of splendid American boys lie buried in the soil of Korea.
Tens of thousands of Korean soldiers have suffered the same fate. My
country is a vast charnel house with ruins and rubble everywhere. I have
termed it a land of the dead and the dying. This it has been for more
than two years now . . . twenty-seven months nearly, to be precise.

(2) Elmer L. Lindseth (President, the Cleveland Electric Illuminat-
ing Company) began an address on "The Price of Prejudice," which
was delivered at an annual conference of the National Urban
League, with a direct reference to the importance of the topic:[2]

Cleveland is grateful to the National Urban League for selecting our
city for this inter-group relations conference at which such important
study is being given to the problems of the Negro citizen in the complex
welter of modern life.

Too few Americans realize how deeply these problems affect all of us—
regardless of who we are or what our occupations may be. In fact, part
of the solution, I believe, is to make this realization so vivid that none
can overlook it.

If I can further that one cause here this morning—if I can in some way
help provide some ideas by which we may portray to all Americans the

[1] *Vital Speeches,* October 15, 1952.
[2] *Vital Speeches,* October 1, 1952.

terrific price of prejudice being paid today—perhaps I can make worthwhile my appearance on your program.

B. Use humor. Although frequently misused, humor can be an excellent method of stimulating favorable interest in the Introduction. Since the opening remarks probably constitute the most conspicuous part of a speech, be especially careful to follow the seven suggestions in Chapter 6 for the use of humor. It is perhaps sufficient here to remind the reader that humor should be fresh, relevant, appropriate, and brief. For a twenty-minute speech humorous introductory material should usually be kept under a minute and a half. As you recall, the average length of the Introduction is about 10 per cent of the total speech. If the Favorable Attention Step takes too much time, either the Clarification Step will be slighted, or the Introduction will be too long. Here are some sample situations in which humor was used to secure interest: (1) A human-relations expert began a talk on courtship in this manner: "Courtship has been semi-seriously defined as that short interlude between lipstick and mop stick." (2) A candidate running for office began a speech at a political barbecue: "I have heard it said that most of our problems in this country could be solved if our politicians in Washington put their heads together—as hard as they possible could." (3) At a meeting of a local bar association a judge introduced his speech ("The Social Responsibilities of the Legal Profession") like this:

According to a story told by the late Judge Hollister, the gate between heaven and hell broke down one day. When Saint Peter discovered the condition of the gate he called to the devil: "Hey, Satan, it's your turn to fix it this time."

"My apologies, sir," replied the boss of the land beyond the Styx. "My men are much too busy to worry about a broken gate."

"Well, then," growled Saint Peter, "I'll sue you for breaking our agreement."

"Yeah?" retorted the devil. "Where will you get a lawyer?"

C. Tell an illustrative story. An example of the effective use of personal experience as a Favorable Attention Step is afforded by a Jew who, at the time of the address, was touring America soliciting contributions for the state of Israel. During World War II his family had been tortured by the Nazis; after the war he had spent several years in a displaced-persons camp, then migrated to Palestine. He began his talk by telling some of his experiences and by showing that they were typical of those of numerous other European Jews who had been uprooted from their prewar homes. It was a compelling indictment of anti-Semitism, moving even to those who opposed the idea of Israel as a homeland for the Jews.

Factual illustrations other than personal experiences can also be used effectively to capture favorable interest. Examples: (1) At the time of his inauguration as president of Stanford University, Dr. J. E. Wallace Sterling began his inaugural address in this manner:[3]

> During the recent war I heard a broadcast by that distinguished reporter, Edward R. Murrow. He had gone along on an air mission over Germany, and was describing the experience. The tension before take-off time seemed to be relaxed once he was air-borne, but as the ship moved across German soil and nearer to the target it occurred to Mr. Murrow how much his courage would have been amplified if only he had been able to leave his stomach at home. The run over the target was made and the bombs released without misadventure. But the flak was heavy. One shell exploded, as Mr. Murrow thought, quite close to the ship and he said to the pilot, "Skipper, that one was pretty close." "Oh, no," responded the Skipper, "when they're really close you can smell 'em." This observation made no sense whatsoever to Mr. Murrow because, as he reported, he had been holding his breath for three hours.
>
> The purpose for which you have been good enough to assemble here today and the peace and beauty of this setting are far removed from the context of war. But I must say that my stomach and breath control are not unaffected by the occasion. For I am deeply sensitive to what is visible and audible in this ceremony and to its symbolism as well.

(2) A speaker soliciting funds for the Red Cross might introduce his subject by relating a specific instance where that organization had provided dramatic assistance to distressed people. (3) If seeking to impress factory workmen with the need for caution in using certain machinery, a foreman might secure attention by telling how a former worker had lost his right arm and left hand only a short time previously because he had ignored the safety devices on a drill press. The foreman should tell specifically how the man was injured through carelessness, and how the accident had worked a severe financial hardship upon his family.

[3] A. C. Baird, *Representative American Speeches: 1950–1951*, pp. 150, 151. Used by permission of Dr. Sterling.

Although the narration of an actual happening is usually much more effective, the relating of an imaginary occurrence can be used to secure attention when a true story is not available. (1) In a speech on the hydrogen bomb, the Favorable Attention Step might describe the dropping of such a bomb on New York City and the resulting chaos. Since no such happening has occurred, the hypothetical story would be necessary. (2) The following excerpt from a student speech demonstrates a different type of fictitious story:

Sometime during childhood we have all read or have been told the enthralling fantasies of the "Arabian Nights." In the story of Aladdin and his lamp, you will remember that Aladdin had lost the magic lamp, the rubbing of which produced a genie bound to carry out all of its owner's wishes. Feeling certain that the lamp had been found by someone in the village, Aladdin conceived an ingenious idea. Disguising himself as a peddler and carrying a basket loaded with bright new lamps, he proceeded from one street to another in the village, crying, "New lamps for old! New lamps for old!" Soon there appeared an old man who sought to trade the battered lamp Aladdin was seeking for a bright, shiny new one.

Perhaps we of America, like the aged man in the fable, have traded an old lamp for a shiny new one! . . .

D. Use a stimulating quotation. A satisfactory method of creating involuntary attention in the Introduction is to use a striking, brief, relevant quotation from a person, book, magazine, or newspaper. The speaker is not limited to quotations taken from written works, but may select oral testimony as well. The flexibility of the quotation as an attention-getter is shown in the following examples. (1) Professor U. G. Dubach, Head of the Political Science Department at Lewis and Clark College, began an address to the Economic Club of Detroit with these intriguing quotations: [4]

More than twenty years ago at Corvallis, Will Durant said: "We stand between two worlds: one dead, and one not yet born; and civilization is chaos for a generation." He said that before the great depression, and those of us who couldn't think, wondered what was the matter with him. Now we wonder what was the matter with us. He was so right.

In this generation I think another truth needs to be repeated which a man expressed about 175 years ago—a great Englishman—"Great empires and little minds go ill together." What a sentence for the hour! "Great

[4] *Vital Speeches*, December 15, 1951.

empires and little minds go ill together." Edmund Burke said something else that brightens me because it is so apropos of the moment. He was talking about his great country: "I fear power—I fear the power of my own nation because who can say that she will not abuse that power." His fears have been borne out in England, and about this I shall speak a little later. But who can say America will not misunderstand or abuse the power and the responsibilities she has at the moment?

(2) A preacher wishing to stimulate his hearers to re-examine their own actions and thinking in the light of Christian doctrines began his sermon like this: "Walpole once said, 'In my youth I thought of writing a satire on mankind, but now in my age I think I should write an apology for them.'" (3) A journalist addressing a woman's club on the role of literature in modern civilization might introduce his topic in this manner:

Books are not dull, inanimate, unimportant sheets of paper attached to cardboard bindings. Without the written recordings of man's thoughts and emotions civilization would be impossible. Clarence Day has expressed well the importance of books in these words: "The world of books is the most remarkable creation of man. Nothing else that he builds ever lasts. Monuments fall. Nations perish. Civilizations grow old and die out— and after an era of darkness—new races build others, but in the world of books are volumes that have seen this happen again and again—and yet live on—still young—still as fresh as the day they were written—still telling men's hearts of the hearts of men—centuries dead!"

E. Mention common relationships, beliefs, interests, and feelings. When addressing audiences which are neutral or favorable toward the speaker's proposal, the speaker can stimulate attention by referring to interests common to both speaker and audience. To illustrate: (1) At the annual meeting of the Inland Daily Press Association, Chicago, Illinois, February 17, 1953, Henry Ford II introduced his topic ("The Free World Can't Trade on a One-Way Street") with this reference to common interests: [5]

I am very happy to be here today. There is something I would like to talk about—and I believe that there is no more appropriate audience for my particular purpose than the newspaper editors and publishers of this great midwest area of the nation—the Inland Daily Press Association.

[5] *Vital Speeches,* March 15, 1953.

We are living in an age when faster and faster communication is being developed between greater and greater numbers of people. In my own lifetime, we have seen some fairly sensational developments. Airplanes have brought the towers of Chicago—including one or two of the ivory variety—within a few hours of London or Honolulu. The telephone has brought us even closer together, and the radio and television have made communication practically instantaneous.

Then, there is that other medium which some people say is even faster than instantaneous on occasion. I mean, of course, the press.

Certainly, therefore, this seems an appropriate time and place to discuss some of the problems that face us in communicating with other people. I say the place is important because, startling as it may seem to many Americans, our often-called "isolationist" Midwest is one of the great trading areas of the world. . . .

(2) A civic leader talking to a boys' club might tell the youngsters of seeing Ralph Kiner hit three home runs in New York the day before, mention that fifteen years earlier he had been a member of this same boys' club, or might refer to his long friendship with the club's director. (3) In his Favorable Attention Step, a commencement speaker might describe his own feelings and emotions at his graduation two decades previously, or state that immediately after the program he was flying to New Haven to attend his son's graduation.

When addressing an audience opposed to his program, the speaker must at once reach common ground with his auditors. As we found in Chapter 2, the psychological set of the "hostile" audience conditions it against the case of the speaker, and very likely against the speaker himself. In such a situation, the first task is to secure an objective hearing. Differences need to be minimized in the Introduction. "Accentuate the positive," as the once popular song goes. If the Favorable Attention Step stresses the basic points of agreement between the speaker and the audience, the points of difference which are presented later may not appear insurmountable. Frequently, if we analyze the situation carefully, we find that the speaker and the audience have the same basic purpose or end result in mind, but that the paths or methods for reaching the objectives may differ. Virtually no situations exist in which there are no elements of common ground between the speaker and his audience. An extreme example of this truism: Only a handful of Westerners have entered the mysterious city of Lhasa. However, Lowell Thomas, who visited the Dalai Lama in Lhasa before the Russian invasion, found powerful bonds linking the interests of Tibet and America.

In order for the speaker to encourage listeners to be fair-minded toward him, he should be fair-minded toward them. A speaker should be thoroughly convinced of the rightness of his cause. He should not forget, however, that the people to whom he is speaking also feel their beliefs are right and just. All of us are fond of our ideas and convictions. We resent any clumsy attempt by a speaker to change our minds. If we did not think we were right, we should have already altered our views. When approached tactlessly, we close our minds to new, unwelcome proposals. However, if approached courteously by a speaker who evidences respect for our beliefs, we feel less on the defensive—hence will possess a more open mind.

There are several requirements you must realize before you can reach common ground with those who disagree with your recommendations.

First, understand that *others view the matter differently from the way you do*, that their beliefs are sincere and genuine, and that they are convinced reason and justice are on their side. *Beware!* It is easy to tell yourself: "Yes, I know they think differently. That's why I'm going to change them." Such a speaker does not really *accept* the fact that his listeners do think differently and do feel that they are *justified* in thinking as they do.

Second, attempt to find the basic reasons for the listeners' objection to your plan. Since we are largely products of our environment, it should not be difficult to trace the causes for their beliefs. Very likely you will discover a surprising amount of logic on their side that you had not thought of before.

Third, what does the *listener* believe the elements of common ground to be? How would you wish to be approached on this problem if you held their beliefs? Of course the speaker cannot mention common relationships, beliefs, interests, and feelings in his Favorable Attention Step and then abandon his courteous, psychological approach during the remainder of the speech.

Let us look at two instances in which speakers were compelled to seek common ground with partially hostile audiences. (1) A college fraternity was being split into two rival groups over the expulsion of a member. At the meeting called to vote upon the question, a leader of the wing favoring expulsion rose to speak. He began by expressing a deep love for the fraternity and stated that he was sorry for the hostility among the members and was ashamed of his own uncharitable actions. He read several letters from prominent alumni urging amicable settlement of the problem. He admitted that both sides desired what was best for the fraternity and that the only real controversy involved the means of attaining this goal. The speaker explained that since the issue was so important to the well-being of the fraternity, he wished to present his arguments as dispassionately as possible, and that he anticipated hearing a spokesman from the other side in order that the differences might be speedily reconciled. This mild, conciliatory approach did much to mollify the opposition. Indeed, the opposition had to agree with everything he had said. With such a gentlemanly, agreeable manner of introducing his case, the other side was much more inclined to listen objectively.

(2) During the Presidential campaign, on September 30, 1952, Dwight D. Eisenhower spoke to a huge crowd at Columbia, South Carolina.[6] The introduction of that address illustrates his highly successful method of reaching common understanding with a traditionally anti-Republican audience.

I am happy to be in the South again and I am proud to be in South Carolina. It is good to be among friends—and it is particularly good to be welcomed here by my close and long-time friend, your distinguished Governor, Jimmy Byrnes.

You know, going South is becoming a habit with me—and a very pleasant one. From what Governor Byrnes says, I gather the habit is beginning to catch on. I know you will give my distinguished opponent a warm welcome when he comes. But you will forgive me if I say I am glad I got here first. It is my aim to continue to keep ahead of him—right through November 4.

Here, close to your lovely Capitol, I am sharply reminded that some ninety years ago, now, South Carolina and the South were a grim and bloody and a tragic battleground. Through good and evil times, you in the South have cherished the heroes and the heroisms of those years.

There, in front of me as I speak, is a monument which illustrates just what I mean. It is a monument "Erected by the women of South Carolina

[6] *Vital Speeches,* October 15, 1952.

to South Carolina's dead of the Confederate Army: 1861–1865." Someone copied for me the words which are carved on it. Let me read part of them:

"Let the stranger who may in future times read this inscription recognize that these were men whom power could not corrupt, whom death could not terrify, whom defeat could not dishonor, and let their virtues plead for just judgment of the cause in which they perished.

"Let the South Carolinian of another generation remember that the state taught them how to live and how to die, and that from her broken fortunes she has preserved for her children the priceless treasure of their memories, teaching all who may claim the same birthright that truth, courage and patriotism endure forever."

Those words, my friends, were written by South Carolinians about South Carolinians. But—North or South—young or old—any American who can read them and fail to be stirred by them has missed something of the heroic meaning of America.

I read, the other day, a newspaper article, written by a Southerner, which said that this year the South is again a battleground—a political battleground. I can only express my hope and my firm belief that you will engage in this political battle in the spirit and with the high motives of the words inscribed on that monument. If you do that, then—whatever the outcome—I will be satisfied with the result.

F. Ask the audience a stimulating question. An easy way to test the "striking" quality of a question is to turn it into a declarative statement. Unless the resulting sentence is stimulating, the question itself will not be so. The query "Do you have sufficient insurance?" when turned into a declaration becomes "You have sufficient insurance." Obviously such a sentence has little attention value. Avoid asking dull, flat, pointless questions or insulting ones such as: Are you Christians? Do you engage in corrupt business practices? Are you unconsciously cruel to your children?

Here are some examples of how the stimulating question can secure favorable attention. (1) A civic leader addressing a group of adults on juvenile delinquency used as his Favorable Attention Step:

What would you do if your son came to you this evening and said, "Dad, I've just killed a man"? What would be your emotions when he poured out his story that he had been drinking and, as he was speeding home, his car struck a pedestrian? Your son a hit-skip driver? A juvenile delinquent? Of course not, you say. But this very situation confronted a neighbor of mine this spring. He didn't think it could happen either— but it did!

(2) A football coach speaking to a rabid collegiate crowd at a bon-fire rally started off his "pep talk" by asking the question "Are you with the team?" (He knew, of course, that the students were frenetically partisan, and that the asking of this question would give them a chance to let off steam. Under ordinary circumstances such a question would lack stimulating qualities.) After the noise had partially subsided, the coach asked, "Do you think we're going to win?" This offered the students another opportunity to participate. (3) A student discussing his experiences at a summer resort in North Carolina began his talk in this manner: "Have you ever found a six-foot-long diamondback rattlesnake in your closet? Well, I did last summer. . . ."

G. Make a pithy, stimulating statement. The striking statement is used in much the same manner as the stimulating question. An ordinary, dull phrase will not gain attention. To catch interest, a sentence must be different, it must be intriguing. Here are some sample illustrations. (1) A student began a talk on the prevalence of prejudice against the Jew like this:

Adolf Hitler is not dead. He is living here in the United States. How do I know Hitler isn't dead? I know because I saw him this afternoon in a hamburger shop on Fifth Street. No, of course, I don't mean Mr. Mustache himself. I mean, I met his spirit. Let me tell you what happened.

He then told the audience of the anti-Semitic remarks which had been made by one of the men in the hamburger shop. (2) The prosecuting attorney leans toward the jury and says with quiet emphasis:

Ladies and gentlemen of the jury: Under this cloth on the table lies the evidence that will send the defendant to prison. [He quickly draws away the cloth.] Look! Here on the table is the hitherto undiscovered typewriter which was used to type the ransom notes. . . .

(3) Public speakers could profitably study the trenchant, interesting methods used by *Time* magazine to introduce its articles. A recent

article about Francois Mauriac and other "confused" Europeans opened with this striking statement:

> The difference between a confused intellectual and an ostrich is that the ostrich cannot manufacture its own sand.

H. Refer to the occasion or purpose of the meeting. Ordinarily a brief reference to the occasion or purpose of the gathering will be made at such speeches as the laying of the cornerstone of a building, the opening of a new bridge, the opening of a new store, the unveiling of a statue, the installation of a new chapter of a lodge, the dedication of a dam, or the awarding of a trophy (see Chapter 15).

If some significant events or accomplishments have produced the reason for the meeting, the audience will expect an early reference to them. For instance, in an address on "The Challenge of Human Relations" (delivered at an Abraham Lincoln celebration of the City Club, Rochester, New York) Dr. Ralph Bunche immediately related the purpose of the meeting to his speech:[7]

> We are gathered here tonight to pay tribute to a man of rare greatness—one of the most stalwart figures of our nation's history. But it is not within our feeble power to do honor to Abraham Lincoln except as we may dedicate ourselves to the fulfilment of the imperative objectives which he sought. . . .
> I have chosen to speak tonight to the topic—"The Challenge of Human Relations"—for two reasons.
> In the first place, it seems to me to be a rather appropriate subject for this occasion. Lincoln, himself, was called upon to save this nation from as great a crisis and conflict in human relations as has ever confronted any nation. . . .
> In the second place, the greatest danger to mankind today, in my view, is to be found in the sordid human relations which everywhere prevail.
> Were Lincoln alive today, he could scarcely avoid taking a dark view of the relations among peoples the world over, not by any means excluding his own country. It would be understandable if even a quick view of the situation should induce in him one of those occasional moods of melancholia which some historians have attributed to him.

[7] A. C. Baird, *Representative American Speeches: 1949–1950*, pp. 142, 143. Used by permission of Dr. Bunche.

I. Compliment the audience. All of us appreciate commendation. If a person is intelligent enough to admire us, we tend to believe he has used similar good judgment in arriving at other ideas, and listen to him somewhat less critically. *Warning:* an audience is quick to sense and to resent flattery. Avoid such fawning expressions as: "I am glad to have the opportunity to speak to such intelligent people"; "Being mentally superior persons, you will approve of my plan"; "I don't believe I have ever talked to such a splendid group."

As in social conversation, frequent opportunities arise in the public speaking situation for the speaker to pay his listeners genuine compliments. Let us look at some sample situations. (1) If you are the guest of a corporation, labor union, university, or social organization, and have been treated courteously and generously, it will be only polite for you to refer to this hospitality in the Introduction. On Herbert Hoover's seventy-fourth birthday some fifteen thousand Iowans gathered in an all-day celebration in his honor. After a picnic dinner and a parade of bands and drum corps, Mr. Hoover rose to speak:

I am deeply grateful for your reception and the honor which you do me today. I deeply appreciate the many thousands of kindly acts and kindly wishes which have marked the day. They come both from those of you who are present and from many parts of my country—which adds to my gratitude. . . .

(2) If you are an outsider speaking in a city or state famed for its scenery, sports, fashion centers, or climate, you may signify your recognition of the prominence for which the community is noted. In a campaign address in Miami, Adlai Stevenson attempted to secure favorable attention with this compliment:[8]

In less strenuous times it has been my good fortune to follow the sun to Florida a couple of times on less urgent business. And, as always, I find myself wondering today if you who live in this well-blessed land fully appreciate your fortunate estate. Or is that a minor compensation reserved for us to whom blue sky, bright sea, and white sand are a benediction after a gray Northern winter?

To me, as to most outlanders, Florida has always seemed a very special

[8] *Miami Herald,* October 12, 1952.

place. As I have come to know this incredible peninsula of yours since I first came here as a boy more than forty years ago, I have understood why every visitor looks upon Florida with a proprietary interest—feeling a personal sense of discovery as though he alone had found a green land rising from the sea. . . .

Here where we stand you have brought forth a world-famous flowering park from a mangrove swamp. Behind it you have erected your shining city of the sun. Seaward you have raised from the waters that fabulous island, Miami Beach. These things you have added to God's bounty in little more than half a century. . . .

(3) If the organization to which you are speaking has had an outstanding record of public service, you are justified in referring to this tradition. On March 31, 1949, the Massachusetts Institute of Technology held its Mid-Century Convocation on the Social Implications of Scientific Progress. The principal speaker, Winston Churchill, spoke to a distinguished audience of fifteen thousand persons. Mr. Churchill began:[9]

I am honored by your wish that I should take part in the discussions of the Massachusetts Institute of Technology. We have suffered in Great Britain by the lack of colleges of university rank in which engineering and the allied subjects are taught. Industrial production depends on technology and it is because the Americans . . . have realized this and created institutions for the advanced training of large numbers of high-grade engineers to translate the advantages of pure science into industrial technique . . . that their output per head and consequent standard of life are so high. It is surprising that England, which was the first country to be industrialized, has nothing of comparable stature. . . . If we are to bring the broad masses of the people in every land to the table of abundance, it can only be by the tireless improvement of all our means of technical production, and by the diffusion in every form of education of an improved quality to scores of millions of men and women. Even in this darkling hour I have faith that this process will go on.

(4) If the listeners have had to wait through several hours of ceremony, oratory, or presentation of awards, or if they have had to combat inclement weather to attend the meeting, you can voice

---

[9] Speech of March 31, 1949, at the Massachusetts Institute of Technology. *In The Balance*, ed. by Randolph Churchill, London, copyright 1951, Cassell and Co., Ltd., and copyright 1952, Houghton Mifflin Company.

your appreciation. Many years ago in Freeport, Illinois, Stephen A. Douglas began a rejoinder to Abraham Lincoln with this deft compliment:

The silence with which you have listened to Mr. Lincoln during his hour is creditable to this vast audience, composed of men of various political parties. Nothing is more honorable to any large mass of people assembled for the purpose of fair discussion than that kind and respectful attention that is yielded, not only to your political friends, but to those who are opposed to you in politics.

(5) If you have been generously applauded upon being introduced, you might thank the listeners for the warmth of their welcome, as did Mr. Hoover on page 176.

PREPARE THE AUDIENCE FOR THE DISCUSSION OF THE SPEECH

A brief orientation of the audience to the speech topic can be secured by following the Favorable Attention Step with a *Clarification Step*. As the term indicates, the function of the Clarification Step is to "clarify," to make clear to the listeners the nature and purpose of the talk, and to give necessary preliminary explanations and definitions. There are three basic methods of achieving the Clarification Step.

A. State the POINT of the speech.   Frequently talks fail to show clearly to the listeners exactly what the speaker wishes them to think, feel, or do. Many times upon asking public speaking classes in industrial organizations as well as in college classrooms to give the purpose of a student's speech, we have discovered that the class had only a vague conception of the POINT. In some cases, members of the audience gave sharply contradictory explanations of the speech purpose. A business letter, a board meeting, a serious social conversation, almost everything in our pattern of daily living has a purpose. Every effective speech not only has a POINT or purpose, but the audience knows what that POINT is.

There can be little doubt of the purpose of a speech if the speaker tells the audience the POINT in a concise, definite statement. If the speaker cannot phrase his intent in one sentence, it is vague in his own mind and therefore will be even less distinct to the hearers. In order to orient the audience to the POINT, one needs only to paraphrase the Specific Speech Purpose. To illustrate: (1) Eugenie Anderson (United States Ambassador to Denmark) prepared her University of Minnesota audience for the Discussion of her speech by saying:[10]

. . . But many people have been asking me questions since I've been home—not always easy questions to answer. Through most of them runs a persistent line that might best be expressed by the question, "Is Our Foreign Policy Working?" It is to that main question that I want to address myself tonight.

(2) Here is the opening sentence of Dean Acheson's address which was delivered at a conference on International Cooperation for World Economic Development (held on the Berkeley campus of the University of California):

I wish to make a report to you about the tensions between the United States and the Soviet Union.

(3) In November of 1951, Robert Ramspeck (Chairman, U. S. Civil Service Commission) used this skillful Introduction in a speech to the Washington Trade Association Executives: [11]

	When John Hulse invited me to speak here today, I more than welcomed the idea. For, in addition to the feeling I naturally have that I am returning to visit old friends and associates in the Trade Association field, I have the firm belief that in talking to this particular
Reference to the Occasion	audience I have an opportunity to reach far beyond the confines of this room and to contact one of the most important elements of our national life. This element, which we broadly describe as business, can do much to solve one of the gravest problems confronting our country today.
Compliment to the Audience	You people are businessmen and women. You represent still greater numbers of business people throughout the country who have banded together in trade associations to further their own particular interests. In the business world, you are key people. Your mem-

[10] *Vital Speeches,* December 15, 1951.
[11] *Ibid.*

bers rely upon you to keep them posted on affairs of
Government. They depend on you for guidance and
leadership.

In part, your jobs consist of smoothing and improving
the relationships between those you represent and the
Reference to Federal Government. As one of your slogans so admi-
Common rably puts it: "Ninety percent of trade association work
Relationships is public relations." In my present position as chairman
of the U. S. Civil Service Commission—the personnel
arm of the Government—improvement of the Government's relations with the public is one of my duties.

So, you see, we're on the same mission. You promul-
gate the interests of your respective groups, striving
always to have those group interests coincide with the
public interest. Government interests *are* the public interest. So our interests are bound to be identical. That's
precisely my point. We're all on the same team. What's
good for business is good for Government, and vice
versa. . . . In today's trying circumstances, there is a
greater-than-ever need for closer-than-ever cooperation. . . .

But are we truly aware of the need for singleness
of purpose in our every thought, word and action in the
life-or-death struggle for survival in which we find our-
Statement selves today? One clear indication that we do not
of the realize the dangers which lurk in the shadows of dis-
POINT unity is the alarming growth of invidious, indiscriminate
smearing of Government employees as a class and the
general disparagement of Government and its functions
which we find on all sides today.

B. State the main heads or arguments of the Discussion. When
it is essential that the audience retain the main arguments of the
talk, the speaker may list them in the Clarification Step before discussing them in the Discussion. This is analogous to looking over
the chapter headings of a book before beginning to read Chapter
One. It gives the listener a preview of what is coming, thereby
orienting him better to the ideas when they are presented later.
Ordinarily the speaker will state the POINT of the speech before
listing the main heads. Examples: (1) An airline representative
wishing to sell his audience on flying might use as his Clarification
Step:

Flying is by far the best method of traveling any distance. There are at least five reasons why you should fly on your next trip. First, air-travel is fast; second, it is dependable; third, it is comfortable; fourth, it is economical; and fifth, it is safe.

In the Discussion of his speech the representative would establish the validity of these contentions. (2) A student who wanted to convince his audience that off-track betting should be legalized stated his POINT and his reasons like this:

I believe that we should legalize off-track betting in our state for several reasons. First, we have to realize that our inability to enforce existing anti-gambling ordinances is making a mockery out of law enforcement. Second, the state is losing at least ten million dollars in revenue a year since there is no tax on illegal gambling. Third, attempts to enforce anti-gambling ordinances cost the state thousands of dollars a year. Fourth, off-track betting is no more immoral than legalized track betting or bingo games. Fifth, the gangster element which now directs off-track betting could be effectively controlled if such betting were legalized and controlled.

(3) In the Introduction of his speech to the American Institute of Mining and Metallurgical Engineers, December, 1952, Max W. Ball listed the major headings of his Discussion:

My subject is oil for the free world's needs. It can be summed up in five short statements:
(1) oil is indispensable;
(2) the world's appetite for oil is insatiable;
(3) the chief risks to an adequate future supply are political;
(4) those risks can only be minimized by a firm foreign policy;
(5) unless they are so minimized the world's oil needs may not be met.
I hope that you will study with me the basis for each of those statements.

C. Provide necessary background explanations. Frequently, definitions will be helpful, if not absolutely essential, in orienting the audience to the topic. Make clear the meaning of any terms which are basically important to the speech. (1) In the preceding illustration concerning off-track betting, the speaker probably should have included in his Clarification Step a definition of this type of gambling. Uninformed persons in the audience might believe that off-track betting included dice, roulette, bolita, and the numbers games. Such misinformation might prejudice them against the speaker's proposal. (2) A debater on Town Hall arguing that basic non-agricultural industries should be nationalized must answer several questions about the topic before he can proceed with his address: What is meant by "nonagricultural industries"? Which industries are included? Which excluded? What is meant by "nationalized"? (3) In a speech designed to convince a Boston audience that "the better educated soldier is a better military man," Arthur S. Adams (President, American Council on Education) began with this definition:[12]

> It is a genuine pleasure, as well as a high privilege, to have the opportunity to meet with you this evening. In speaking to the topic, "Education for National Strength," I think it necessary that our understanding of "strength" not be a narrow concept of force or power. Webster defines strength as "the quality or state of being strong." I should like to expand upon that definition by saying that I regard strength as the ability to apply resources effectively to the solution of problems.

(4) In December, 1951, William H. Joyce, Jr. (Economic Cooperation Administration official) opened his address to the First International Conference of Manufacturers with this definition:[13]

> The very term "productivity" which we have all been thinking and talking about, particularly in recent weeks, derives originally from the Latin verb *produco* which means to lead forth. The meaning of this Latin word has, I think, a very direct and genuine significance for every person in this audience. For, as I see it, the underlying purpose of our international Management Productivity Mission, and the underlying purpose of this splendid first International Conference of Manufacturers, are one and the same. That purpose is to stimulate the businessmen of the free world to lead forth not merely as the custodians of free enterprise, but rather as the proponents of the kind of free enterprise which is both free and enterprising, which can constantly renew itself, and win evergrowing respect and support, by means of fresh contributions to the community, local, national and international.

In order to understand the present significance or meaning of a topic, an audience may require some explanation of previous events

---

[12] *Vital Speeches,* January 1, 1952.
[13] *Ibid.*

pertinent to the subject. (1) A world traveler speaking about modern Japan would need to trace briefly the history of Japan in order that his listeners might understand better the present patterns of thought and behavior. (2) In discussing the submarine as a modern sea fighter, the speaker might preface his remarks with a brief narration of the developmental history of the submarine. (3) In a radio address to the nation, December 15, 1950, Mr. Truman declared that a state of emergency would be proclaimed on the following day. During the Introduction, the President found it desirable to explain briefly the events which had necessitated such a speech: [14]

Statement of the POINT

Reference to Significance of Topic

Historical Background Information

I am talking to you tonight about what our country is up against, and what we are going to do about it.

Our homes, our nation, all the things we believe in are in great danger. This danger has been created by the rulers of the Soviet Union.

For five years we have been working for peace and justice among nations. We have helped to bring the free nations of the world together in a great movement to establish a lasting peace.

Against this movement for peace, the rulers of the Soviet Union have been waging a relentless attack. They have tried to undermine or overwhelm the free nations, one by one. They have used threats and treachery and violence.

In June the forces of Communist imperialism broke out into open warfare in Korea. The United Nations moved to put down this act of aggression, and, by October, had all but succeeded.

Then in November, the Communists threw their Chinese armies into the battle against the free nations.

By this act, they have shown that they are now willing to push the world to the brink of a general war to get what they want. This is the real meaning of the events that have been taking place in Korea.

Reference to Significance of Topic

That is why we are in such grave danger. The future of civilization depends on what we do—on what we do now, and in the months ahead.

We have the strength and we have the courage to overcome the danger that threatens our country. We must act calmly, wisely and resolutely.

[14] *Vital Speeches,* January 1, 1951.

Statement   Here are the things we will do:
of the   First, we will continue to uphold . . . the principles
Main Ideas   of the United Nations . . .
of the   Second, we will continue to work with the other free
Discussion   nations to strengthen our combined defenses.
                     Third, we will build up our own army, navy and air
                     force and make more weapons for ourselves and our
                     allies.
                     Fourth, we will expand our economy and keep it on
                     an even keel.
                     Now, I want to talk to you about each one of these
                     things.

Sometimes the audience needs general background information on the subject before it is competent to follow the speaker easily. (1) A spokesman for the civilian defense program, in addressing a typical metropolitan audience about the radar protection system for New York City, would have to explain the basic principles of radar detection in his Clarification Step. (2) Some time ago a young man told a social organization about attending a national weight-lifting contest. Very few individuals present possessed even a rudimentary knowledge of weight-lifting. However, the speaker prepared the audience for the Discussion by supplying background explanation. He began with a brief history of the sport, told of the relatively widespread interest in weight-lifting throughout the world, revealed the terrific strength of champion lifters, and then explained the nature of the three Olympic lifts used in American Amateur Athletic Union competition: the press, the snatch, and the clean and jerk. As a result of this Clarification Step, the audience was well oriented toward the subject.

THE FOUR MOST COMMON SINS OF THE INTRODUCTION

A. Do not apologize. If you imply that you are going to do poorly, the audience will be conditioned to expect an ineffective speech and will tend to believe (even though unjustifiably) that it *is* unsatisfactory.

B. Do not be long-winded. Get to the point. Do not bore your listeners with a wordy, rambling Introduction. As you will remember, the average length of the Introduction is about 10 per cent of the total speech. Time yourself in your rehearsal periods; and unless there is a genuine need for a longer Introduction, keep within the 10 per cent limit.

C. Do not antagonize or offend. Do not mention unnecessary controversial material; do not be dogmatic with groups which might disagree with you; do not make offensive, slighting remarks; do not make false assumptions about your audience; do not be patronizing; do not use unsavory humor.

D. Do not use irrelevant material. Not only must all material have a direct application to the subject, the audience, or the speech occasion, but the application must be obvious to the audience.

SUMMARY

The speech Introduction serves two important purposes: to secure favorable attention for the speaker and his message and to orient the audience to the speech. The Favorable Attention Step can be accomplished by (1) referring to the significance of the subject; (2) using humor; (3) telling an illustrative story; (4) using a stimulating quotation; (5) mentioning common relationships, beliefs, interests, and feelings; (6) asking an intriguing question; (7) making a pithy, stimulating statement; (8) referring to the occasion or purpose of the meeting; (9) complimenting the audience. The Clarification Step can be achieved by: (1) stating the POINT of the speech; (2) listing the main heads or arguments of the Discussion; (3) providing necessary background explanations.

In planning the Introduction the most common errors the inexperienced speaker is likely to commit are to apologize, to be longwinded, to antagonize or offend, and to use irrelevant material.

EXERCISES AND ASSIGNMENTS

1. Analyze the methods used by various news commentators to begin radio broadcasts or telecasts. Notice that frequently a program begins with the reporter's listing the main items of news; then, following a commercial, he discusses each of the items in detail. In such cases would the original listing serve as a Favorable Attention Step as well as a Clarification Step? Why, or why not?

2. Read the Introductions of several speeches to discover in each case the speaker's methods of capturing attention and of preparing the listeners for the Discussion. In what ways do you think the Introductions could be made more effective?

3. Attend a sermon by a minister who is recognized as being an outstanding speaker. What does he do to get your attention at the outset? If a text is read, observe how it serves as a partial Clarification Step. Can you think of any way in which his Introduction could be improved?

4. In the Introduction of his keynote address to the Democratic National Convention of 1952, Paul A. Dever characterized certain prominent Republicans as "fossils." Do you think the use of this expression was effective for the audience in the hall? Would it be as effective for the T.V. and radio audience? Why, or why not?

5. What methods of achieving favorable attention are found in the following excerpt from the Introduction of General MacArthur's keynote address to the Republican National Convention of 1952?

"I speak with a sense of pride that all of my long life I have been a member of the Republican party, as was before me my father, an ardent supporter of Abraham Lincoln. I have an abiding faith that this party, if it remains true to its great traditions, can provide the country with a leadership which, as in the days of Lincoln, will bring us back to peace and tranquillity."

6. Begin your next speech with the relating of a short personal incident which has a close relationship to your speech subject. (Possibly you will experience less nervousness when beginning a speech in this way.)

7. In future speeches in class attempt to use more than one method of achieving favorable attention in the Introduction. By carefully planning what you are going to say, you need not exceed the recommended 10 per cent limit.

8. In a short talk to the class explain the "Yes Technique" in the Introduction as used by the persuasive speaker.

9. Why should you avoid beginning a speech by stating the title in a fragmentary sentence?

10. In general, would the speech to convince or the speech to stimulate require the more carefully planned Clarification Step?

CHAPTER 8

Developing the Conclusion

Even the simplest forms of social communication require some sort of "conclusion." When closing a conversation with an acquaintance whom you chance to meet, do you cease talking abruptly, turn your back, and walk off? Some concluding phrase is necessary, such as: "Well, I'll be seeing you, Harry," or, "It was nice to see you again, Charlie. Bring your wife and drop over some evening soon." When leaving a party, do you get up from the bridge table without a word to anyone, pick up your hat and coat, and walk out? Or are there certain social amenities you must follow? When telephoning a client, don't you conclude by saying something like this: "Thank you very much for your order, Mr. Primrose. I'll see that you get the papers by tomorrow morning. Good-bye."

A "conclusion" is even more important in public speaking than in social situations. The final impression you give your listeners is perhaps even more important than the initial one. *The Conclusion is your last chance to achieve your Specific Speech Purpose. It is the final opportunity to tie up any loose threads of thought, to make clearer the materials previously discussed, to reinforce what has gone before, to vitalize the implications of the speech, and to impel the auditors to action.*

If you treat the Conclusion as a perfunctory duty, it will sound that way to the audience. Your speech must not grind to a dull, uninteresting stop. An impotent, mumbled close may nullify a previously established favorable speaker-audience relationship. The Conclusion must "pack a punch"; it must wind up the speech strongly; it must leave the listeners with the conviction that you have presented effectively a message of significance. The power of the Conclusion was shown following the first Alger Hiss trial when a juror explained that she had been uncertain as to Hiss's guilt until the summation of the State's case by the prosecutor, Thomas Murphy.

How long should a Conclusion be? Perhaps the most effective answer is to refer the student to the reply made by Abraham Lincoln when asked how long a man's legs should be: "Long enough to reach to the ground." A speech Conclusion should be long enough to crystallize the thought of the speech, to promote the proper mood, and to stimulate the desired action on the part of the audience. No arbitrary length can be established. In the typical speech, however, the Conclusion will occupy about 5 per cent of the total speech length. Of course, upon occasions the Conclusion might be either shorter or longer than this average figure. Since a speech *to entertain* contains no vital information to be retained by the listener, no profound philosophy to be driven home, there is no need for an extended Conclusion. Usually one or two well-turned phrases will suffice. An effective ten-minute entertaining talk which described a student's adventures in shooting the rapids of the Colorado river was concluded in this simple fashion:

> With the final bend of the canyon we were out of the swirling, crashing, dangerous waters of the Colorado River canyon. My brother Tom and I were now among the handful of men who had successfully shot the rapids. But I can promise you that I will never do such a crazy fool stunt again.

Usually, though not invariably, speeches *to inform* and *to persuade* will have longer Conclusions than speeches *to entertain*. The nature of the speech itself, the material covered in the Discussion, and the knowledge and attitude of the audience will help determine the length of the Conclusion. If the talk is relatively simple, or if the material has been presented in a clear, logical manner, an extended close is unnecessary. Andrew Kaul III once concluded a lengthy high-school graduation address (entitled "The Great Delusion," a warning against accepting the programs of "Socialism") with the following brief summary:

> In closing, I appeal to you young men and women, for your own sakes, to *keep* America the land of opportunity.
> Don't be taken in by the "Great Delusion."
> Your future is in your own hands: hang on to it.

The purposes of the Conclusion can be realized by means of one or both of these steps: the *Summary Step* and the *Action Step*. Let us now analyze the relationships which these steps bear to each other and to the remainder of the speech.

SUMMARIZE THE SPEECH

Frequently the Conclusion is a dull recapitulation, producing stifled yawns instead of animated attention. However, the Summary Step can be, and must be, a vital, stimulating reinforcement of the Specific Speech Purpose. Although lines of demarcation cannot always be drawn, the basic methods of summarizing a speech are: statement of the POINT; formal listing of the main ideas of the talk; informal review; and indirect summary by quotation, comparison, or example. As we shall see, a speaker may use more than one type of summary in his Summary Step.

A. Statement of the POINT of the speech. As you will recall from Chapter 7, the stating of the POINT during the Introduction insures that the audience will clearly understand the speaker's Specific Speech Purpose. Sometimes it is advisable to repeat in the Conclusion the purpose of the speech so as to focus final attention upon the essential point or message. Not infrequently the central theme of a speech becomes partially submerged under the accumulation of examples, quotations, statistics, and reference to authorities. To restate the POINT concisely in the Conclusion promotes clarity, but offers little interest appeal. Here are some examples.

(1) At a recent national convention of the Speech Association of America, James McBurney concluded his presidential address [1] ("The Plight of the Conservative in Public Discussion") in this way:

In conclusion, I wish again to make it clear that I do not present this analysis to plead the cause of the conservative, nor do I mean to question the ability and integrity of the conservative. It is my purpose rather to point out that conservatives generally are not doing their cause justice in public discussion and debate, explain why this is the case, and suggest some of the ways in which this weakness can be corrected. . . .

(2) Benjamin Fairless, President of the United States Steel Corporation, restated the POINT of his address ("Detour Ahead") before the Baltimore Association of Commerce like this:

[1] *Vital Speeches*, March 15, 1950.

Seriously, gentlemen, make no mistake about it, U. S. Steel has been singled out as the target for this present attack on "bigness"—but only temporarily, and if our Washington jugglers now succeed in placing U. S. Steel on trial before the court of public opinion, then they also will have managed to put every successful, growing business in America on trial beside it.

(3) A student ended a talk advocating a program of federal aid to education by restating his POINT:

In the ten minutes allotted me I have endeavored to show you convincing, powerful reasons why the federal government should shoulder part of the burden of supporting the public school systems of our nation. America must adopt a program of federal aid to education.

B. Formal listing of the main ideas of the speech. A clear, concise method of summarizing in the Conclusion is to list the main ideas of the speech in a formal "one, two, three" order. There is no better way of enabling the audience to remember specific points than to list them in the Introduction, analyze them in the Discussion, and relist them in the Conclusion. However, most authorities agree that a formal stating of main points in the Conclusion tends to be too obvious, too much like an academic lecture, and too stilted and monotonous. A safe generalization would be: Use this method only when it is essential that the audience retain specific points, arguments, phases of a program, or important directions. In the following examples the speakers have clarified the thought of their respective speeches by a formal listing of main ideas.

(1) The late spring of 1950 was a period of sordid mud-slinging between Republicans and Democrats over the alleged presence of Communists, fellow travelers, and sex perverts in the State Department. On June 1, the Senate's only woman member, Mrs. Margaret Smith of Maine, delivered a stirring indictment of such irrational behavior. Speaking directly to her Senatorial colleagues, and indirectly to the American public, she summarized her message by presenting a definite statement of her main contentions. After hearing this formal listing of major points, which Mrs. Smith called "a Declaration of Conscience," no one could be in doubt as to the nature of her views: [2]

[2] *Vital Speeches,* July 1, 1950.

It is with these thoughts that I have drafted what I call a Declaration of Conscience. . . .

1. We are Republicans. But we are Americans first. It is as Americans that we express our concern with the growing confusion that threatens the security and stability of our country. Democrats and Republicans alike have contributed to that confusion.

2. The Democratic administration has initially created the confusion by its lack of effective leadership, by its contradictory grave warnings and optimistic assurances, by its complacency to the threat of communism here at home, by its oversensitiveness to rightful criticism, by its petty bitterness against its critics.

3. Certain elements of the Republican Party have materially added to this confusion in the hopes of riding the Republican Party to victory through the selfish political exploitation of fear, bigotry, ignorance, and intolerance. There are enough mistakes of the Democrats for Republicans to criticize constructively without resorting to political smears.

4. To this extent, Democrats and Republicans alike have unwittingly, but undeniably, played directly into the Communist design of "confuse, divide, and conquer."

5. It is high time that we stopped thinking politically as Republicans and Democrats about elections and started thinking patriotically as Americans about national security based on individual freedom. It is high time that we all stopped being tools and victims of totalitarian techniques—techniques that, if continued here unchecked, will surely end what we have come to cherish as the American way of life.

(2) Speaking at a convocation of the Wood Junior College of Mathison, Mississippi, Charles T. Morgan concluded his analysis of the future of the "church-related college" with this formal listing:[3]

In closing may I summarize. What I have said may fall under these headings:

1. We are living in a confused, complex, cruel, and a divided world.
2. America needs both private and tax-supported higher education.
3. *The church-related college must be Christian.*
4. *The church-related college must be discriminating in its choice of students.*
5. The church-related college must produce Christian citizens and religious workers.

(3) Senior statesman Bernard Baruch used a formal listing to summarize his address of August, 1950, in which he urged the

[3] *Vital Speeches,* July 15, 1950.

Senate Banking and Currency Committee to endorse a program of immediate total mobilization: [4]

To sum up my recommendations:

1. Organize America for all-out mobilization, with a general ceiling over the entire economy to prevent further inflation and an all-embracing system of priorities to strengthen our defenses and minimize dislocations.

2. The very least that must be done is to amend this priorities legislation to provide for effective price and wage control and rationing authority. To do less is to invite cruel suffering and possible disaster.

3. Taxes high enough to eliminate profiteering and to cover *all* defense costs. These taxes should take effect for at least the second half of this year.

4. Continued rent controls with provision for clearly justifiable increases.

5. Prompt creation of an over-all mobilizing agency to synchronize all our efforts.

6. Postpone less essential expenditures. As an aid to that a Capital Issues Committee should be established under the Secretary of the Treasury to review all capital issues, public and private, deferring less essential projects to make sure housing, schools, hospitals and other more essential needs are met first.

7. Strengthen the United Nations by coordinating our efforts with it in common defense of peace.

8. Speedier assistance in the rearming of those nations ready to resist aggression, along with the expansion of our own defense forces.

C. Informal review. Perhaps the most widely used method of summarizing a speech is to review informally the major ideas presented in the Discussion. In most cases an informal review is preferable to a formal listing of points: it sounds less academic and teaches without appearing so obviously to teach. In the following examples the informal review summarizes the thought of the respective speeches effectively and interestingly. Notice that the speeches from which these selections were taken would not lend themselves readily to a formal listing of main heads.

(1) A student's speech entitled, "A New State of Mind," concluded in this way: [5]

[4] *Vital Speeches*, August 15, 1950.
[5] Sander Vanocur, "A New State of Mind," *Winning Orations, Northern Oratorical League Contests, 1945-1950*, Minneapolis, copyright 1951 by The Northwestern Press, p. 168.

The battle for freedom will not be fought in the Pentagon. It will be fought with food and ideas in the rice paddies of China and the fields of Indonesia. It will be fought wherever men seek freedom from oppression.

For what force has blinded us to is that the peoples of the world are stirring and seeking their freedom. My plea is that we subordinate the philosophy of force to the philosophy of freedom; that we adopt a new state of mind—one that will support a positive program of aid for all men who will seek freedom and a better life.

But if we are to remain blind and continue to rely primarily on the philosophy of force, then Communism will spread, freedom will fall, and we will fall with it.

We *must* have a new state of mind. I think that you and I must choose *our* states of mind, for *together* they are the state of mind of this nation. We must make our choice:

It is human dignity or human misery.

It is freedom or it is force.

It is all a state of mind.

(2) Abraham Lincoln typically closed his speeches by means of an informal review. The Conclusion of his First Inaugural Address tells us vividly that the basic purpose of the speech was to help preserve the union and to cast odium upon the Southerners if they seceded:

My countrymen, one and all, think calmly and well upon this whole subject. Nothing valuable can be lost by taking time. If there be an object to hurry any of you in hot haste to a step which you would never take deliberately, that object will be frustrated by taking time; but no good object can be frustrated by it. Such of you as are now dissatisfied, still have the old Constitution unimpaired, and, on the sensitive point, the laws of your own framing under it; while the new administration will have no immediate power, if it would, to change either. If it were admitted that you who are dissatisfied hold the right side in the dispute, there still is no single good reason for precipitate action. Intelligence, patriotism, Christianity, and a firm reliance on Him who has never yet forsaken this favored land, are still competent to adjust in the best way all our present difficulty.

In your hands, my dissatisfied fellow-countrymen, and not in mine, is the momentous issue of civil war. The government will not assail you. You can have no conflict without being yourselves the aggressors. You have no oath registered in heaven to destroy the government, while I shall have the most solemn one to "preserve, protect, and defend it."

I am loath to close. We are not enemies, but friends. We must not
be enemies. Though passion may have strained, it must not break our
bonds of affection. The mystic chords of memory, stretching from every
battle-field and patriot grave to every living heart and hearthstone all
over this broad land, will yet swell the chorus of the Union when again
touched, as surely they will be, by the better angels of our nature.

(3) Dr. James R. Killian, Jr., President of the Massachusetts
Institute of Technology, concluded an address on the status of universities in a period of international uncertainty with this informal
review: [6]

Such, gentlemen, are some of our responsibilities. Such, then, some of
our hopes. If we can keep our eyes on the ball and resist the siren call
of immediacy; if we can resist communism without warping our freedom;
if we can keep our universities financially strong without having them
become wards of the Federal Government and thus nationalized by de-
fault; if we can keep them citadels of altruism and high standards,
beacon lights high above the shoals of mediocrity;—if we can do these
things, then we shall have met the challenge posed by the present
dangers, and turned a period of crisis into a time of opportunity.

(4) At times the speaker may wish to use in his Conclusion both
a formal listing of main points and an informal review. Mr. Baruch,
in the speech referred to earlier, wished to emphasize the significance of his message; so, after listing his arguments in a formal
"one, two, three" order, he also summarized informally. Here is
the informal review portion of Mr. Baruch's talk:

Nearly three years ago I clipped an item from a newspaper which
seems ominously prophetic today. It told of a boast made by a Soviet
General. This general boasted that the Western Democracies were bound
to be defeated by the Soviet Union because they would not make the
sacrifices necessary to arm themselves. They prized their standards of
living too highly. They would not be willing to accept the disciplines
to put "guns" over "butter." In Russia, though, this general boasted, the
people were inured to hardship. The Soviet government would force the
sacrifices to mobilize. A lean, hungry, but mobilized Russia would overrun a Western world which couldn't bring itself to mobilize—in time.

This is the test which confronts us—not only this country but all of the

[6] *Vital Speeches*, February 1, 1950.

free peoples of the world. It. is the choice of "peace" or "butter," of mobilizing our strength now, while peace can still be saved, or of clinging to petty wants and petty profits, imperiling our freedom and our civilization.

No outside enemy can defeat us. We *can* defeat ourselves. Gentlemen, yours is the decision. Which shall it be—discomfort or defeat?

D. Indirect summary by means of quotation, comparison, or example. As its name implies, the indirect summary recapitulates in an oblique, indirect manner. When a quotation, comparison, or example is used in the Conclusion as an indirect summary, it must help crystallize the thought of the speech in a stimulating manner. Rarely used as the sole method of reiteration, the indirect summary is almost invariably inserted either after a statement of the POINT, after a formal listing of the main ideas of the Discussion, after an informal review, or into the framework of an informal review. Of the three methods of summarizing indirectly, the quotation is the easiest to apply and is by far the most frequently used.

1. *Quotation following a statement of the* POINT *of the speech:* James McBurney, in the speech previously referred to, stated his speech purpose formally in the Conclusion of his address on "The Plight of the Conservative in Public Discussion." Wishing to accentuate the importance of his message, McBurney followed the statement of the POINT with a quotation:

Statement of *the* POINT	In conclusion, I wish again to make it clear that I do not present this analysis to plead the cause of the conservative, nor do I mean to question the ability and integrity of the conservative. It is my purpose rather to point out that conservatives generally are not doing their cause justice in public discussion and debate, explain why this is the case, and suggest some of the ways in which this weakness can be corrected. . . .
Use of *Quotation*	As Aristotle put it, over two thousand years ago: "Truth and justice are by nature more powerful than their opposites; when decisions are not made as they should be, the speakers with the right on their side have only themselves to thank for the outcome."

2. *Quotation following a formal listing of the main points of the speech:* William N. Brigance delivered his "Backwash of War"

speech more than forty times during and following World War II.
Here is the Conclusion of this address: [7]

*Formal Listing
of Main Ideas
of the
Discussion*

These, then, are the especial problems that face us
in this backwash of war: First, the problem of the returning soldier adjusting himself to civilian life; second,
the danger of transferring our hatred of the Japanese
and Germans to other groups; third, the danger that in
fighting against militarism, we ourselves shall become
militaristic; and finally, the danger of permitting too
much of a moral holiday now that we are relieved from
the Spartan discipline of war.

*Use of
Quotation*

We do not face these problems with fear. We do
not face them with hesitation. To the timid and faint-
hearted who long for security and repose, we quote the
answer of Mr. Justice Oliver Wendell Holmes: "Security
is an illusion, and repose is not the destiny of man."
We shall meet these problems as a people who are conscious of their destiny.

3. *Quotation in conjunction with informal review.* An example
of a speaker's weaving several quotations into an informal review
is found in the following Conclusion of a speech by George W.
Maxey, Chief Justice of the Supreme Court of Pennsylvania. This
address (delivered on the 103rd anniversary of Thomas Edison's
birth before the Edison Pioneers and Associates in New York City),
was an appeal to resist what the speaker considered to be a trend
toward statism: [8]

*Informal
Review*

We have learned at last that static right is no match
for dynamic wrong, that a nation not ready for war is
ripe for subjugation. Not only are the lawless hordes
without the gates getting ready to destroy our country
but the lawless hordes *within* our gates are getting ready
either to devour, or to trample underfoot, the hus-
bandry of our civilization. As we face this situation we
had better become a little more dynamic and a little
less static. We had better use our eyes for seeing and
our strength for action.

When the Constitution was signed in 1787 a woman
who met Benjamin Franklin coming out of Independ-

[7] *Vital Speeches,* December 1, 1945.
[8] *Vital Speeches,* March 15, 1950.

ence Hall, asked: "What have we got, Dr. Franklin?"
He replied: "A republic, if we can keep it." When
Use of
Quotations
James Russell Lowell was minister to Great Britain in
1882 he was asked: "How long will the American Republic endure?" He replied: "As long as the ideas of
the men who made it remain dominant." The ideas of
the men who made this republic are dominant no
longer. . . .

Informal
Review
I believe that if Lincoln or Edison were here they
would tell us dynamically to defend the American way
of life and perhaps their summons to us would be in
somewhat the same tenor as the summons of Henry V,
when on the eve of the battle of Agincourt he declared
to his archers and men-at-arms:
He who hath no stomach for this fight,
Let him depart; his passport shall be made.
I would not either live or die in that man's company.
This day is call'd the feast of Crispin;
He that outlives this day, and comes safe home,
Will stand a tip-toe when this day is nam'd.
Use of
Quotation
He that shall live this day, and see old age,
Will yearly on the vigil feast his neighbours,
And strip his sleeves and show his scars,
And say, 'These wounds I had on Crispin's Day.'
And gentlemen now a-bed
Shall think themselves accurs'd they were not here,
And hold their manhood cheap while any speak
Who fought with us on Crispin's Day.

4. *Quotation following informal review.* A student closed a philosophical address on "happiness" with this brief informal review and
quotation:

Informal
Review
Happiness, one of God's best gifts, is bestowed upon
us freely. There is plenty for all. It does not announce
itself with blaring trumpets, for it is a quiet element
that is found in the simple things of life. It is true, as
Ruskin wrote: "All the real and wholesome enjoyments
possible to man have been just as possible since first
Use of
Quotation
he was made of the earth—to watch the corn grow, and
the blossoms set; to draw hard breath over a plowshare
or spade; to read, to think, to love, to pray—these are
the things that make men happy."

5. ***Comparison following a statement of the*** **POINT.** A student in an adult class in public speaking once used the following analogy for its emotional appeal as well as for its help in clarifying the purpose of the speech. In view of the vivid quality of the comparison and the total length of the speech, this Conclusion is not exceedingly long:

Statement of POINT

Use of Comparison

> Let me leave but one thought with you: have a care and give to Care—C-A-R-E. Before you retire tonight, take a few minutes to stand by the bedside of your youngsters. (If you are like me, you have a towheaded little boy of four named Jackie, and a black-eyed girl of two named Susan.) Look beyond those beds across several thousand miles of ocean and land to the country of South Korea. In your mind's eye see what I saw this summer. See a skinny little boy, just about the age of my Jackie, shuffling along a country road, helping his mother carry water from a neighbor's well because the well at his home is polluted. Notice the lad's protruding cheek bones; see his torn, ragged clothes. Look at his toes sticking through those home-made shoes of straw and burlap. Now, pass your gaze to the mother. She's in her late thirties, but she looks twenty years older. Why doesn't the father help carry the water? He can't. He's dead. Bayoneted by Communist soldiers. There used to be a little girl in this family, but she died from malnutrition and overexposure. Tragedy has deeply marred this family, as it has thousands of families throughout Korea. They need your help. How generous the Lord has been to you and your families! Take another look at your wonderful little kids, safe and healthy. If they should be in the same position as those innocent Korean children, wouldn't you want some good Samaritan to give them aid?

6. ***Example following a statement of the*** **POINT.** A student used the following example to make more vivid the basic message of his speech:

Statement of POINT

> In summation, let me ask you once again not to drive an automobile if you have been drinking. Don't be another Frank Hollis. Frank was my roommate last year in the dormitory. He liked to drink his way from

*Use of
Example*

bar to bar, and then, about two in the morning, would drive home singing and having a great time. One morning Frank didn't come in. When I left the room to go over to Louie's cafe to get breakfast, I thought he had spent the night with some buddy. Frank didn't come to his 8:30 class. I didn't know it at the time, but at the hour Frank should have been taking notes in history, the state police were pulling his body out of his partially submerged car in the river. He had turned a corner too fast and his car had skidded out of control into the river. The pathetic thing was that only the front seat was covered with water. But poor Frank˙ drowned in three feet of water because he was too drunk to know enough to crawl into the back seat. My sincere advice to you is not to take the chance of becoming another Frank Hollis.

PROMOTE ACTION

The beginning speaker should remember four significant points: (A) Only speeches to actuate require an *Action Step*; (B) A close relationship exists between the *Summary Step* and the *Action Step*; (C) The *Action Step* must clearly indicate the response desired from the audience; (D) The *Action Step* must constitute an effective appeal to the emotions as well as to the intellect.

A. Only speeches to actuate require an Action Step. As you will remember, speeches *to inform* attempt "to give intellectual comprehension, to widen mental horizons, and to bring the unknown or misunderstood into the realm of correct interpretation"; speeches *to entertain* endeavor to give pleasure and enjoyment; speeches *to convince* and *to stimulate* or *impress* are designed to produce intellectual agreement or emotional feeling. None of these four types is primarily designed to produce immediate, specific, observable action. Only speeches *to actuate* have as a principal purpose the stimulation of the listeners to definite activity, i.e., to buy, sell, lend, veto, contribute, vote, work harder, sign a petition, eat less, join the National Guard, and so forth.

B. A close relationship exists between the Summary Step and the Action Step. Although the Action Step is sometimes the only step in the Conclusion, ordinarily it is used in conjunction with the

Summary Step. One of the most effective methods of impelling an audience to action is to recapitulate previously discussed reasons why they should act. The Summary Step consists of restatement of what has already been said. The Action Step is a direct appeal to the audience to perform the action desired by the speaker. The difference between the two steps is clearly illustrated in the Conclusion of Daniel Webster's summation speech in the White-Knapp murder case. Although this passage may seem long, in reality it constitutes only about 2 per cent of the total speech length.

Summary Step by Means of Informal Review

Gentlemen, I have gone through with the evidence in this case, and have endeavored to state it plainly and fairly before you. I think there are conclusions to be drawn from it, the accuracy of which you cannot doubt. I think you cannot doubt that there was a conspiracy formed for the purpose of committing this murder . . .; that you cannot doubt that the Crowninshields and the Knapps were the parties in this conspiracy; that you cannot doubt that the prisoner at the bar knew that the murder was to be done on the night of the 6th of April; that you cannot doubt that the murderers of Captain White were the suspicious persons seen in and about Brown street on that night; that you cannot doubt that Richard Crowninshield was the perpetrator of that crime; that you cannot doubt that the prisoner at the bar was in Brown street on that night. If there, then it must be by agreement, to countenance, to aid the perpetrator, and, if so, then he is guilty as principal.

Action Step

Gentlemen, your whole concern should be to do your duty, and leave the consequences to take care of themselves. You will receive the law from the court. Your verdict, it is true, may endanger the prisoner's life, but then it is to save other lives. If the prisoner's guilt has been shown and proved beyond all reasonable doubt, you will convict him. If such reasonable doubts of guilt still remain, you will acquit him. You are the judges of the whole case. You owe a duty to the public, as well as to the prisoner at the bar. You cannot presume to be wiser than the law. Your duty is a plain, straightforward one. Doubtless we would all judge him in mercy. Towards him, as an individual, the law inculcates no hostility; but towards him, if proved to be a murderer, the law, and the oaths you have taken, and public justice demand that you do your duty. With consciences satisfied with the discharge of duty, no consequences can harm you. There is no evil that we cannot either face or fly from but the consciousness of duty disregarded. A sense of duty pursues us ever. It is omnipresent, like the Deity. If we take to ourselves the wings of the morning, and dwell in the uttermost parts of the sea, duty performed or duty violated is still with us, for our happiness or our misery. If we say the darkness shall cover us, in the darkness, as in the light, our obligations are yet with us. We cannot escape their power, nor fly from their presence. They are with us in this life, will be with us at its close; and in that scene of inconceivable solemnity, which lies yet farther onward, we shall find ourselves surrounded by the consciousness of duty, to pain us whenever it has been violated, and to console us so far as God may have given us grace to perform it.

C. The Action Step must clearly indicate the action desired from the audience. The content of the Action Step depends upon the character of the response desired, the exigencies of the speech occasion, the audience, and the nature of the materials previously presented. In general, however, the Action Step should answer these questions: What is the action desired? How is it to be accomplished? Where is it to take place? When is it to be consummated? Obviously the Action Step of speeches on important social, political, or philosophical themes cannot make as specific an appeal for overt response as can the Action Step of speeches with limited themes, such as contributing to the cancer drive, purchasing a gas refrigerator, or voting for a particular candidate. As a persuasive speaker, always focus your attention on motivating the audience to *do,* to *act,* to *perform.* Make the action as easy to accomplish as possible. Avoid a vague, trite request like "write to your Congressman." Many people don't know their Congressman. Do you? If someone should ask you to write to your city commissioner, state representative, U. S. Representative, or U. S. Senator, would you know the man's full name and his mailing address? Wouldn't you be more likely to write the desired letter if the speaker gave you and the rest of the audience stamped and addressed envelopes?

Perhaps the following examples will help clarify the nature of the Action Step.

(1) In a speech on scouting (delivered to the Kansas City Chamber of Commerce, February, 1953), William H. Fetridge concluded with this Summary Step and Action Step: [9]

Summary
Step

Well, that's my sales story on Boy Scouting—the great boy movement that serves not only the boy but the man, the community and the nation as well.

Some of you sales executives here are probably saying, "He hasn't asked for the order." I intend to do that now.

Action
Step

I ask you leaders of Kansas City to give more support to Boy Scouting than you have ever done in the past. Those of you who have been too busy for Scouting, I ask you to find some time for it. Get into it actively. See that more troops are organized so that more boys may come to know and benefit by the adventure of Scouting. If you cannot serve as Scoutmasters or in some other capacity, see that men in your company are encouraged to do so and that they are given the time and encouragement so they can do the job well. Finally, see that the coffers of the Kansas City Council are never so light that this movement cannot operate at top effectiveness.

Do these things and I will assure you this: Years hence when you are resting from your life's labors, you will look back with pride and satisfaction in the part you played to make this great boy movement greater.

(2) Several hours before a disastrous hurricane struck southern Florida, a student in an adult public speaking course in Miami brought a packing box full of Sterno stoves to class and attempted to sell them. Here is his Conclusion:

Summary
Step

During my talk I have demonstrated to you how simple it is to operate the Sterno Cook Stove. I even fried an egg and brewed a pot of coffee. As I have told you, the 10:30 advisory from the weather bureau states that a severe hurricane will strike the Miami area sometime this evening. You need a Sterno Cook Stove because electricity possibly will be cut off during the storm to avoid electrocutions from fallen wires. You can't go out to a restaurant during the hurricane. The storm may last through the night and through tomorrow. If the storm doubles

[9] *Vital Speeches,* March 15, 1953.

*Action
Step*

back as the one did on the west coast of Florida this summer, it may last even longer. What's more, electrical service in some parts of the city may be off for ten days to two weeks. Buy a Sterno Cook Stove from me for seventy-five cents, and you can have as many cups of coffee as you want during the storm. On this little stove you can heat the baby's formula, cook a pan of beans, or prepare an entire dinner. Seventy-five cents is a small investment. This morning I started out with twenty-five stoves, and I've sold fifteen already. Don't wait until this afternoon or tonight to buy a stove from me; I doubt that I'll have any left. I have only ten stoves here. Let me see the hands of those who want one. If you don't have the money with you, you can pay me the next class period. Now, how many of you want stoves?

(3) Perhaps the most famous Action Step in the history of American public address is found in the Conclusion of Lincoln's Second Inaugural Address:

With malice towards none; with charity for all; with firmness in the right, as God gives us to see the right, let us strive on to finish the work we are in; to bind up the nation's wounds; to care for him who shall have borne the battle, and for his widow and orphans; to do all which may achieve and cherish a just and lasting peace among ourselves and with all nations.

(4) Ministers hope by means of their sermons to influence the future conduct of their parishioners. The Action Step of one preacher went something like this:

The Christian way of living is not a one-day-a-week manner of behaving. It is a day-to-day, every-day process. It is a standard of conduct for every day of every week of every month of every year. I don't say to you: "Go out and be a Christian for the remainder of the Sabbath, and then on Monday you can revert to selfish self-seeking." No. That's not the way the Lord intended you to act. A one-day-a-week Christian, a fifty-two-day-a-year Christian is not a true Christian. Be a Christian 365 days a year. If the true spirit of Christ dwells in your heart, your pattern of existence will not vary from one day to the next. Put your trust in Jesus. Depend on Him for guidance, and He will lead you safely through the perils and temptations of life. He will never desert you. He is the master shepherd and we are His flock. Be faithful unto Him. Set for yourself a daily goal to be worthy of the sacrifices Christ endured for you. May we pray that we all follow closely the path of righteousness until we meet in the name of the Lord again next Sunday.

D. The Action Step must constitute an effective appeal to the emotions as well as to the intellect. As psychologists have long known, man is not primarily a rational being. Only a small fraction of our beliefs and judgments is determined through strictly logical processes. Everything which has genuine meaning in our lives is colored with emotional overtones. Every stereotyped word or phrase contains connotative, emotional values as well as denotative, intellectual meanings. We eat, sleep, love, hate, marry, beget offspring, and strive to excel largely upon a physiological-emotional basis. In the words of Woodrow Wilson, "We speak of this as an age in which mind is monarch, but . . . mind is one of those modern monarchs who reign but do not govern." The cerebrum (that portion of the brain devoted to thinking, remembering, and learning) is physically only a small proportion of the human body. Its dominance over the body's activities is frequently theoretical rather than actual. For example, if a small amount of epinephrine is sent into the blood stream from the adrenal glands, the human organism may become so upset that it will curse, fight, or murder—perform actions which the individual under "normal" circumstances would not commit.

An appreciation of the emotions is necessary for an understanding of the Action Step. Audiences are *not* stimulated to action by purely intellectual appeals. William James has shown that we accept a new belief, or judgment, only when the new idea possesses sufficient emotional appeal. The inexperienced speaker should be warned, however, that maudlin, affected, overdone, insincere appeals to the emotions are generally ineffective. Listeners will be resentful, and rightly so, of any obvious play on their feelings. Never use an emotional plea because you think it is a good rhetorical "trick." In using emotional materials exercise a discriminating judgment based upon a genuine respect for the intelligence of your audience. Only well-reasoned appeals will constitute a persuasive Action Step.

As we have seen in Chapter 6, an effective address to the feelings of the audience should be integrated into the continuum of the entire speech. However, it is probably in the Action Step that a skillful emotional plea is most important as a motivating factor. Notice that almost all of the examples of the Action Step given in this chapter contain an emotional charge, and that none relies upon an abstract, exclusively intellectual statement of the action desired by the speaker.

THE FIVE MOST COMMON SINS OF THE CONCLUSION

A. Do not apologize. As in the Introduction, to offer excuses in your Conclusion is a reflection of inadequate self-confidence. If you have conscientiously planned your speech, and have delivered it to the best of your ability, you are entitled to the sincere appreciation of the audience.

B. Do not be abrupt or long-winded. A basic purpose of the Conclusion is to "round off" the talk. Many speakers halt their talks abruptly, as though they were being called to the telephone, or drone on and on, overlooking various possible opportunities to close.

C. Do not introduce important new points of view. No major point should be introduced for the first time in the Conclusion. The place for it is in the Introduction or Discussion.

D. Do not include irrelevant material. Irrelevant material will hinder your efforts to focus final attention on the specific message of your speech.

E. Do not lose the attention of the audience. As we have stated previously, the final impression may be even more important than the initial one. If you wish to be persuasive, avoid permitting a let-down in interest during the Conclusion.

SUMMARY

The Conclusion, which constitutes about 5 per cent of the total speech, represents the speaker's final opportunity to accomplish the Specific Speech Purpose. The basic elements of the Conclusion are the Summary Step and the Action Step. The methods of summarizing are to: state the POINT; relist formally the main ideas of the Discussion; review informally; and summarize indirectly by means of quotation, comparison, or example. The Action Step is an effort to motivate the audience to overt, observable response. Remember that: (1) only speeches to actuate require an Action Step; (2) a close relationship exists between the Summary Step and the Action Step; (3) the Action Step must clearly indicate the action desired; (4) the Action Step must make an effective appeal to the emotions as well as to the intellect. In preparing the Conclusion the novice should be especially careful to avoid apologizing, being abrupt or long-winded, introducing irrelevant or important new material, or losing the attention of the audience.

EXERCISES AND ASSIGNMENTS

1. General MacArthur concluded his address to the joint meeting of the Houses of Congress, April 19, 1951, in this way:

"The world has turned over many times since I took the oath at West Point, and the hopes and dreams have all since vanished, but I still remember the refrain of one of the most popular barracks ballads of that day which proclaimed most proudly that old soldiers never die; they just fade away.

"And like the old soldier of that ballad, I now close my military career and just fade away, an old soldier who tried to do his duty as God gave him the light to see that duty. Good bye."

Contrast the immediate with the long-range influence of this appeal.

2. For your next speech in class prepare two different Conclusions. In one follow a statement of the POINT with a formal listing of the main ideas of the Discussion. In the second state the POINT, and then give an informal review of the material covered in the Discussion. Record the two Conclusions and determine which one is superior.

3. Attend an evangelistic service. The nearer the close, the more emotional the speaker is likely to become. Why?

4. A student once stated that most radio commercials consist exclusively of an Action Step. Was his reasoning valid?

5. Study the Conclusions of at least five printed speeches. Which methods of summarizing seem to predominate? In what ways could the Conclusions be improved?

6. Should emotional appeals to action in the Conclusion always be avoided when speaking to the well educated? Why or why not?

7. In a set of speeches in class pick out the best and the poorest Conclusions. Be prepared to defend your judgment before the class.

8. Keep a written record of the most common "sins" of the Introduction and of the Conclusion which you hear in speeches on the campus and in the community.

9. Deliver a sales talk in class in which you close with an Action Step. Do your hearers agree that your Conclusion is impelling? Does it answer the questions: what, how, where, and when?

10. Close one of your class speeches with an indirect method of summarizing, i.e., quotation, illustration, or comparison. Make sure that your material is relevant and interesting.

Delivering the Speech

Essential Purpose of Section III: to enable the student to deliver his speeches with effectiveness.

CHAPTER 9: *An Introduction to Delivery*

I. Basic principles of delivery
  A. Effective delivery makes full use of both the visible and audible codes
  B. Effective delivery is adapted to the total speaking situation
  C. Effective delivery is sincere
  D. Effective delivery is modest and unassuming
  E. Effective delivery is confident and assured
  F. Effective delivery does not attract attention to itself
  G. Effective delivery is enthusiastic and animated
II. Modes of expression
  A. Memorizing
  B. Speaking impromptu
  C. Reading from manuscript
  D. Speaking extemporaneously
III. Platform etiquette and conduct
  A. Before the speech
  B. Beginning the speech
  C. During the speech
  D. After the speech
IV. Dress and appearance
V. Use of a public address system

CHAPTER 10: *Using the Body in Delivering the Speech*

I. The importance of bodily action
  A. Facilitates adjustment

B. Helps to secure and maintain audience interest and attention
C. Helps to clarify meaning
D. Helps to attain emphasis
II. The use of bodily action
   A. Facial expression
      1. Cultivate direct eye contact
      2. Reduce inhibitions
      3. Determine facial expression according to meaning
      4. Avoid the most common sins in the use of facial expression
   B. Posture
      1. Placement of the feet
      2. Positions for the hands
      3. Importance of good posture habits and sufficient practice
      4. Most common sins in the use of posture
   C. Movement
      1. Importance of effective movement
      2. Characteristics of effective movement
      3. Most common sins in the use of movement
   D. Gestures
      1. Descriptive gestures make meaningful such concepts as distance, size, shape, and direction
      2. Emphasis by use of gestures may be secured by the pointed finger, clenched fist, open palm, and so on
      3. Most common sins in the use of gestures

CHAPTER 11: *Using the Voice in Delivering the Speech*

I. The six attributes of the effective voice for public speaking are audibility, pleasantness, variety, animation, fluency, and clarity
II. Audibility and pleasantness are the products of proper habits of breathing, phonation, and resonation
   A. An explanation of the basic processes of breathing, phonation, and resonation
   B. The application of knowledge of the basic processes to the acquisition of proper habits
III. Variety, animation, and fluency necessitate a flexible voice
   A. Flexibility in pitch

B. Flexibility in force
C. Flexibility in rate
IV. Clarity depends upon distinctness and correctness of speech

CHAPTER 12: *Using Language in Delivering the Speech*

I. The nature of language
   A. Words are symbols having meaning only in terms of the associations established between the symbol and the object or concept to which it refers
   B. Words never tell everything about the ideas or concepts they symbolize
   C. Meaning cannot be transmitted, but can only be stirred up in the listener
   D. Word meanings are constantly changing
II. Specific guides for the effective use of language
   A. Language should be designed primarily to be heard, not read
   B. Language should be adapted to the audience, the occasion, and the speaker's personality
   C. Language should possess clarity
   D. Language should be objective
   E. Language should be vivid and impressive
   F. Language should include a large stock of connective and transitional words and phrases
   G. Language should be arranged into clear and varied sentences
   H. Language should be chosen from a constantly increasing *speaking* vocabulary

CHAPTER 13: *Rehearsing the Speech*

I. Where to rehearse
   A. First, in a private room
   B. Second, in the room where the speech will be delivered, if possible
II. When to rehearse
   A. Not until materials are gathered and outline completed
   B. Not after entering the room at the time the speech will be given

III. How to rehearse
  A. The preliminary phase in rehearsing is to fix the speech in
     mind
  B. The second phase in rehearsing is to polish the delivery of
     the speech

CHAPTER 9

An Introduction to Delivery

The preceding section dealt with the problem of speech preparation, including choice of subject and specific purpose, discovery of materials, and the development of the Introduction, Discussion, and Conclusion. We are now ready to discuss the principles of speech presentation.

How important is delivery in determining the total effectiveness of a speech? Occasionally, an audience will be attentive to a speaker with inferior delivery—if he has a significant message. With sound, interesting ideas and a strong desire to share them with others, one may move an audience in spite of violating many of the rules for good presentation. We have heard awkward, unsophisticated students hold classes spellbound by presenting inherently interesting ideas. A speaker in a position of authority may also find his audiences attentive despite poor delivery. Any man holding the office of President of the United States, for example, will command at least reluctant attention, even though he speaks ineffectively. Although isolated instances indicate that a speech may be well received without good delivery, we cannot conclude that presentation is therefore unimportant. Because of inadequate delivery, many speeches of genuine significance are failures.

As noted in Chapter 1, some students mistakenly believe that to pursue the development of good delivery is fruitless—that some speakers are "naturally good," while others are doomed to permanent ineffectiveness. Of course, some individuals possess aptitudes which permit some degree of effectiveness without training. Those with pleasant voices, good articulation, quick minds, fluent tongues, and attitudes of confidence will need a minimum of training in delivery. Others less generously endowed will need to spend long hours in study and practice to achieve the same measure of ability.

In the chapters in Section III, we shall discuss the techniques of effective speech delivery. These principles should be used as guides, not as arbitrary rules. Delivery is intimately related to personality and, within certain bounds, the rules should be interpreted to fit the individual. For example, in the matter of gesture, the naturally demonstrative person will gesticulate far more frequently than the less effusive speaker. While gestures aid anyone addressing a visible audience, all speakers cannot be expected to use the same kinds of gestures or to gesticulate with equal frequency.

BASIC PRINCIPLES OF DELIVERY

A. Effective delivery makes full use of both the visible and audible codes. Many of you have read in your morning paper the text of a speech which you watched on television the previous evening; conversely, some of you may have examined the text of a speech before you heard it delivered. In either case, you were probably struck by the difference between your reactions to reading the speech and to hearing it. In one instance, the printed text may seem clearer and more persuasive; in another, listening to the speech may be more rewarding. The factor of delivery chiefly accounts for the differences.

Delivery consists of that visible and audible activity by which the speaker communicates his ideas and his feelings to his listeners. The successful performer neglects neither the visible nor the audible code in attempting to secure a response. The voice can do more than simply produce the sounds which in various combinations become language; it can emphasize significant ideas by changes in pitch, intensity, and duration; it may convey delicate nuances of meaning through the use of inflection; and it may enhance emotional appeal by a judicious use of pause, stress, pitch variability, and modification of timbre. The visible code, consisting of posture, movement, gesture, and facial expression, may also aid in pointing up specific meanings and in strengthening emotional appeals.

Admittedly, some successful speakers do not use voice and diction to best advantage, and others fail to make the most of bodily expressiveness. The discerning student, however, will recognize that the difference between an indirect, lifeless, uninspiring performance and a meaningful, stimulating message often may be the full and varied use of both the visible and audible codes. Because these codes are so essential to good delivery, Chapter 10 will discuss the use of bodily action and Chapter 11 the use of the voice.

B. Effective delivery is adapted to the total speaking situation. The audience, the occasion, the subject, and the speaker are the four major components of the speaking situation. It may be necessary for the speaker to adjust his delivery to any one or all of these constituents in a given appearance. (1) *Adaptation to the audience*: Academic or intellectually inclined groups seem to prefer the restrained and dignified delivery of an Adlai Stevenson, while ebullient delegates to a political or labor convention respond to the more vehement and dynamic presentation of an Alben Barkley or a Walter Reuther. The heterogeneous radio audience was moved by the intimate, confident, and straightforward delivery of Franklin D. Roosevelt, while a large segment of the television audience has been captivated by the dramatic presentation, both vocal and visual, of Bishop Fulton J. Sheen. Small audiences expect a quieter and more informal manner than do large gatherings in spacious surroundings. (2) *Adaptation to the occasion*: While the pep rally and demonstration may be addressed with great informality, the dedication or convocation will call for considerable dignity and solemnity in presentation. A nominating speech at a political convention will undoubtedly call for more vigorous projection than will a lecture on Victorian poetry to a women's study club. (3) *Adaptation to the subject*: Your General Purpose may influence to some extent your manner of delivery. Although it is difficult to generalize, it may be concluded that a speech to entertain may be presented with informality and a maximum of gesture, movement, and vocal dynamics; the speech to persuade requires an earnest, direct, and sincere speech personality; the speech to inform must be delivered distinctly and perhaps a bit more slowly, but with sufficient animation to retain interest. Your Specific Purpose also will help determine what delivery adaptations may be desirable. (4) *Adaptation to the speaker*: Audiences expect youthful speakers to be more informal, dynamic, and vigorous than middle-aged performers. Listeners also expect men to speak with greater volume, bolder gestures, and less restraint than women. One's profession may also influence the manner of presentation. For example, most of us look for more formality and restraint from a physician, a clergyman, or a college professor than from a professional football player, a famous comedian, or a gossip columnist.

The speaker should adapt his delivery to meet the peculiar demands of a particular audience, occasion, and subject.

C. Effective delivery is sincere. Among the speakers heard by the authors during the past year were (1) a student, notorious for neglecting school work in order to participate in nearly every campus social activity, who argued that scholastic attainment should be the primary goal of every college student; (2) a well-known gambler who pleaded for better enforcement of the law; (3) a "big-time" football coach who declared that his task is to build character, and that winning games is of secondary importance; (4) an account executive in a successful advertising agency who claimed that the most important function of advertising is to educate the public; and (5) the president of a large corporation who developed the thesis that satisfied employees are more important to him than making large profits. In each of the above cases, the speaker was considered insincere by many of his listeners.

Listeners are far more likely to believe what a speaker says if they are convinced that he believes it. Even a suggestion of insincerity may result in failure. For example, one student ruined what was otherwise a moving speech on the value of prayer by winking slyly as he said, "Even sophisticated intellectuals find solace in prayer." From that point on, his listeners doubted his sincerity. The best way to give the impression of sincerity is to *be sincere*. Do not plead causes concerning which you remain unconvinced.

Apparent insincerity is a problem almost as serious as actual insincerity. Although completely in earnest, the novice speaker may give the impression of insincerity by poor eye contact, furtive glances, and other manifestations of insecurity. By developing confidence, avoiding affectation, and improving eye contact, the sincere speaker may eliminate the common signs of insincerity.

Closely related to sincerity is the concept of the *ethical responsibility* of the speaker. In a materialistic civilization where many believe in achieving personal ends at any cost, effective speaking, like atomic energy, may be used to further evil causes. With many unethical persons eager to use their persuasive powers to make the worse cause appear the better, it is the obligation of the responsible citizen to use his speaking ability in the interest of good causes.

The character of the speaker carries much weight in influencing conduct and belief. The speaker with a reputation for honesty, reliability, and dependability may succeed where a more polished and experienced performer will fail, if the motives or character of the latter are subject to suspicion. If you are to maintain a reputation for integrity, avoid taking any side of any question for the sake of momentary personal gain. Otherwise, audiences may become convinced that you are without principle, and then you will find it difficult to secure acceptance of those ideas in which you really believe.

D. Effective delivery is modest and unassuming. To the unsure, stumbling beginner, modesty is not a problem. With increased confidence and added experience, however, he may develop an exalted opinion of himself. If this is apparent to listeners, it will surely alienate them. The overly confident beginner, of course, has this opinion of himself at the outset. Great speakers, like most great men, recognize that modesty is an important asset in interpersonal relationships. Therefore, they avoid making a show of superior knowledge, and disdain both pomposity and obvious cleverness.

E. Effective delivery is confident and assured. We have discussed in Chapter 1 the problem of controlling nervous tension and alleviating stage fright. When the speaker has learned to adjust to the speaking situation, he has made an important move toward assurance in manner. Thorough preparation and accumulated experience also promote confidence. Overt overconfidence, of course, must be avoided.

F. Effective delivery does not attract attention to itself. Speakers sometimes are tempted to exhibit for audience approval their resonant voices and well-turned gestures, often at the expense of communicating ideas. Some years ago, grade-school students memorized and declaimed (but scarcely understood) orations originally delivered to the ancient Romans. Some people attended the Chautauqua lectures of William Jennings Bryan primarily to admire his magnificent delivery. Today, however, we attend a speech primarily because the speaker has something to say which interests us. Conscious audience reaction to the successful speaker should be focused on what he has to say, not his manner of saying it. In short, good delivery does not attract attention to itself, but rather to the speaker's ideas.

G. Effective delivery is enthusiastic and animated. Enthusiasm is infectious. If the speaker is alert, animated and "on fire," his listeners probably will reflect to some extent similar enthusiasm. A dull, lifeless speech personality rarely engenders an ardent response. Animated delivery results primarily from a *desire to communicate*. If you believe in your ideas and are strongly motivated to share them with others, your presentation is likely to be alert, vigorous, and dynamic.

Modes of Expression

Several modes of delivery are available to the speaker. He may (1) *memorize*, (2) speak *impromptu*, (3) *read* from manuscript, or (4) speak *extemporaneously*, with or without notes. We recommend that you avoid the first mode, use the second only when no other method is possible, and employ the third primarily when exactness of language or careful timing is essential. The extemporaneous mode should be most effective in the majority of situations.

A. Avoid the memorized speech. Because the beginning speaker fears he will be unable to find the right words and remember his ideas, he is tempted to memorize his entire speech. He reasons that this will relieve him of the necessity to think on his feet during a period of emotional strain.

For three reasons, we believe it is unwise to memorize: (1) Although a student may find time to memorize an oration for an annual contest, the busy person who speaks often is unable to devote enough time to commit speeches to memory. (2) He who memorizes is in constant danger of forgetting. If he forgets his lines, he is lost unless able to extemporize, an ability the habitual memorizer usually has not developed. (3) Memorized speeches usually sound mechanical; the speaker is concentrating upon remembering the next word or phrase rather than upon his ideas and his audience. His delivery and speech personality suffer as a result.

Frequently it may be desirable for the speaker to memorize a joke, a punch line, a sentence or two at the beginning or end of a speech, or a crucial passage in which exactness of language is paramount. However, we recommend that you do not memorize an entire speech.

B. Make the best of the situation if you are forced to speak impromptu. The impromptu speech is treated in detail in Chapter 15 as a special type. Because it is one of the modes of expression available to the public speaker, brief reference to it is made at this point.

The impromptu mode is that used when one is asked unexpectedly to "say a few words." In the absence of time for leisurely preparation, the speaker is forced to utilize the short period between the request to speak and his first words in quickly organizing his thoughts. Impromptu speaking requires that most of one's thinking be done while speaking. This is not as difficult as it may appear, since everyone is forced to do so consistently when engaging in conversation. However, in public speaking it is a frightening prospect to many, because the situation is more formal and one is more subject to nervous tension.

Remember that you are not completely unprepared for the impromptu speech. You are aware of the occasion and its demands, you have listened to the previous speakers, and you may draw upon your general knowledge. Attempt to control your nervous tension, forget yourself, and concentrate on communicating your thoughts.

C. Read from manuscript when exactness of language or careful timing is important. Detailed advice on the preparation and delivery of the manuscript speech is given in Chapter 15. Like the impromptu speech, the reading of a manuscript is a mode of expression. Hence, we include a brief reference to it in this section.

The precise timing required by radio and television and the frequent stipulation that manuscripts be submitted for examination before delivery on the air are in part responsible for the prevalence of this mode of delivery. Also, some occasions, such as the presentation of a professional paper, require precise phraseology to minimize the possibility of misinterpretation. Moreover, busy people who have not had proper training and sufficient experience in extemporaneous delivery find it easier to read from manuscript.

The greatest objection to the practice of reading is that frequently it is poorly done. In writing a manuscript, work from a completed outline. Be certain to write a speech, not an essay (see Chapter 12, "Using Language in Delivering the Speech"). In rehearsal, concentrate on becoming familiar with the ideas and language, and practice to acquire facility in reading and handling your manuscript. During delivery, endeavor to re-think and re-create the ideas. Attempt to achieve a maximum of spontaneity, eye-contact, animation, and enthusiasm.

D. Use the extemporaneous mode of delivery for the majority of your speeches. In this mode of delivery, language is coined, for the most part, at the moment of utterance. Successful use of this mode, therefore, depends largely upon the degree of language facility possessed by the speaker.

You may extemporize with or without notes. In either case, use your outline during rehearsal to aid in fixing your ideas and their sequence firmly in mind. (1) *Delivery without notes*: Although it is perfectly acceptable to use notes, some advantages accrue from eliminating their use. It is easier to be direct and communicative when relieved of the necessity of referring to notes. However, delivery without notes makes mandatory the careful memorization of the sequence of ideas and their supporting points. The novice often is mistakenly convinced that he cannot talk without notes. Nonetheless, he should attempt to deliver some of his early speeches without them. Such experience should convince him that it is possible to extemporize without difficulty in their absence. (2) *Delivery with notes*: Using notes will detract little if any from effectiveness, provided they are referred to only infrequently and do not become a barrier between speaker and audience. Put your notes on a lectern, if one is available; or you may prefer to hold them in your hands. Do not place them on a low table; for some, this will necessitate bending down in order to read them. Use small, inconspicuous cards, but make no attempt to hide the fact that you are using them. If you need more than one card, number each and write on one side only. Be so familiar with the sequence of your ideas that only rarely will you need to refer to your notes to remind you of the next point. Unless you have a good reason for an extended pause, try to anticipate the need to look at your notes so that this can be done while speaking the last few words of a sentence. Thus, you can avoid a long hesitation before beginning the next point.

PLATFORM ETIQUETTE AND CONDUCT

A. Before the speech. When several speakers are to appear on a program, the principal speaker should lead the procession to the platform, and the chairman should be last in line. If the seating arrangement is determined in advance, confusion will be avoided.

Although your speech may be first on the program, your obligations are not completely discharged upon concluding your talk; subsequent speakers deserve courteous attention, and the audience will be quick to notice lack of interest or distracting behavior on your part. If your speech occurs near the end of the meeting, the same rule for courteous attention holds. Excessive random action or preoccupation with your notes prior to and during the other speeches will be resented by the listeners, who expect you to listen as attentively as they do.

As the time for your speech draws near, attempt to relax and control nervous tension. Breathing deeply and slowly a number of times usually helps.

B. Beginning the speech. Upon introduction by the chairman, rise and walk briskly but calmly to the speaker's stand. Wait until the chairman has finished his introductory remarks, however, before leaving your seat do not "jump the gun." At the speaker's stand, pause a moment, acknowledge the chairman with the words, "Mr. Chairman," and address the audience in most cases with the words, "Ladies and gentlemen," or "Friends." It is usually unnecessary to acknowledge a number of individuals or groups in your opening greeting. An opening statement such as, "Mr. Chairman, Governor Brown, Senator Smith, Mr. Mayor, Members of the Board of Trustees, distinguished guests, and ladies and gentlemen," may be a bit ludicrous.

Avoid random action at the outset. If it is necessary to button your coat, adjust your tie, or clear your throat, do so at your seat, not upon reaching the speaker's stand. Such activity will distract your listeners at a point when you are making a strong bid for attention to your subject matter.

Even if the chairman does not announce the title of your speech, begin with the first sentence of your introduction. Do not begin a speech by announcing the topic in an incomplete sentence, such as, "How to swing a golf club."

C. During the speech. Concentrate on your ideas and your audience in an attempt to make your delivery enthusiastic and communicative. Do not worry about how well you are doing, or whether the audience approves of you. Whether reading or extemporizing, think primarily of the ideas and emotions you wish to convey.

If you lose your trend of thought, pause a moment and attempt to go on with an elaboration of the preceding idea. If you find this difficult, glance at your notes and move on to the next major point. Do not worry about omitting some material; unless it is a vital point the audience probably will be unaware that you have done so. If you make a mistake in pronunciation or diction, or if you hesitate, cough, or drop your notes, do not pause to apologize; this will only emphasize the distraction. Only serious mistakes which alter the meaning you wish to convey should be corrected in the course of the speech.

D. After the speech. Although prominent speakers sometimes conclude with "Thank you," it is unnecessary to thank a group for listening unless your appearance was at your own request. If you have done well, they should thank *you*. When your final word has been spoken, pause a moment, give a slight nod of acknowledgement if you wish, and return to your seat.

DRESS AND APPEARANCE

A neat, well-groomed appearance is essential to the speaker. In a formal speaking situation, clothes should be well fitted and pressed, shoes should be shined, and hair should be trimmed and combed. Audiences tend to regard the speaker's grooming as some evidence of the kind of person he is.

Dress should be appropriate to the occasion and should not attract attention to itself. An open-necked sport shirt would hardly be appropriate for a Community Chest dinner speaker. A girl wearing a party dress for a speech at a pep rally would be the subject of unfavorable comment. The male speaker will find that a business suit of conservative cut and color and a white shirt will be correct on the majority of occasions. Listeners notice sharp contrasts, clashing colors, and extremes in the cut and style of clothing. The man who wears a blue suit should be careful to avoid bright green socks, and should save his dazzling Christmas tie for another day. The woman who is to address a meeting of the Parent-Teacher Association should put aside her eye-arresting frock for more appropriate occasions and choose either a more conservative dress or a suit.

USE OF A PUBLIC ADDRESS SYSTEM

Webster, Clay, Bryan, and others who spoke prior to the electronic age were forced to depend solely upon vocal projection to reach the back rows of audiences. Because most large auditoriums and meeting halls today are equipped with public address systems, such strenuous vocal activity is unnecessary. However, amplifying systems require that some adjustments be made if the speaker is to use them to best advantage.

A. If present, a public address system should be used. If the sponsors of your meeting have installed an amplifying system, experience has probably indicated that it is needed by most speakers in that particular room when a large audience is in attendance. Although you may be fairly certain that your voice will carry without amplification, it will be better for you to use the public address equipment. The audience will expect you to do so, and will appreciate hearing you without effort. Furthermore, by disdaining its use, you may hurt the feelings of those who provided it.

B. Keep within close range of the microphone. Microphones are usually secured to the speaker's stand or placed near it. Speak directly into the mike from your position behind the lectern. More than one step to either side or backward will cause a noticeable decrease in amplification. To avoid distracting variations in volume, keep a fairly consistent position in relation to the microphone.

C. Maintain normal volume and projection. Although a large audience and a spacious room ordinarily require increased volume and projection, remember that the amplifier makes this unnecessary. Avoid sharp increases in volume, which will overload the amplifier. Your rate will need to be a trifle slower with a large audience, even though using a public address system. Do not be disturbed by the fact that you can hear your voice as it leaves the amplifier; use what you hear as a guide in adjusting your volume and projection.

SUMMARY

Certain principles and practices are basic to the achievement of effective speech delivery. Good delivery (1) makes full use of both the visible and audible codes, (2) is adapted to the total speaking situation, (3) is sincere, (4) is modest and unassuming, (5) is confident and assured, (6) does not attract attention to itself, and (7) is enthusiastic and animated.

Among the various modes of delivery, the extemporaneous is the most effective in a majority of situations. Reading from manuscript may be employed when exactness of language and timing is required, if sufficient care has been exercised in preparation and rehearsal. The impromptu speech may be successful if the speaker is able to organize quickly and think on his feet. Memorized speeches are usually ineffective.

The speaker should be aware of the essentials of platform conduct and etiquette before, during, and after his speech. His dress, appearance, and manner should be correct and appropriate. If a public address system is provided, he should use it skillfully.

EXERCISES AND ASSIGNMENTS

1. During a round of speeches write a short analysis of the delivery of each of your classmates, using as a guide the basic principles in this chapter. Include both assets and liabilities. Put each analysis on a separate sheet of paper and do not sign your name. Hand the papers to your instructor, who will read them, sort them, and return to each student the various analyses of his delivery. How do your classmates' estimates of your delivery compare with your own? Are there points upon which there is substantial agreement? How will these evaluations help you in future work on techniques of delivery?

2. From among the well-known speakers you have heard select the three who, in your judgment, are most effective in delivery. Be ready to defend your choice in class discussion.

3. Can you name several recognized speakers who are consistently well received by audiences even though their delivery is only average? Report orally to the class your analysis of the reasons for their effectiveness.

4. Prepare a two- or three-minute speech for extemporaneous delivery and record it on wire or tape. Then write out the speech verbatim, and read it into the mike. Play back both versions and evaluate the two pres-

entations. Which mode of delivery seems more effective? Why? Do your classmates agree?

5. Make one speaking assignment a "work session," in which each speaker may be stopped at any time by either classmates or instructor to point out deficiencies in delivery and to suggest improvements. Following each interruption, attempt to remedy the deficiency noted as you resume speaking.

6. Write two speech topics on separate pieces of paper. Each topic should ask for an opinion or point of view on some common subject matter area. Be certain that your topic is general enough to permit any student to speak on it from his general knowledge. Place these topics along with those of your classmates on a table at the front of the classroom. Each student will choose one as he goes before the group and speak on it for two or three minutes. Compare the delivery of each student in this impromptu session with his delivery of prepared speeches.

7. Arrange to use a public address system in one speaking assignment. If your school does not own one, your city library probably makes such equipment available for rent at a nominal fee. In presenting your speeches, observe the rules noted in this chapter for the effective use of such equipment.

CHAPTER 10

Using the Body in Delivering the Speech

In this chapter, we shall discuss the visible code in delivery—what the listener *sees* when the speech is presented. The visible code includes every observable action on the part of the speaker. The major components of visual communication are posture, movement, facial expression, and gesture. Skill in the use of each is essential to the public speaker. The visual aspect of delivery is frequently called *bodily action*.

THE IMPORTANCE OF BODILY ACTION

Before considering the principles of bodily action, it is necessary to dispose of certain misconceptions about its place in the speech situation. (1) *Visible action is not a distinct and separate activity to be employed or ignored as the speaker sees fit.* It is impossible to speak to a visible audience without communicating visible meaning. Even the comparatively inactive person does so, possibly without being aware of it; his inactivity in itself gives his audience some clue to his personality and his attitude toward speaking. Moreover, such a speaker inevitably shifts his weight now and then, moves his eyes and head from time to time, and is forced to move his mouth to form words. Inescapably, the visible code is an integral part of the face-to-face speaking situation. (2) *The speaker is not concerned with visible action as an end in itself.* A gesture inserted for its own sake in a speech is exhibitionism. Bodily action which calls attention to itself at the expense of the speaker's ideas will hinder the achievement of the Specific Speech Purpose. (3) *Visible action does not replace the audible code; it supplements it.* In attempting to communicate meaning, inarticulate speakers sometimes try to substitute movement, facial expression, and gesture for words. Carried to extremes, this behavior approaches pantomiming and

226

the sign language of the speechless. (4) *Effective visible action is not artificial or unnatural.* The statue-like, "poker-faced" speaker who asserts that gesture and movement are artificial and unnatural to him usually unconsciously punctuates his own conversation with appropriate gestures and facial expression. Upon adequate adjustment to the speaking situation, he is sometimes surprised to discover that he is using the visible code freely and naturally.

Effective bodily action helps the speaker in (1) adjusting to the speaking situation, (2) securing and maintaining interest and attention, (3) clarifying meaning, and (4) attaining emphasis.

A. Bodily action facilitates adjustment to the speaking situation. It was noted earlier that a major component of stage fright is muscular tension. One of the best ways to achieve partial relaxation of a muscle is to use it. For example, a cramp in a leg muscle can be relieved by "walking it out." Muscular tension at the outset of a speech may be alleviated by moving about the platform and gesturing. The resulting partial relaxation will aid in controlling muscles which previously may have been too rigid. Recovery of control will increase your confidence and help put you at ease. Moreover, movement and gesture will provide a constructive outlet for the excess energy accumulated as a result of being "keyed up." Otherwise, this energy may find its release in such distracting random action as coin-jingling, nose-rubbing, head-scratching, and so forth.

B. Bodily action helps to secure and maintain interest and attention. As you know, a major problem at the beginning of a speech is to secure the favorable attention of the listeners. Much of your effort in choosing and organizing material for the Introduction is directed toward that end. The use of some bodily action, such as a gesture, will enhance your chances of attaining interest, since we are ordinarily attracted more quickly to a moving object than to a stationary one. Animation will invite audience interest.

Attention once acquired must be maintained. While holding audience interest is largely a matter of speech content and organization, bodily action may aid measurably in this respect. The fact that most of us are unable to focus our attention on any one object for any length of time poses a genuine problem for the speaker. Action will enable the listener to shift his attention periodically and yet keep it focused primarily upon the speaker and his ideas.

C. Bodily action helps to clarify meaning. Words alone are often insufficient to communicate full meaning. For this reason, speakers and writers often augment words with visual aids such as pictures, maps, diagrams, and charts (Chapter 6). Experienced speakers know that descriptive bodily action also serves admirably in clarifying meaning. The concepts of distance, size, shape, direction, and speed are frequently more meaningful and vivid to an audience if illustrated by descriptive action. The optimum *distance* from a microphone, the *size* of a dent in a fender, the *shape* of a modernistic end table, the *direction* taken by a cue ball in a three-cushion billiard shot, and the *speed* of a boxer's left jab was typical of concepts which may be pointed up by descriptive action. Moreover, the lift of an eyebrow, the curl of a lip, or the shrug of a shoulder may convey the meaning of hundreds of words.

D. Bodily action helps to achieve emphasis. A series of points may be emphasized by enumerating them on your fingers. Your fist may strike the table to drive a point home. Position on the platform also may influence audience reaction. For example, standing some distance from the audience and on a higher level emphasizes formality; a position at floor level close to the audience results in less formality and greater intimacy. Appropriate facial expression also aids in emphasizing specific meanings and emotions.

The Use of Bodily Action

The visible code may be divided into four major aspects: (1) facial expression, (2) posture, (3) movement, and (4) gesture. Although each is treated separately, remember that all are closely integrated in the actuality of speaking.

A. Facial expression. Perhaps most important to the speaker in the use of facial expression are the eyes. Your eyes are the means by which you achieve direct contact with your listeners. Most of us like people who "look us in the eye" when addressing us, either in conversation or from the speaker's platform. We dislike and even distrust those who avoid looking at us while conversing; as members of an audience, we lose interest in the speaker who looks constantly at his notes, the floor, the ceiling, out the window, or anyplace rather than at his audience. *Except for necessary reference to notes* *or to visual aids, keep your eyes on your listeners, or you may lose them.*

Single out some individual in the audience, speak briefly to him, and then shift to another. Repeat this procedure throughout the speech. Avoid merely looking in the general direction of the audience without focusing your eyes upon the group. Listeners are quick to detect a blank stare or a "far-away" look and will react negatively. Each member of an audience likes to believe the speaker is talking directly to him.

The rest of the face also aids in clarifying meaning, in revealing the speaker's attitudes and personality, and in attaining emphasis. As previously stated, we are all aware of the meaning which can be revealed by a smile, a set jaw, a frown, or a knit brow. Two principles should guide you in acquiring effective facial expression: (1) free yourself of inhibitions to the extent that facial expressions can manifest themselves naturally; and (2) do not plan and rehearse facial expressions in advance, but let them be governed by the meaning inherent in your words. Your natural expressiveness will probably be sufficient if you *think* and *feel* the meaning behind your words.

The most common sins in the use of facial expression: (1) *The "poker face":* Nervous tension often inhibits facial expression. While an inexpressive face may help the poker player, it limits the effectiveness of the public speaker. (2) *The "mugger":* This frustrated actor accompanies each word with exaggerated facial grimaces (sometimes called "mugging"), thus calling attention to himself rather than to his ideas. Except in some speeches to entertain, acting has little place in public speaking. (3) *The facial contortionist:* This speaker releases pent-up tension by random activity of the facial muscles bearing little relation to his intended meaning. Achievement of a degree of adjustment will permit him to release his energy more profitably, and make possible meaningful facial expression.

B. Posture. Although there is no single correct way to stand while delivering a speech, keep these general suggestions in mind: Your body should be erect without the exaggerated stiffness of the soldier-at-attention. Relax sufficiently to be comfortable, but not so much that you appear on the verge of collapse from fatigue. You will be most comfortable if your feet are placed from six to twelve inches apart, with your weight resting on the balls of your feet, and your toes pointed slightly outward. Place one foot slightly behind the other and rest most of your body weight on the rear foot, if you wish. In adopting the latter suggestion, be sure that your body is not thrown excessively out of line by the transfer of weight. Your arms may hang naturally at your sides, unless you are using them for gesticulation. Occasionally you may wish to grasp the lectern with your hands, but avoid leaning on it for any length of time. Other acceptable hand positions are (1) both hands in pockets, (2) either hand in a pocket, and (3) hands clasped behind you. Avoid maintaining any of these for an extended period, because they inhibit gestures. Vary your hand positions periodically while speaking.

Good posture while speaking will be most easily attained if you practice proper bearing at all times. Like the six-day-a-week thief who tries to be pious in church on Sunday, the speaker with habitually bad posture will be uncomfortable in attempting good bearing while on the platform. Make good posture a habit, and you will not need to worry about it when speaking.

The most common sins in the use of posture: (1) *The "sloucher":* Audiences get the impression that the "sloucher" is too tired to stand up and that he lacks interest in both his ideas and his listeners. Members of the audience find their attention wandering from his ideas to his appearance. (2) *The "leaner":* Overly enamored of tables, lecterns, and the backs of chairs, this speaker clutches at any object which will support much of his weight and clings to it doggedly throughout his speech. Audiences wonder how he would survive a speech on an empty platform, and as a result sometimes are not sure what he talked about. (3) *The "ramrod":* With stomach in, chest out, shoulders back, and chin in, the "ramrod" gives the impression that at any moment he might click his heels and salute. Audiences wish he would relax, so that they could do likewise.

C. Movement. We refer here to gross movements of the entire body, such as walking about the platform; activity by parts of the body for the purpose of gesticulation is treated in the following section.

Movement is important to the speaker for two reasons: to attract attention and to convey meaning. It was previously noted that we are attracted more quickly to a moving object than to a stationary one. Changing positions on the platform—moving from behind the lectern to the right or left, or walking forward a few steps toward the audience—will often bring drowsy listeners to life. Such movements should be executed smoothly and naturally. Walking about the platform stiffly or awkwardly will attract negative attention. Various meanings can be conveyed by movement. For example, a pause accompanied by a few steps to either side will indicate transition; a move forward may mean you are about to make an important point, perhaps the climax, of the discourse.

How much movement should you engage in? A categorical answer cannot be given; your subject, your physical surroundings, the occasion, and other factors will influence your mobility on the platform. In general, it will be wise to avoid extremes. Do not remain in one spot throughout the speech (unless you are using a public address microphone); on the other hand, avoid continuous movement. A two-minute announcement will probably need no movement about the platform. In a five-minute speech, feel free to move several times.

Many speakers forget that effective movement is also important in approaching and leaving the platform, since first and last impressions occur at these times. Moderation is again the keyword. Move at a normal rate, avoiding both nervous rapidity and exasperating slowness. Shun the manner of the timid soul afraid to be seen, or that of the swaggering show-off bidding for attention.

The most common sins in the use of movement: (1) The *"statue"*: Like his stone counterpart, the "statue" appears to be riveted to the floor and incapable of movement. A step or two either forward or to the side might revive the attention and interest of his listeners. (2) *The "pacer"*: Like the proverbial caged lion, the "pacer" walks with determination from one side of the platform to the other and then back. His audience longs for the speech to end so that both he and they can rest. (3) *The "swayer"*: The "swayer" rhythmically moves his body from side to side or forward and backward as his weight shifts. He joins the "pacer" in forcing audience attention to focus on his mannerism rather than on his message.

3. Gestures. A gesture is a purposive movement of some part of the body to convey meaning and secure emphasis. As stated earlier, a *descriptive* gesture will make more meaningful concepts such as distance, size, shape, and direction. These gestures usually involve the use of the hands and arms. For example, the size of "the fish that got away" is indicated by holding the hands a good distance apart. A gesture of *emphasis* is used to strengthen the impact of an idea upon the listener so that it will be accepted and remembered. (1) A pointed finger may emphasize accusation or warning, but should be pointed slightly above rather than directly at the audience. (2) The clenched fist may pound the table to reveal anger or determination, but should be used with restraint to avoid startling the audience and diverting attention from the speaker's point. If you are moved to pound the table, weaken the force of the blow just before striking the surface so that the movement of force is apparent but distracting noise is prevented. Banging the speaker's stand may offend listeners. (3) Rejection and disapproval may be reinforced by "pushing away" with the open palm. (4) Emphasis may also be achieved by head and shoulder gestures, the most common of which are shrugging the shoulders and shaking or nodding the head. The animated speaker does not have a stiff neck. His head is in almost constant movement.

Gestures, facial expression, movement, and posture should be practiced and checked before a full-length mirror, preferably under the guidance of an instructor, until awkwardness, stiffness, and ungracefulness are removed, and execution becomes uninhibited and natural.

When practicing gesticulation, check for the following characteristics: (1) The effective gesture consists of the *preparation,* the *stroke,* and the *return.* The preparation takes the arm or hand to the point where meaningful action, or the stroke, takes place. The return brings the arm back rather slowly to a position of rest. (Do not watch your gestures except when practicing). (2) The stroke should possess vigor and strength. It should not be a vague, meaningless sweep of the arms. (3) A gesture should be timed so that it occurs simultaneously with the word or phrase to be emphasized. Much of the effect is lost if the stroke noticeably "jumps the gun" or lags behind. Of course, a gesture may occasionally stand alone, unaccompanied by words. (4) Keep gesticulation within the gesture zone. The speaker has an effective gesture area much like the baseball strike zone, except that the gesture zone extends from the shoulders to the waist, the strike zone from the "letters" to the knees. Gestures should usually occur within this area, and should be brought in toward the front of the body. (5) Practice a variety of gestures so that you will not rely exclusively on one or two habitual favorities. Remember that both hands should be used at various times; do not favor one hand at the expense of the other.

Do not plan specific gestures to be executed at a certain place in a speech. To do so usually results in artificial, unmotivated activity. Let the stimulus for gestures arise from within; meaningful activity will spring from the speaker's enthusiasm and emotion, and his desire to make a point clear and strong. Remember that a gesture is made by the *whole body,* not just the extremities. If you have practiced gestures until you can execute them easily and gracefully, and if you feel strongly enough about your subject, effective gestures will come naturally.

Two valuable projects in the development of effective bodily action are the pantomime and the speech of demonstration. The pantomime restricts communication to the visible code, and the speech of demonstration usually demands an abundance of bodily action. These activities will develop patterns and habits of action which may be called upon in other speaking situations.

The most common sins in the use of gestures: (1) *Random action:* Speakers frequently substitute distracting random activity for purposive gesture. Such activity includes fidgeting with notes, pencils, buttons, coat lapels, pockets, bracelets, and beads; it embraces wiggling like a jitterbug, performing a tap dance with the soles or heels, rubbing the nose and chin, running fingers through the hair, taking ones' glasses off and putting them on, and the like. Such movements serve no purpose other than to distract the listener from the content of the speech. Developing facility in gesticulation will drain off the excess energy which prompts such activity. (2) *Perpetual motion:* Perpetual motion is as monotonous as perpetual immobility. The speaker who constantly uses his hands will soon lose the reinforcement of meaning and the emphasis which gestures can provide. Gestures should punctuate ideas at appropriate points rather than serve as ever-present accompaniment to words. Persistent gesticulation without relation to the words spoken is purposeless. (3) *The abortive gesture:* This movement is usually well motivated but inadequately or incompletely executed. A potentially full-blown, vigorous movement of the arm falls short of realization and becomes only a slight twitch of the arm or a cramped, jerky movement of the fingers or wrist. Sufficient practice to "get the feel" of gesturing should make it a natural and an uninhibited activity, and should put an end to abortive gestures.

SUMMARY

Visible activity facilitates adjustment to the speaking situation; helps the speaker to secure and maintain audience interest and attention; aids the speaker in clarifying meaning; and gives added emphasis. The values of bodily action will be realized by the effective use of (1) facial expression, (2) posture, (3) movement, and (4) gestures.

EXERCISES AND ASSIGNMENTS

1. Deliver a three- or four-minute speech demonstrating (1) good and bad posture, (2) properly and improperly executed movement, (3) the most common sins in the use of facial expression, or (4) effective and ineffective use of gestures.

2. *Project in Individual Pantomime:* Choose for class presentation a subject well adapted to pantomime. The following suggestions may give you some ideas: (1) Teach an imaginary person to play golf, to dance the tango, to box, to apply cosmetics to the face, to use several wrestling holds, to drive an automobile. Make your choice of subject as original and unusual as possible. Your instructor and classmates will attempt to identify what you are doing. (2) Tell a story without the use of words. Then ask a classmate to retell the story in words. (3) Impersonate a well-known comedian, actor, or public official.

3. *Project in Group Pantomime:* With two or three of your classmates select a narrative or playlet which you can produce in pantomime, with each student playing one part. Your selection should call for considerable action on the part of each character. Detective stories, adventure stories, and melodramas lend themselves well to group pantomime. Write your own production, if you wish. Limit the presentation to ten minutes.

4. Choose a subject upon which you have strong feeling—something which arouses your indignation or your anger. Exhort your audience to

"do something about it." In giving vent to your feelings, make a real attempt to "let yourself go." Move freely about the platform, let your face reflect your emotions, pound the lectern, shake your fist; approach expressive action with abandon, and do not worry about overdoing it.

5. Check your use of the visible code in a full-length mirror.

(1) Note your relaxed and habitual posture from both front and side views. If you are slouching, straighten up and get the feeling of "standing tall." Are you putting approximately equal weight on both feet? What is your habitual head position?

(2) Execute the types of gestures noted in this chapter. Are they cramped and awkward? Practice various types of hand and arm gestures (include preparation, stroke, and return) until they are easily and gracefully executed.

(3) Deliver a portion of a speech you have prepared which calls for a variety of facial expressions. Does your face express the emotions you feel and the meaning you wish to convey? If not, practice creating facial expressions until they approximate what you want.

(4) Practice in front of a mirror until you are approaching effectiveness in the use of the visible code. When you are satisfied with what you see, repeat until you "get the feel" of a given gesture or facial expression. You will then be well on the way to building a useful habit. Although some actions may seem awkward at first, this reaction will disappear in time. In doing this exercise, remember that your purpose is to build habits; do not plan specific gestures and facial expressions for use in a particular speech.

6. Watch a well-known speaker on television. Give particular attention to his use of the visible code. Did he commit any of the common sins of posture, movement, facial expression, or gesture? In what ways did his use of bodily action contribute to or detract from his effectiveness? Report to the class.

7. *Project in Motion Picture Photography.* An excellent device for observing one's use of the visible code is to photograph on motion picture film each student's delivery both at the beginning and the end of the term. This project will be easy to arrange if your school owns a motion picture camera and projector and if funds are available to purchase a roll of film. If funds for a film are not available, members of the class may be able to raise the money by contribution. If your school does not own motion picture equipment, it may be available for rental at the local library.

(1) Plan to film about thirty seconds of each speaker's performance.

(2) The camera operator should not make obvious to the speaker the exact moments during which the camera is activated.

(3) If you wish, record the speeches at the same time.

(4) In showing the film, run the projector at a speed identical with that of the camera in taking the pictures. This will enable you to synchronize the recording and the film, although this is admittedly somewhat difficult.

(5) Stop the film after each speaker's performance for comment by the instructor and the class.

(6) If possible, repeat the project at the close of the term. Compare the pictures taken at the beginning of the course with those taken at the end.

Although this project is a bit elaborate and somewhat expensive, motion pictures are of considerable value in showing the speaker how he appears to others. The Speakers' Division of the Cleveland Advertising Club has made this an annual project, with encouraging results.

CHAPTER 11

Using the Voice in Delivering the Speech

The vocal aspects of delivery are singularly important in the effective presentation of a speech. The speaking voice produces those sounds (words) which represent the speaker's thoughts, thus audibly conveying his ideas to his listeners. The voice also carries many other messages. It ordinarily reveals the sex of the speaker, and gives a general idea of his age; it provides some clues to his state of health and reflects his emotional condition; it is so intensely personal that one can identify even casual friends by a phrase or two spoken over the telephone.

Successful speakers recognize that a sensitive, well-trained vocal instrument permits the communication of delicate nuances of meaning, helps create favorable attitudes toward the speaker, and aids in achieving audience acceptance of his ideas. Inadequate voice production, however, may result in irritation, loss of attention, misunderstanding, and, in severe cases, total loss of meaning. A beautiful voice and perfect diction will not be sufficient to guarantee speaking effectiveness; inferior vocal usage, however, can be responsible for complete failure. On the speaker's stand and in everyday conversation the use of one's voice is basic to successful communication. In this chapter, we shall note the attributes of the effective voice, and discuss those principles of vocal production, articulation, and pronunciation which aid in developing these attributes.

Six Attributes of an Effective Speaking Voice

A. Audibility. It is obvious that a speaker cannot make himself intelligible unless he can be heard. Every spoken word should be clearly and effortlessly heard by every member of an audience.

Because beginning speakers are usually accustomed only to informal talk in small groups, their voices are not always easily heard in the periphery of audiences. Occasionally, the novice speaker will overcompensate by almost blasting his listeners from the room with excessive loudness. A good speaker will adjust his volume and force to the size of the room and audience and to the acoustical requirements of the situation.

B. Pleasantness. Since pleasantness is a highly subjective concept with a multitude of meanings, it is difficult to define. Perhaps it will be best understood by noting those characteristics of voice generally agreed upon as undesirable. Unpleasant voices may be harsh, raspy, guttural, shrill, nasal, or breathy in quality; they may be pitched too high or too low, or may lack variability in rate or force. The concept of pleasantness is also related to the speaking situation and to the other attributes of voice discussed in this section. In general, we prefer those patterns of voice, articulation, and pronunciation to which we have become accustomed.

C. Variety. Monotony, or inflexibility, is frequently a characteristic of the untrained voice. In the beginning speaker, this defect can be attributed to his intense preoccupation with himself and the problem of putting his ideas into words; he is unable to give adequate attention to voice production and has not developed habits of vocal variety. A well-trained voice varies in pitch, rate, quality, and loudness with every change in the speaker's mind, attitude, and purpose, with every shade of meaning to be conveyed, and with every discernible listener-reaction.

D. Animation. An animated voice is lively, spirited, and vibrant; it possesses flexibility in pitch, rate, and force. Animation is most likely to occur when the speaker sincerely believes in what he is saying, and strongly desires to communicate those ideas to his listeners.

E. Fluency. Fluency refers to smoothness in the flow of words. Lack of fluency may be the result of nervousness, faulty breathing, or poor preparation. It manifests itself in frequent hesitations and vocalized pauses, during which the speaker hunts for the next word. When words finally come, they are sometimes spoken much too

logical condition or structural abnormality, the cause is probably improper use of voice. Chronic harshness is usually caused by uncontrolled exhalation and excessive muscular tension in the throat. It can be corrected by learning to expel breath evenly and smoothly, rather than all in one burst, and by attempting to relax neck and throat muscles. (4) *Nasality*, paradoxically, can be the result of either too much or too little nasal resonance. An example of nasality caused by too much nasal resonance is the voice quality of cleft-palate speech. This condition makes it impossible to close the nasal chambers to the passage of air during exhalation. Nasal quality caused by insufficient nasal resonance may result from adenoidal obstruction, congestion from a head cold, etc. If this unpleasant quality exists without organic cause, it is probably attributable to an established habit pattern. In such cases, the problem is that of learning to use nasal resonance. Although only the *m, n,* and *ng* sounds are primarily nasal, a number of other sounds in our language are ordinarily produced with a small amount of air escaping through the nose, thus providing a *slight* degree of nasal resonance. Hum the *m* sound until you can feel the vibrations in your nose; then, with the soft palate partly relaxed, try the *ah* sound until you feel some vibration in both the nose and mouth. This will give you the feeling of nasal resonance. With a sufficient nasal component in the vowel sounds, your voice will acquire a ringing brilliance not otherwise possible. Be careful not to relax the palate too much; to do so will result in the common nasal whine. To help achieve proper balance, check with your instructor and listen carefully to recordings of your voice.

B. Variety, animation, and fluency necessitate a flexible voice. An adequately supported tone, clearly produced and richly resonated, will nevertheless be monotonous and dull unless it possesses *flexibility*. We were concerned in the previous section with the development of a pleasing voice; in this section we shall examine those characteristics of voice which give it variation, animation, expressiveness, and responsiveness. Flexibility increases interest values, reveals the speaker's personality, and clarifies meaning. The most important variable attributes of voice are *pitch, force,* and *rate.* Although the three work in combination and in close relation to each other, they may be examined and practiced separately.

1. *The effective speaking voice has flexibility of pitch.*   Pitch refers to the location of the sound on a musical scale. Variation of pitch is accomplished by moving up and down the scale, either by a clear stop followed by a new pitch, or by a continuous slide from one pitch to another. A discussion of pitch usage should include general pitch level, pitch variations, and pitch or melody patterns.

General pitch level should be appropriate to the age and sex of the speaker. The adult male voice is expected to be lower in general pitch level than the adult female voice; the voice of a child is ordinarily pitched higher than that of the adult. Any extreme variation from these expectations will startle listeners and may hinder effective communication. General pitch level also reflects the emotional state of the speaker. During anger, most voices will maintain an average pitch higher than normal; during grief, the opposite effect is common.

The optimum general pitch level for the speaker is usually determined by the size of his vocal cords, the structure of his larynx, and the size of his resonators. Little can be done about these anatomical characteristics—you cannot make a tenor out of a bass, although you can increase the active pitch range of both. Habitual pitch, however, may not always be optimum pitch. Attempt to find that level which is resonated most effectively. Your optimum level will probably be about one-fourth of the way up your total range. This placement will enable you to raise or lower your pitch without strain.

Flexibility in pitch will give animation, interest, and meaning to your speaking. Without it, speech is monotonous and dull, and may convey little meaning. We noted previously that variations in pitch or inflection occur in two ways: the *step*, an abrupt change in pitch either upward or downward, occurs between phonations; the *glide*, a continuous, gradual change in pitch in either direction, occurs during the production of a sound. Your goal should be the normal inflections of animated conversation, in which the meaning and emotion to be communicated dictate the nature and extent of pitch variation. Avoid extremes such as the lifeless monotone or the exaggerated inflections of "affected" speech.

Minimize melody or pitch patterns. Pitch variations are sometimes arranged into patterns which are repeated monotonously in the course of extended utterance. One is the "sing-song" up-and-down pattern, in which a few words are repeated with a slowly rising inflection, followed by another group delivered with a gradually falling inflection. Beware, also, of ending each sentence with an upward inflection—this makes every sentence sound like a question. Moreover, shun the pattern in which each sentence begins with a sharply rising inflection and ends with a slowly receding inflection. Check with your instructor periodically on the possible development of undesirable patterns and listen for them in recordings of your voice. Again, the meaning and mood of what you say should govern your pitch variations; avoid using the same inflection pattern to express a variety of different meanings and emotions. Keep the natural patterns of conversation. Public speaking should be like conversation, except formalized a bit and usually somewhat louder.

Practice reading and speaking with appropriate inflections until lively and animated expressiveness becomes a habit. When you reach the platform, forget the techniques and permit the habits you have established to provide the vocal variety necessary to stir up desired responses.

2. The effective speaking voice has flexibility of force. We are aware that a fundamental requirement of the speaker's voice is that it be heard by all listeners. Minimum requirements are that the speaker use sufficient force or loudness to be heard without effort in the periphery of the audience, that he avoid excessive force in the small room, and that he make adjustments in volume to fit the mood of the occasion and subject. He should also speak with enough force to impress his audience with his desire to speak and his interest in his subject. Moreover, force should be used with variation. Continuous use of any level of volume—soft, medium, or loud—will bore listeners and eliminate variation in force as a method for conveying meaning. Variation in force may also be used to achieve emphasis. It is possible to underscore a word or point by markedly *increasing* or *decreasing* force. While sharply increasing volume is a well-known device for securing emphasis, many speakers do not realize that decreasing volume may secure a similar effect. The latter device, that of "underplaying," is useful in regaining lagging attention or in driving a point home.

Greater vocal force may be achieved by increasing the power and speed of exhalation. This results in greater air pressure on the vocal cords, causing them to vibrate with greater amplitude. Reduction in force is accomplished by the opposite process—exhalation with less force and speed.

Practice delivering words, phrases, and sentences with a variety of force to develop the habit of flexibility. During delivery concentrate on meaning and let it dictate the amount and type of variation needed.

3. *The effective speaking voice has flexibility of rate.* The speed with which words are spoken affects the intelligibility and general effectiveness of the speaker. The average rate of speaking is between 120 and 150 words per minute. If your average rate is slower than 110 or faster than 160 words per minute, it may need some adjustment. An important consideration for the speaker is the concept of *apparent* rate. Audiences do not sit with stop watches to check the speaker's rate of utterance; their judgment is subjective and is colored by factors such as pause, vocalized pause, hesitation, and prolongation of vowel sounds. Although Franklin D. Roosevelt spoke more slowly than average, the majority of his listeners were probably unaware of it; his *apparent* rate was near the average. Conversely, some effective speakers may attain a rate of 175 words per minute without giving the impression of excessive speed.

Rate should be varied to fit the material presented and the mood of the occasion. Light, joyful, or exciting content usually demands a relatively rapid rate, while ponderous material and solemn occasions require a slower rate. A sports announcer giving a play-by-play description of a game ordinarily uses a faster rate than a minister delivering a funeral sermon.

Other than varying the number of words spoken per minute, the most important factors in rate variability are *pause* and *duration of sound*. *Pause* should be differentiated from *hesitation*. *Hesitation* is that interruption of utterance which occurs when the speaker is unable to think of the proper word or loses his train of thought. Since it reveals uncertainty and interrupts communication, it should be avoided. *Pause* is a purposeful interruption of utterance which serves to punctuate what the speaker says, as the period or comma in an essay sets off words into thought groups. *Pause* also helps to emphasize important ideas by allowing them to "sink in." Beginning speakers are usually guilty of excessive hesitancy, but have not developed effective use of pause. *Duration of sound* refers to the amount of time consumed in producing a sound, particularly the vowel sounds. Prolonging the vowel sound in the word "bad," for example, will aid in securing emphasis. Duration of sound should vary with the material presented and the mood of the occasion. Solemn or depressing occasions will usually demand greater duration of sounds to accompany the slower rate; light or exciting situations or ideas are more appropriately handled by shortening the vowel sounds and increasing the rate.

Variety in rate will aid in holding attention, making effective transitions, and attaining emphasis. How can an appropriate rate be acquired? First, listen to yourself and consult with your instructor on your apparent rate; second, learn through practice to vary the duration of sounds to achieve emphasis, and attempt to incorporate the use of pause; third, practice to minimize vocalized pause and hesitation; finally, attempt to adjust these variable factors to your material and to the occasion.

Variety, fluency, and animation in voice usage can be achieved by the speaker who acquires flexibility in pitch, force, and rate.

C. Clarity depends upon the distinctness and correctness with which you speak. Delivery of a speech in a clear, pleasant voice with sufficient variety in pitch, force, and rate may still be ineffective if articulation and pronunciation are inadequate. In a broad sense articulation and pronunciation are the processes which are involved in the production of the sounds of a language.

The concepts of articulation and pronunciation are closely related and occasionally overlap. A sound or combination of sounds habitually produced improperly, resulting in impaired intelligibility and comprehension, may be classified as an articulatory problem. Most articulatory difficulties occur in the formation of the consonants, individually or in combinations. A pronunciation error occurs when the sounds of a word are given values, sequences, or accents which are unacceptable to listeners and consequently are judged incorrect. Articulation, then, is primarily concerned with *intelligibility;* pronunciation is a matter of *acceptability,* which is determined by conventional standards of correctness.

Unacceptable pronunciation frequently does not interfere with intelligibility. For example, although many people find "theeayter" an unacceptable pronunciation of the word "theater," this pronunciation is undoubtedly almost universally comprehended. On the other hand, "Sgoweet" for "Let's go eat" is an example of a common slurring error which may impair comprehension.

1. *Use distinct articulation.* Indistinctness may cause speech to be unintelligible or misunderstood. Many words in our language depend upon a single sound for identification; if that sound is improperly produced or if another is substituted, the word may be lost to the listener, or he may mistake it for another. If articulation errors are frequent, listeners will be irritated or repelled, and will wonder why the speaker has not made some effort to improve. The result may be a failure in communication.

Common difficulties in articulation are: (1) *mumbling* or *muffling*, (2) *slurring*, and less frequently (3) *overprecision*.

a. Mumbling or Muffling. This occurs when the jaws, lips, and tongue are not active enough to allow precise formation of a given sound. Habitual laziness in the use of these articulators causes general indistinctness. Tongue and jaw laziness hinders vowel production; difficulty with consonants is encountered when lips and tongue are inactive.

b. Slurring. This fault takes place when a series of sounds and words are run together so that syllables are indistinctly formed or omitted altogether. *What are you doing tonight?* is commonly slurred so that it becomes *Whutchadoontnight?* Slurring is frequently caused by excessive speed. Many combinations of sounds require a considerable amount of movement by the articulators; unless sufficient time is allowed, it is unlikely that these sounds will be precisely produced. Slurring may also be caused by carelessness and habit.

c. Overprecision. While overprecision is not as common as indistinctness, it is sufficiently prevalent to warrant a word of warning. When a speaker is unduly conscious of his enunciation, he may make excessive use of his articulators, resulting in an affected manner. Overprecision calls attention to itself at the expense of ideas.

How may distinctness be improved? Begin by analyzing your speech to discover its weaknesses. Many articulatory problems remain unsolved because the speaker does not know they exist. Record your voice and check your mistakes with the help of your instructor. If your problem is general indistinctness, resulting from lazy articulators or excessive speed, begin your program for improvement by slowing down and increasing jaw, lip, and tongue movements. If the problem is limited to certain sounds, begin by learning to distinguish between correct and incorrect production of the sound in question; next, find out how well you produce the sound in isolation; finally, and most difficult, develop the ability to produce the sound correctly in combination with others to form various words. Continued practice will build the new habit.

More serious problems affecting voice and articulation, such as stuttering, lisping, the inability to produce particular consonants, cleft palate, and spastic paralysis, are beyond the scope of this book. Defects of this kind usually respond to treatment by a specialist in speech rehabilitation.

2. *Use acceptable pronunciation.* Mistakes in pronunciation may irritate or distract the audience. Such errors can be avoided if the speaker is sensitive to the standards of pronunciation prevalent in the community, and if he is aware of the common types of pronunciation errors.

a. FOLLOW THE PRONUNCIATION PRACTICES OF RESPECTED AND EDUCATED PEOPLE IN YOUR COMMUNITY OR REGION. We are all aware that different regions produce different dialects. The speech of a native Bostonian, for example, differs markedly from that of a Nebraska farmer. Such variations do not constitute pronunciation errors, provided the majority of the intelligent people in the region involved adhere to them. Extreme dialects and other pronunciations below the standards of a region should be modified, because audiences may not find them acceptable. Modification of a dialect may also be required when an individual moves to a new region, if intelligibility is impaired. Foreign dialects are acceptable unless so obvious that they are distracting or prevent instant intelligibility. Regional and foreign dialects tend to become modified as the individual consistently associates with people in a new environment. In the majority of cases, educated persons will use those pronunciations recorded in a recently published dictionary. If in doubt about the correct pronunciation of a word during rehearsal of a speech, the speaker should check the latest edition of a well-known dictionary. Do not shift from one pronunciation to another, even if a word has more than one acceptable pronunciation. Make your choice and stick to it, at least throughout the course of a given speech.

b. AVOID PRONUNCIATION ERRORS SUCH AS OMISSIONS, ADDITIONS, INVERSIONS, SUBSTITUTIONS OR MISPLACED ACCENTS. *Omission* of sounds occurs most frequently at the ends of words (*kep* for *kept, slep* for *slept,* etc.), although it is also common in the middle of words (*libary* for *library, govment* for *government, probly* for *probably, hep* for *help*). Common examples of *additions* are *acrost* for *across, stastistics* for *statistics,* and *athalete* for *athlete. Inversion* of sounds results in *hunderd* instead of *hundred, intregal* instead of *integral,* etc. Common examples of *substitution* are *ast* for *ask, miyyuns* for *millions,* and *liddle* for *little. Misplaced accents* often occur in such words as *precedence, exemplary, inexplicable, exquisite,* and *ignominy.*

SUMMARY

An effective speaking voice possesses the attributes of (1) audibility, (2) pleasantness, (3) variety, (4) animation, (5) fluency, and (6) clarity. Audibility and pleasantness are the products of proper habits of breathing, phonation, and resonation. Variety, animation, and fluency necessitate a voice flexible in pitch, force, and rate. Clarity depends upon distinct articulation and acceptable pronunciation.

EXERCISES AND ASSIGNMENTS

EXERCISES TO IMPROVE HABITS OF BREATHING

To promote relaxation:
  Since the relaxed, confident speaker is less likely to experience breathing difficulties, attempt to create a healthy mental attitude toward the prospect of speaking (Chapter 1). Such an attitude is abetted by achieving general relaxation of the body musculature. Students have found the following to be helpful in reducing muscular tensions:
  1. Play a game or two of table tennis before going to speech class.
  2. Walk briskly to the building in which you are to speak.
  3. Before entering the room in which your speech will be given, stretch, yawn, and roll your head in a circular manner to aid in relaxing the muscles of the face, throat, neck, and shoulders.

4. During the last minute or two before you rise to speak, breathe slowly and deeply ten or fifteen times to aid in general relaxation.

To promote control of exhalation:

1. Lie on your back and place a hand on your abdomen. Breathe deeply so that the hand is moved upward by inhalation and downward by exhalation. Get the feel of the action of the diaphragm and abdominal muscles.
2. Stand and place your hands on your sides below the ribs and above the pelvis. Thumbs should extend backward and fingers forward on the abdomen. Breathe deeply several times, noting the feel of frontal and lateral expansion.
3. With hands in the same position, pant sharply and cough. Repeat a number of times, again attempting to "'get the feel" of the frontal and lateral abdominal muscles in regulating vocal dynamics and in supporting vigorous projection of voice.
4. Take a deep breath and count as far as you can before again inhaling. Count in unison with your classmates to discover who can count furthest.
5. Choose a page from this book and read aloud as far as you are able on a single exhalation. Do not exceed your normal rate, preserve normal inflections, and maintain volume sufficient to be heard easily by an audience of at least forty people. Repeat this exercise periodically, noting whether your control of exhalation increases. With practice, you should be able to reach at least fifty words.

Exercises to Improve Habits of Phonation and Resonation

1. Hum the sound *ng*. Touch your lips, nose, and cheekbones lightly with your finger. You should feel a slight vibration.
2. Vocalize the following words a number of times, prolonging the *ing* in each case: *sing, swing, cling, spring, bring, ring.*
3. Whisper the sound *ah,* gradually increasing loudness; as you increase volume, change the whisper to a phonated sound with eventual full resonance; at that point, reverse the process, ending with a whisper. Do the exercise in one breath.
4. Select a prose or poetry reading and attempt to deliver it in (1) a tense whisper, (2) a nasal whine, (3) a shrill, metallic tone, (4) a harsh, raspy quality, and (5) the most pleasing quality you can attain.
5. By changing your vocal quality, read the sentence, "I wonder if it's true," so as to reflect the following emotional states: (1) fear, (2) exultation, (3) grief, (4) pity, (5) anger.

6. Select one of your favorite poems which possesses a single predominant mood. Read it aloud with appropriate vocal quality.

EXERCISES TO IMPROVE VOCAL FLEXIBILITY AND EXPRESSIVENESS

1. Say "Are you sure?" with (1) an upward inflection, (2) a downward inflection, and (3) a double inflection (rise followed by fall, or *vice versa*).
2. Choose a poem or the text of a speech which requires a maximum of flexibility in pitch, force, and rate to express adequately its meaning. Practice reading it aloud, attempting to increase vocal expressiveness.
3. Read aloud the following, attempting to express the meaning and mood of each. Do not worry about "overdoing" your interpretation.

   a. Your attention, ladies and gentlemen. The main event of the evening, fifteen rounds, for the heavyweight championship of the world. Introducing, in this corner, weighing 189½ pounds, wearing white trunks, from Brockton, Massachusetts, the heavyweight champion of the world, Rocky Marciano.

   b. The sneer is gone from Casey's lips, his teeth are clenched in hate.
   He pounds with cruel vengeance his bat upon the plate;
   And now the pitcher holds the ball, and now he lets it go,
   And now the air is shattered by the force of Casey's blow.

   Oh, somewhere in this favored land the sun is shining bright,
   The band is playing somewhere, and somewhere hearts are light;
   And somewhere men are laughing, and somewhere children shout,
   But there is no joy in Mudville—mighty Casey has struck out.

   c. Oh the *gladness* of her *gladness* when she's *glad,*
   And the *sadness* of her *sadness* when she's *sad,*
   But the *gladness* of her *gladness*
   And the *sadness* of her *sadness*
   Are as *nothing,* Charles,
   To the *badness* of her *badness* when she's *bad!*
4. Read aloud the following selection without pausing except at the end of each line. Do you agree in all cases with the suggested phrasing? If not, what are your reasons for disagreement?
   HAMLET: Speak the speech,
              I pray you,
              as I pronounced it to you,
              trippingly on the tongue:
              but if you mouth it,
              as many of your players do,

I had as lief the town-crier
spoke my lines.
Nor do not saw the air
too much with your hand,
thus;
but use all
gently:
for in the very torrent,
tempest,
and, as I may say,
whirlwind
of your passion,
you must acquire
and beget
a temperance that may give it
smoothness.
O, it offends me to the soul
to hear a robustious
periwig-pated fellow
tear a passion to tatters,
to very rags,
to split the ears of the groundlings,
who, for the most part,
are capable of nothing
but inexplicable
dumb-shows
and noise:
I would have such a fellow
whipped
for o'er doing
Termagant;
it out-herods
Herod:
pray you, avoid it.

I PLAYER: I warrant
your honor.

HAMLET: Be not too tame
neither,
but let your own discretion
be your tutor:
suit the action
to the word,

the word
to the action;
with this special observance,
that you o'erstep not
the modesty of nature;
for anything so overdone
is from
the purpose of playing,
whose end,
both at the first
and now,
was
and is,
to hold,
as 'twere,
the mirror up to nature;
to show virtue
her own feature,
scorn
her own image,
and the very age
and body of the time
his form
and pressure.
Now this overdone
or come tardy off,
though it make the unskillful laugh,
cannot but make the judicious
grieve;
the censure of the which
one
must
in your allowance
o'erweigh a whole theater
of others.
O, there be players
that I have seen play,
and heard others praise,
and that highly,
not to speak it profanely,
that neither having the accent
of Christians

nor the gait of Christian,
pagan,
nor man,
have so strutted
and bellowed,
that I have thought some of nature's journeymen
had made men,
and not made them well,
they imitated humanity
so abominably.

5. Say, "Good morning. How are you today?" so as to express a variety of feelings, such as: *eagerness, gaiety, pathos, romance, haughtiness, hurry, disinterest,* etc.

EXERCISES TO IMPROVE HABITS OF DISTINCTNESS AND CORRECTNESS

1. Write a paragraph which will contain as many as possible of the sounds in English speech. If possible, use each sound in initial, medial and final positions. Try to include words you habitually mispronounce or find difficult to articulate. Your instructor may check your articulation and pronunciation as you read your composition. (Sentences for a complete articulation examination may be found in Grant Fairbanks, *Voice and Articulation Drillbook* (New York, 1940), pp. xii-xv.)

2. During one round of speeches jot down every word misarticulated or mispronounced by each speaker. Indicate the nature of the error. Use a different sheet of paper for each speaker. Give each his list at the conclusion of his performance.

3. Carry with you a note pad for a period of one or two weeks. Listen carefully to your friends, family, and business associates for slurring, mumbling, sound omissions, additions, substitutions, and inversions. Note each error on your pad. Arrange the list of words under the headings above and bring to class. In cooperation with your classmates, make a master list of the most commonly mispronounced words. Practice the list and read it aloud to your classmates, who will check for errors.

4. Read to the class the following commonly mispronounced words:

abdomen	battery	children
accidentally	because	combatant
ally	boundaries	comely
amenable	certainly	comptroller
arctic	chastisement	consummate
athlete	chauffeur	detail

different	interesting	recognize
diphtheria	intricacies	research
drought	irrelevant	romance
efficacy	laboratory	route
executor	lamentable	sonorous
exemplary	larynx	sophomore
experiment	leisure	statistics
exquisite	library	superfluous
extant	literature	superintendent
family	livelong	surprise
film	maintenance	sustenance
finance	miniature	synthesis
flaccid	miserable	temperature
forehead	naturally	tortoise
formidable	nominative	tremendous
frailty	obligatory	trough
generally	onerous	umbrella
gesture	orgy	unctuous
gratis	particularly	usually
height	patronage	vagary
heinous	perspiration	vegetable
history	picture	vehemence
hundred	precedence	where
impious	precedent	white
impotent	prelate	why
infamous	pronunciation	worsted
insurance	quantity	zenith
integral	really	zoology

Additional words may be found in Edward L. Thorndike, *The Teacher's Word Book* (New York, 1921), and in Fairbanks, *Voice and Articulation Drillbook,* pp. 105–132. For an excellent treatment of the problem of correcting pronunciation difficulties, see Gladys L. Borchers and Claude M. Wise, *Modern Speech* (New York, 1947), pp. 93–190.

5. Bring to class a "tongue-twister." Place on the speaker's table face down. Each student should choose one, glance through it, and then read it aloud. Do it slowly the first time, gradually increasing speed in subsequent readings. Here are some examples which require nimble use of the articulators:

a. Six slim, sleek saplings.

b. Stop at the shop at the top of Schram Street.

c. In January and February there are few athletic exhibitions.

d. Some shun sunshine; some shun shade.

e. He whittled a white whistle from the willow wand which he cut.
f. Shoes and socks shock my shy sister Susan.
g. Fill the sieve with thistles; then sift the thistles through the sieve.
h. The freshly dried flesh of flying fish is fine eating.
i. Much whirling water makes the mill-wheel work well.
j. She sells sea shells; does he sell sea shells too?

CHAPTER 12

Using Language in Delivering the Speech

Many speakers give only slight consideration to the words they use to express ideas. Subscribing to the "say what you have to say quickly and be done with it" school, they exhibit little interest in developing an effective oral style, preferring to leave that to the Websters and the Churchills. Understandably, these speakers reflect the age in which they live—a highly efficient and accelerated society which puts a premium on simplicity and brevity. It is true that superfluous ornamentation and "style for the sake of style" belong to speakers of the past. However, if the modern speaker limits his concern with language to grammar and glibness, he misunderstands the nature and functions of language in speech.

Language is at the heart of communication. Spoken words symbolize the speaker's thoughts, just as printed words represent the writer's thinking. Together with the visual language of gesture, movement, and facial expression, the speaker's words stir up meanings and emotional responses in the minds of his listeners. Ineffective word choice may inhibit or break down completely the process of oral communication: ideas may be misunderstood; structure may seem confused; and emotional appeals may fail. Since language is so inextricably interwoven with the other speech processes, it is difficult to overestimate its importance.

In this chapter, we shall inquire into the nature of language and offer suggestions for developing an effective oral style.

THE NATURE OF LANGUAGE

A mature oral style is based upon a knowledge of certain characteristics of language. The first principle to remember is that *words are only symbols*. Although this observation seems obvious after a moment's reflection, many people react to words as though they were actually the objects, ideas, or nonverbal facts to which words refer.

To clarify the process of symbolization, let us turn again to the nonverbal world of the baby or small child. Unable to use words, the baby communicates his feelings as best he can by crying, screaming, or cooing. Later on, he depends largely upon the visual code for communication—fondling and exhibiting his new toy for approval, pointing to the food he wants, nodding his head in assent, turning away in rejection, and "showing off" to gain attention. In time, he comes to associate certain sounds with particular objects, ideas, and desires, much as his parents do; thus, he eventually refers to the object which contains milk by saying "bottle"—it is no longer necessary to point to it. The word "bottle" has come to "stand for" the glass container which holds his milk; the child believes that his parents have the same association when they hear or speak this word. He will soon discover, however, that his symbols do not always clearly represent his thinking. For example, "bottle$_1$" may refer to "bottle of milk," "bottle$_2$" to "bottle of castor oil," "bottle$_3$" to "bottle of ink," and so forth. Furthermore, he discovers that not only liquids are "bottled"; traffic may be "bottled," a football team's attack may be "bottled," and a military offensive may be "bottled." In such cases, the word "bottle" denotes "restraint" or "encompassment," a somewhat broader concept. As the child becomes older and his language facility increases, he will find the problem of symbolization markedly more complex when dealing with words considerably more abstract than "bottle," "baby," "toy," "book," and "dog." More difficult to pin down will be the precise definition of a word such as "democracy." Does this word mean "the form of government we have in the United States"? Possibly so, although some aspects of our form of government do not seem "democratic," at least to some; the child may not even be sure what "our form of government" means. Further confusion may arise when he finds that Soviet Russia labels herself a "democracy" and calls the United States a "dictatorship," while the United States claims the exact reverse! It is clear that the word "democracy" has a multitude of meanings—that the term is highly abstract.

It is apparent, then, that words have relative rather than absolute meanings, that *language has meaning only in terms of the associations established by individuals between the verbal symbol and the object or concept to which it refers.* The thoughtful person further realizes that *a symbol never tells everything about the object or concept to which it refers.* Even ten thousand words would be insufficient to reveal all that could be said about the chair in which you may now be sitting.

Of what significance to the speaker is an understanding of the process of symbolization? It points up the pitfalls we may encounter in attempting to communicate ideas; it helps to explain why we are misunderstood so frequently when talking or writing, why we misinterpreted a recent speech by the President, and why we failed to get the point of an editorial in last night's *Globe.* Upon knowing that words are not the objects to which they refer but only symbols "standing for" them, one can appreciate more fully the importance of careful word choice.

Stemming directly from the foregoing discussion is another important related principle: *thought cannot be "transmitted"; it can only be stirred up in the listener.* When you say the word "honor," your vocal mechanism sets up a series of sound waves. These sound waves, when they impinge upon the hearer's neuro-muscular system, stir up meanings. The nature of these meanings, however, depends largely upon his previously developed associations concerning the word "honor."

Constant changes in word meaning further complicate communication. While meanings are dynamic, words remain static. What you presently believe to be "morally right" may resemble only faintly what was considered so in the eighteenth century—possibly your concept of morality has undergone change within the past week. Transportation at the speed of 25 m.p.h. was undoubtedly "fast" in 1850; today it is considered "scarcely moving." Ten years ago an airplane which attained a speed of 300 m.p.h. was "fast"; today's jet plane is not "fast" unless it exceeds 700 m.p.h., and this rate is rapidly becoming commonplace. Fifty years was considered a "ripe old age" in 1850; today the half-century mark signals the beginning of middle age. With almost every object, idea, or principle constantly in the process of change, it is clear that *no arbitrary, timeless meaning can be ascribed to any verbal symbol.* Thus, the changing nature of meaning further complicates the problem of oral communication.

Despite its complex nature, effective oral communication can be achieved by the average speaker. Greater understanding of these principles will enable you to develop sound language habits. Thus, knowledge that "the word is not the thing" is a reminder to choose words which express as specifically, clearly, and faithfully as possible the concepts you have in mind. Awareness that meanings can never by "transmitted" should sharpen your sensitivity to the intelligence, experience, background, and language skills of your auditors; such knowledge may enable you to stir up predictable meanings in their minds.

In short, be certain, first, to choose words whose meanings are clear *to you*; second, to the best of your ability select words and arrangements of words which will call forth in your listeners' minds meanings as close to yours as possible.

SPECIFIC GUIDES FOR THE EFFECTIVE USE OF LANGUAGE

In developing an effective oral style, keep in mind the following principles: (1) language should be chosen for its oral qualities; it is primarily meant to be *heard*, not read; (2) language should be adapted to your own personality, your audience, and the occasion; (3) language should possess *clarity*; (4) language should be *objective*; (5) language should be *vivid* and *impressive*; (6) language should include an abundant stock of connective and transitional words and phrases; (7) language should be arranged into clear and varied sentences; and (8) language should be chosen from a constantly increasing *speaking* vocabulary.

A. Language should be chosen for its oral qualities; it is primarily meant to be *heard*, not read.   Language meant to be heard possesses certain characteristics differentiating it from language designed primarily for reading, although written and oral style have much in common (occasionally, essays are effective when delivered orally and, conversely, speeches sometimes become permanent literary works). (1) *Oral language should be personal and direct.* While the writer aims at a comparatively indefinite and scattered audience, the speaker talks to a specific, well-defined group. He is closer to his audience both physically and mentally than the writer; even the television and radio audience keenly feels the personality and—particularly the television audience—the physical presence of the speaker. To achieve directness, make extended use of personal pronouns such as "I," "me," "we," "you," "mine," "ours," and "yours." Be conversational and idiomatic, rather than stilted and formal. Employ short sentences, contractions, and appropriate idioms to promote directness and to personalize your style. Moreover, use direct and rhetorical questions. The direct question is answered by the speaker. For example, the question "Do you know how many teen-age dope addicts were arrested last month in Chicago?" would be followed by an answer provided by the speaker. The rhetorical question allows the audience to provide an answer, one which is usually obvious and represents commonly held belief. For example, the question "Would you elect to the office of President of the United States a man who would deliberately lead us into another World War?" should elicit a prompt but silent "no" response from almost every listener. (2) *Oral language should provide for instant comprehension of meaning.* While the reader who does not fully understand a sentence or paragraph may reread it, the listener obviously does not have that opportunity. Instead, new words and sentences strike his ear while he is trying to comprehend what has been said previously. If bombarded with a series of concepts which are not clear, he soon becomes hopelessly lost, and may give up listening altogether. Clearly, the speaker must insure that what he says is immediately understood. Speed of comprehension will be enhanced by developing these language habits: use concrete words to express abstract ideas; let short, simple sentences predominate; avoid unusually long, involved constructions; repeat and restate important ideas to insure their eventual comprehension and retention.

B. Language should be adapted to your own personality, your audience, and the occasion. Choose words which fit your particular personality, interests, attitudes, and background. A freshman student should not attempt to impress his instructor with a large assortment of polysyllabic words which he scarcely understands and which do not fit his personality, background, or his subject; a middle-aged dowager should not couch her ideas in current collegiate slang. Do not attempt to copy closely the style of some well-known speaker; probably it will not fit your personality or background. (However, we urge you to study the speeches of great orators to aid in developing your individual style).

Careful analysis of the audience will enable you to adjust your language patterns to fit the intelligence, backgrounds, attitudes, and interests of your auditors. On the basis of such an analysis together with your knowledge of the occasion, decide the degree of formality to be used, the extent to which certain technical terms might be understood, the type of idiomatic usage you might include, and how much and what type of humor might be effective.

C. Language should possess *clarity.* Clarity is that attribute of language which facilitates close correspondence between the speaker's meaning and that stirred up in the minds of his auditors. Language will be clear if it is (1) accurate, (2) simple, and (3) concrete.

(1) Language will be clear if it is *accurate.* Only words which "say what they mean" are accurate. Understand clearly the concept you wish to express. Then choose words which correspond as closely as possible to that concept. If there is a chance that a word may not represent accurately and precisely a given concept, define the word. Consider, too, the possibility that a term may convey no meaning whatsoever. Such may be the case if you use foreign terms, technical jargon, or uncommon words beyond the vocabularies of most persons. In general, avoid such usages as *Q. E. D., vis-a-vis, puissant, quid pro quo,* and the like. Technical jargon and slang such as the following may convey no meaning to the average person: (1) logic: *non sequitur, circulus in probando, post hoc ergo propter hoc, petitio principii, ignoratio elenchi;* (2) philosophy: *sophistic, pragmatism, logical positivism;* (3) medicine and nursing: *D. O. A., I and D, T and A, gone out, carcinoma, hysterectomy, lobotomy, colostomy;* (4) college life: *point average, finals, midterms, rush week, pinned, cramming;* (4) football: *buttonhook, draw, trap, bootleg, spread, double-team, statue of liberty, protection pocket;* (5) college slang: *out of this world, sent, gone, dig, terrific* (*horrible, wonderful, exotic, different, frightening, competent, attractive, unusual* are only a few of the meanings which this word may have!). Inaccuracy also may result from careless use of every-

day words with multiple meanings. Many speakers recklessly use abstract words and phrases such as *love, honor, right, wrong, big business, the moneyed interests, socialism, the American way,* and *the common man* without definition and without recognizing that these words may have many meanings. Be certain to clarify words with multiple meanings so that listeners understand in which sense you use them. Then stick to that definition.

(2) Language will be clear if it is *simple.* The concept of simplicity is closely related to that of accuracy. Fight the temptation to use a pretentious polysyllabic word when a simple and universally understood word will suffice. Use *fire* instead of *conflagration, fight* instead of *altercation, home* instead of *domicile.* In public speaking use the straightforward, informal wording of spontaneous conversation, not the ornate, stilted, and verbose style of the old-fashioned orator. Keep in mind that your goal is to make ideas meaningful, not to display oral style for approval.

(3) Language will be clear if it is *concrete.* Concreteness contributes to clarity by substituting particularization and specificity for generalization and abstraction. Concrete language is replete with names, dates, figures, examples, illustrations, proper names, and qualifying adjectives and adverbs. To illustrate, the comparatively abstract sentence, "We spent a lot of money on the war effort," would be considerably more concrete if it read, "The United States spent a total of fifty-two billion dollars for planes, tanks, guns, and other weapons in 1952." In general, concreteness may be achieved by employing a variety of examples, illustrations, and statistics (Chapter 6), and by couching them in words which represent your thought as specifically as possible.

The striking difference between effective oral language and a verbose, esoteric, and turgid style may be noted by comparing Lincoln's Gettysburg Address with the following rewritten version, done in fun by a professor "so that professors can understand it":

Eight and seven-tenths decades ago the pioneer workers in this continental area implemented a new group based on an ideology of free boundaries and initial conditions of equality. We are now actively engaged in an over-all evaluation of conflicting factors in order to determine whether or not the life expectancy of this group or of any group operating under the stated conditions is significant.

We are met in an area of maximum activity among the conflicting factors. The purpose of the meeting is to assign permanent positions to the units which have been annihilated in the process of attaining a steady state. This procedure represents standard practice at the administrative level.

From a more comprehensive viewpoint we cannot assign—we cannot integrate—we cannot implement this area.

The courageous units, in being and annihilated, who were active in this area have integrated it to the point where the application of simple arithmetical operations to include our efforts would produce only negligible effects.

The reaction of the general public to this colloquium will be nonessential and transitory but the reaction to the impingement of the combat group is invariant. It is for this group in being rather to be integrated with the incomplete activities for which the combat groups who were active in this area have so comprehensively effected the initial implementation.

It is preferable for this group to be integrated with the incompleted implementation—that from the standards set by these respected deceased units we take accelerated intensive effort—that we here resolve at a high ethical level that the deceased shall not have been annihilated without furthering the project—that this group under divine leadership shall implement a new source of unhampered activity—and that political supervision composed of the integrated units, for the integrated units, and by the integrated units shall not perish from the superficial area of this planet.[1]

D. Language should be *objective*. Objective language is grounded in fact and comparatively undistorted by emotionalism. Emotionalism in language is exemplified in the slogans and stereotypes of the advertiser and by the "loaded" words of some speakers who seek to persuade. Such a style evokes responses predominantly emotional rather than reasoned. In persuasive speaking, be aware of the power of such words to secure your response. Use them with care, however, and never as a substitute for sound evidence and argument. If your purpose is to inform, objective language is essential in securing understanding. Compare each of the following "loaded" terms with the more objective usage appearing opposite it:

[1] Richard D. Fay, "Gettysburg Address Translated into Faculty English by Machine Methods." Copyright 1951, *Harvard Bulletin, Inc.*; reprinted by permission of the *Harvard Alumni Bulletin* of February 24, 1951.

LOADED	COMPARATIVELY OBJECTIVE
socialized or political medicine	compulsory health insurance
the Truman war	the United Nations police action in Korea
economic royalists	those who make over $50,000 annually
reactionaries	those who belong to the Republican party
communists	those who refuse to take anticommunist oaths
the welfare state	a government which provides social security, old-age pensions, unemployment compensation, etc.
racketeer	one who has been sentenced to prison for gambling
bureaucrats	those who hold positions in government

Objective language need not be dull, lifeless, and colorless. All words call forth some emotional response, and colorful words heighten interest. We urge, however, that the use of highly emotional language be tempered by a healthy respect for adequate evidence and valid reasoning.

E. Language should be *vivid* and *impressive*. Language possessing clarity will be understood; but if language is to hold attention, maintain interest, and create a lasting impression it must be vivid and impressive. Vividness results from words and phrases which arouse sense imagery in the listener. Impressions of our environment are received through the senses—sight, hearing, taste, smell, and touch. When the stimulus which calls forth a particular response is not present, the response may be elicited by reliving a former experience. Thus, we can remember how good the sirloin steak tasted last Tuesday; we recall the extravagant coloring of a beautiful sunset in the Rocky Mountains; we relive the rhythmic sensation of dancing at the Junior Prom; we hear again the blending of the various instruments in the symphony orchestra's rendition of Brahms' *Fourth Symphony*. Complex combinations of imagery resulting in new concepts beyond the scope of past experience may be called imagination.

Imagery and imagination may be stimulated by words. Coupled with visual aids, facial expression, and the speaking voice, language helps the listener to relive old experiences and to create new ones through imagination.

Vividness also may be sought by the use of figures of speech. Probably the most commonly used figures are the *simile* and the *metaphor*. Both are devices to compare objects or concepts basically unlike; each calls forth sharp, vivid imagery which clarifies and emphasizes (Chapter 6 discusses comparison as a form of support). A simile states a likeness between two objects of a different class, and usually, though not always, connects the two with the word "like." For example: "The old man stood before us, gaunt and weatherbeaten, like a gnarled oak"; "She appeared to be fragile and unreal, like a china doll." A metaphor also compares two objects or ideas which are fundamentally different, but does so by a direct identification of the two on the basis of a common likeness. Thus, a *sharp-tongued woman* "is" a *cat*; *highways* "are" *arteries*, an *initial speech in a campaign* "is" the *opening gun; establishing a basis for promoting communism* "is" *sowing the seeds of communism;* and *flames spreading to the second story of a building* "are" *tongues of flame licking at the second story*. Many metaphorical expressions have become so universal in use that we accept them as part of our regular language patterns. Since such metaphors have lost much of their power to create imagery, it is wise to choose figures which are fresh and unusual if you are to stimulate the sharpest, most vivid imagery.

Another useful figure is *personification*, in which ideas or inanimate objects are given certain characteristics of living beings. *Time marches on* is a commonly used example of personification. The previously cited figure, *tongues of flame licking at the second story*, utilizes personification as well as metaphor.

Vividness is closely related to impressiveness. Figures rich in imagery may elicit an emotional response sufficient to make a lasting impression. Impressiveness also may be secured by the frequent use of a number of the methods for supporting ideas discussed in Chapter 6. Striking facts, statistics of a personal nature, pithy quotations and epigrams, sharply etched descriptions, and vivid illustrations are particularly effective. Originality in the choice of words also lends force and impressiveness. Most of us are addicted to the use of hackneyed, trite phrases; in extemporizing, these words usually come to mind first. Unfortunately, listeners have heard them too often to be impressed. An attempt to avoid these terms and to develop fresh, original usages will be rewarded by attentive and retentive listening. Impressive, also, are the techniques of surprise, climax, suspense, and conflict.

Note that the attributes of clarity, vividness, and impressiveness are not mutually exclusive, but overlap at many points. A word or phrase chosen because it possesses one of these attributes may actually possess all of them, under some circumstances and with certain audiences. For example, parallel structure, commonly the recurrent use of a particular phrase or sentence, lends both clarity and impressiveness to oral discourse (repetition as a form of support is discussed in Chapter 6).

F. Language should include an abundant stock of connective and transitional words and phrases. The beginning speaker, though seemingly well prepared, frequently finds in rehearsal and delivery that his language effectiveness breaks down perceptibly when moving from one point to another. Even the experienced extemporizer with considerable language facility often connects ideas awkwardly and abruptly. The sixth suggestion for effective language usage, therefore, is to "stock up" on connective words and phrases so that transitions may be made smoothly, clearly, and with variety.

Many speakers are limited to the use of only a few connectives. Among the most common are *another thing, my second point is, also, now, for example,* and *in other words.* For the sake of freshness and variety, such speakers should incorporate into their speaking vocabularies the following connective words and phrases, as well as many others: *furthermore, moreover, meanwhile, nevertheless, nonetheless, whereas, on the contrary, in consequence, at the same time, in contrast to, inasmuch as,* and *on the other hand.*

Connective words and phrases will also enable you to achieve greater clarity and unity by indicating the relationship among ideas and by tying each idea to the Specific Purpose. Such connective phrases as the following will be helpful: "The third reason for adopting a national sales tax is . . ."; "The last step in building a model airplane is . . ."; "Now that we have established the advantages of constructing the St. Lawrence Seaway, let us examine . . ."; "Not only were we pleased with the conversation; in addition, we were impressed by . . ."

G. Language should be arranged into clear and varied sentences. While the writer may rework a sentence until it is polished to his satisfaction, the extemporaneous speaker has only one opportunity to compose a given sentence. "On-the-spot" construction frequently results in: (1) the stringing together of a number of ideas in one long, cumbersome, complex-compound sentence (note the rewritten Gettysburg Address earlier in the chapter); (2) faulty sentence structure, resulting in uncertainty of meaning; and (3) lack of variety in sentence structure, resulting in monotony.

Sentence composition in extemporaneous speaking will be improved by observing these suggestions while developing an oral style: (1) Keep sentences relatively short, for the most part—no more than ten or twelve words, on the average; shorter sentences usually are more easily and quickly understood. (2) Occasionally, use longer sentences (thirty words or more) to provide variety and to avoid choppiness and lack of rhythm. (3) Secure freshness and interest by employing a variety of sentence types. While the majority of your sentences will undoubtedly begin with the subject and end with the predicate, do not neglect the periodic structure, in which the order is reversed with the conditional elements appearing first. For example, the following construction is loose: "Inflation could be curbed if every citizen would buy only what he needs, avoid excessive installment buying, and invest in government bonds." Inverting such a sentence provides greater interest and suspense: "If every citizen would buy only what he needs, avoid excessive installment buying, and invest in government bonds, inflation could be curbed." A third type, the balanced sentence, uses antithesis for emphasis. To illustrate, "If I go to a movie, I'll fail the exam; if I stay home and study, I'll pass." (4) Make liberal use of interrogative, exclamatory, and imperative sentences to add balance, variety, and persuasiveness. While declarative sentences predominate in a written style, interrogative, exclamatory, and imperative sentences appear in great numbers in an effective oral style. Direct and rhetorical questions have been discussed earlier in this chapter. Exclamatory sentences are attention-getters; for example, "He dares to claim that!" "Vacations are wonderful!" "We must be on guard!" Listeners sometimes react strongly to the command in imperative sentences, such as "Throw the rascals out," "Do it now," "Vote for our candidate," "Drive carefully," and "Rid yourselves of prejudice."

Of course, the speaker can rarely be conscious of the principles of sentence structure while delivering an extemporaneous speech; his primary concerns during delivery are, of necessity, his ideas and his audience. However, we advise the use of the foregoing principles in your long-term development of an effective oral style. By so doing, sentence structure in extemporaneous speaking will be improved.

H. Language should be chosen from a constantly increasing *speaking* vocabulary. Since all the foregoing advice for developing an effective oral style basically depends upon your choice of individual words, our final suggestion is to build a consistently larger *speaking* vocabulary. Although dictionaries list hundreds of thousands of words, most of us are fortunate if we can count 35,000 of these in our reading vocabularies. Our writing vocabularies are much smaller, and our stock of words available for facile use in speaking is smaller yet.

While it is obviously important to enlarge one's basic vocabulary by wide reading, by a close familiarity with a good dictionary and thesaurus, and by developing "word consciousness" and "word interest," of even greater importance to the speaker is the growth of his active speaking vocabulary. Your primary effort, therefore, should be directed toward the consistent transfer of words from your reading and writing vocabularies to your active speaking vocabulary for use in expressing thoughts clearly, vividly, and impressively.

SUMMARY

Keep these general principles in mind in developing an oral style: (1) words are symbols having meaning only in terms of associations established between symbols and the objects or concepts to which they refer; (2) words never represent completely the objects or ideas they symbolize; (3) meaning cannot be "transmitted"; it can only be stirred up in the listener; and (4) word meanings are constantly changing.

The following principles should guide the speaker in developing an effective oral style: (1) language should be designed primarily to be heard, not to be read; (2) it should be adapted to the speaker's personality, audience, and occasion; (3) it should be clear; (4) it should be objective; (5) it should be vivid and impressive; (6) it should include a variety of connective and transitional words and phrases; (7) it should be arranged into clear and varied sentences; and (8) it should be chosen from a constantly increasing *speaking* vocabulary.

EXERCISES AND ASSIGNMENTS

1. Examine carefully the language used in a published essay, a theme you have written for English composition class, or a newspaper article. Is the language better adapted to reading or listening? Rewrite the selection to conform more closely to the requisites of oral style. Hand to your instructor the original and your rewritten version.

2. List ten words whose meanings have undergone considerable change in the last fifty years. Trace each change by a series of short written definitions.

3. Make a list of the hackneyed words and phrases used in a debate, discussion, or on a radio or TV panel show. Opposite each on your paper write a more original usage.

4. Evaluate the language in a speech from A. Craig Baird's *Representative American Speeches*, Harold Harding's *Age of Danger, Vital Speeches*, or James M. O'Neill's *Models of Speech Composition* (New York, 1921), for (1) clarity, (2) objectivity, and (3) vividness and impressiveness. Support your judgments with examples from the text of the speech. Give an oral report of your findings to the class.

5. Rewrite a speech made by a public official or a faculty member. Attempt to make the style more informal, idiomatic, and colloquial.

6. Examine for the use of loaded words the language used in several newspaper, radio, or TV advertisements, or in a political address. Have these words or phrases been used to mask faulty reasoning? Rewrite, substituting a more objective term for each loaded word. Does this weaken the persuasive power of the advertisement? Discuss in class.

7. Bring to class a written list of ten unusual figures of speech. A student committee may be appointed to combine the individual lists into one large one, which may be mimeographed for distribution to the class. Attempt to use several of these figures in your remaining class speeches. Save the list for future use.

8. In your next speech, attempt through careful word choice to arouse vivid sense imagery involving at least two of the senses.

9. Record a three-minute extemporaneous speech. Listen carefully to the playback for (1) a rough estimate of average sentence length, (2) the possible predominance of one type of sentence structure at the expense of others, (3) long, involved sentences, (4) an excessive number of short, choppy sentences occurring in succession, (5) needless repetition of some words and phrases, and (6) an insufficient variety of connective and transitional words and phrases. It may be necessary to listen to the playback several times in order to complete these observations. Take notes rather than relying on memory. Attempt to improve your extemporaneous style on the basis of this analysis.

10. Make a list of one hundred words whose meanings you know, but which you rarely if ever use in extemporaneous speaking. Attempt to include at least three of them in your next speech. Add several others from the list to each future speech until you have used each at least once and preferably several times before the end of the course.

CHAPTER *13*

Rehearsing the Speech

The last time you witnessed a collegiate or professional football contest weren't you impressed by the deceptive ball handling, the hard, efficient blocking and tackling, and the smooth, integrated operation of the offensive and defensive units? Do you remember that right-end sweep during the third quarter? How the man in motion drifted out to the left side of the line, as though getting in position to go down field for a pass? How the quarterback faked a handoff to the fullback, who plunged into the line? How the quarterback then faded farther to the rear, apparently to toss a long aerial down field, only to turn suddenly and throw a short bullet pass to the right half? Recall how that back sprinted for the right side of the line, how blockers cleared a path for him, and how beautifully the runner timed his stride to avoid tacklers as he swivelhipped his way to a first down? It is a genuine thrill to watch a well-integrated football team in action. We realize only vaguely the tremendous time and effort that goes into the training and conditioning programs of such a team. If you had been present for the initial meeting of spring practice, you would have found a group of disorganized, slightly bewildered individuals—not the smooth-functioning juggernaut the squad was later to become. The efficient execution of buck laterals, buttonhook passes, trap plays, spread formations, and other intricate patterns came gradually as the result of scores of hours of hard practice.

Just as in football and all other sports, practice is essential in dramatics. The first time a cast runs over the lines of a play the rendition is uninspiring. There will be many rehearsals before the curtain can be raised on a finished performance. We are also aware of the innumerable hours of rehearsal necessary for successful concert appearances by singers, pianists, and violinists.

273

It is perhaps unnecessary to add that almost all effective speakers rehearse their speeches in some form before delivering them. A sample roll call of distinguished speakers who have utilized speech rehearsal might include: William Jennings Bryan, Albert J. Beveridge, Benjamin Disraeli, Franklin D. Roosevelt, Thomas E. Dewey, Eric Johnston, and General Douglas MacArthur. Only an extremely limited few are so talented, like Clarence Darrow, that they can speak with maximum effectiveness without some rehearsal. Much of what passes for impromptu shafts of oratory has been carefully rehearsed. The famed eighteenth-century English orator, Richard Brinsley Sheridan, worked out almost all of his "impromptu" wit and rebuttals in advance of utterance. Winston Churchill is known to have rehearsed a crushing rejoinder as much as a month in advance.

Conceivably, some readers may protest: "I've been talking since I was two and a half. Why should I rehearse my speech? I get plenty of practice in speaking every day." We would answer by explaining that ordinary conversation differs from public speaking in several essential ways. Unlike public address, conversation is a face-to-face situation with all parties contributing; there are no silent rows of auditors. Being largely non-purposeful and disconnected, conversation does not present the need for logical, meaningful continuity delivered by one speaker for a continuous period of five to twenty minutes or longer. The conversational speaking situation does not provide the same strains and stresses as does public speaking. It does not present quite the same problems of poise, projection, clarity of articulation, accuracy of phrasing, posture, or bodily expression. As you well know, there are many adequate conversationalists who are not effective public speakers.

The average speaker cannot present with maximum effectiveness a speech of five or ten minutes without rehearsal. The first time you give a particular speech you are apt to ramble, and to be hesitant, repetitious, and awkward in phrasing. By rehearsing you will be able to avoid the disconcerting breaks in your thinking process which are apt to occur when facing an audience. Through practice you will be able to reduce verbiage, prevent redundancy, smooth out delivery, acquire more self-confidence, and put more of the dynamic quality into your presentation.

Now that we are agreed that you should practice your speech

before delivery, let us examine the three basic factors in your rehearsal: where to rehearse; when to rehearse; how to rehearse.

WHERE TO REHEARSE

Effective speakers make use of a wide variety of places for speech rehearsal. One student practices his talks in the shower. A preacher who drives some thirty miles to his pulpit rehearses en route, striking the steering wheel in his efforts to drive home important points. A business executive rehearses in his parlor before the analytical eyes of his wife and father. Lincoln as a young man delivered speeches to lonely fields of corn and pumpkins. Daniel Webster rehearsed even while fishing. John Pastore, United States Senator from Rhode Island, sometimes practices his speeches in his bedroom while dressing. Probably the best place for you to practice is some private room at home or in the dormitory, where you can work undisturbed. If possible, arrange at least one practice period in the room where the speech is to be delivered (as did Governor Paul A. Dever prior to his keynote address before the Democratic National Convention in 1952), or in a similar location. If you are accustomed to the physical surroundings of the designated hall, you will possess somewhat better poise at the time of actual presentation. Test the acoustics; find how much volume is necessary to carry to the back row. If you are to speak from a raised platform, climb the stairs to the dais and become accustomed to looking out at the seats. If a lectern is present, stand behind it; walk to the side; become accustomed to its physical presence. Even a golf professional like Sam Snead will play several practice rounds to get the feel of a course before engaging in competition.

WHEN TO REHEARSE

The rehearsal period should not begin until the outline has been completed and all materials gathered. Although a few individuals may succesfully violate this rule, the average beginner should complete his speech at least a day in advance of the delivery date. The longer the speech and the more demanding the situation, the longer this interval should be. If you are to give a twenty-minute address at the annual banquet of the interfraternity council, a thirty-minute eulogy of the recently deceased president of your company, or a fifteen-minute summary of the month's activities of your personnel department, you would be wise to finish your talk a minimum of two days before the time for delivery. Allow a period for your speech to "jell" in your mind. Give yourself sufficient opportunity to rub off some of the rough spots in delivery. Experience will demonstrate the optimum length of the rehearsal period for your particular needs. Perhaps we should add a point of caution: in your zeal to leave sufficient time for rehearsal, do not finish the organization and development of your talk so far in advance that the speech loses its warmth and vitality.

For most individuals, the rehearsal period should stop before the beginning of the program at which the speech is to be given. Of course, there are exceptions. For instance, President Roosevelt at times rehearsed major radio addresses at the banquet table after completing his dinner and before being introduced. However, for most beginning speakers, last-minute practice will tend to increase tension and may decrease effectiveness. If you follow carefully the suggestions given in the remainder of this chapter, you will have no reason to be concerned about remembering the speech. When waiting to be introduced by the chairman, do not worry about your talk. Try to relax by concentrating your attention on the chairman, on other speakers, on something in the auditorium, or by engaging someone in conversation.

How to Rehearse

The following methodology is offered not as an arbitrary program, but as an effective procedure for the beginning speaker. We will consider the rehearsal period under two heads: (A) the preliminary program of fixing the speech in the mind; (B) the final program of polishing the delivery of the speech.

A. The preliminary phase in rehearsing is to fix the speech in the mind. A generation or so ago speakers typically committed to memory entire speeches, which were sometimes more than an hour in duration. However, in our jet propulsion age, few individuals can afford the time for such extensive memorization. (Indeed, many of our civic and political leaders do not even bother to prepare their own speeches, being content to assign the task to secretaries or other subordinates. Recently an official of the Community Chest asked one of the authors to have his speech composition classes write talks for others to use during the local campaign.) Even if sufficient time were available, few speakers could deliver effectively a memorized talk. The authors suggest that as a general rule you memorize only the sequence of the ideas you wish to present. Fix firmly in your mind the outline of the speech, even when planning to use notes during the actual presentation. If you follow carefully the suggestions contained in the previous chapters on organization, your outline will contain a logical progression of ideas and will be much easier to remember than a jumbled assortment of points. If your speech structure adheres closely to the ten requirements for the logical partitioning of materials (Chapter 4), you will find it relatively simple to learn and retain the outline of even a long speech. (For instance, if you have used parallel phrasing for main heads, memorization of the outline will be greatly facilitated.) Usually, when a student complains that he cannot remember his speech, the authors have found that he either has not obeyed the canons of good speech organization or has not rehearsed adequately.

Here is a recommended program for fixing the speech in the mind.

(1) Read over the entire outline *silently* one or more times, endeavoring to concentrate on each point as you go along. Go straight through. Do not stop or retrace any portion.

(2) Read the outline *orally.* Continue through the entire outline without stopping or repeating any section.

(3) Now attempt to give the speech without any recourse to notes. If you cannot remember specific points, go on as best you can. Do not give up until you have made every effort to complete the entire talk. Do not worry if you stumble and falter. As one student said: "It's better to mess up the speech in private than before an audience."

(4) Reread the entire outline silently, then orally. *Think* while you are doing it.

(5) Try again to give the speech completely from beginning to end without reference to notes.

(6) Review the outline, silently and orally, and deliver the speech extemporaneously, without notes, until you have the sequence well in mind.

Notice that the emphasis in the preliminary phase of rehearsing has been to give you a firm grasp of the *total sequence* of the speech. Every time you interrupt the continuity during this phase of the rehearsal period you encourage forgetting at that particular point during the actual presentation.

B. The second phase in rehearsing is to polish the delivery of the speech. Practice makes permanent as well as perfect. Unless you follow an intelligent program of polishing your delivery, practice may do more harm than good. Admittedly, rehearsing for a particular speech may not correct major, constant faults; however, conscientious application of the following nine points will greatly improve your speech presentation.

(1) If possible get a sympathetic but analytical friend or relative to attend at least one rehearsal and make suggestions. You will be wise, however, to accept with reservation the advice offered by your observer, unless he is a competently trained critic. If no one is available, place several chairs in a row and address the chairs as though people were sitting in them. For at least part of your practice, try to construct in your mind the audience and the situation with which you will be confronted during the actual speech presentation, and rehearse accordingly. We suggested earlier that if possible at least one practice period should be arranged in the room (or close approximation) where you will speak. Try to prepare yourself for the total speaking situation.

(2) Spend part of your practice period rehearsing before a full-length mirror. Notice your facial expressions, posture, and gestures. The value of such practice is endorsed by the most effective evangelist of our era, Billy Graham, who rehearses each new sermon in front of a mirror.

(3) *A tape or wire recorder is highly desirable for adequate speech rehearsal.* Listen critically and make notations along the margin of the speech outline at the appropriate places where improvements in vocal delivery are needed. Do not erase the recordings each time, but check improvement by playing back the various attempts.

(4) Spread your rehearsal over various intervals instead of concentrating your practice in one or two sessions. Four fifteen-minute periods will be more valuable than a single period of an hour and a half.

(5) The number of times one should practice the speech in the second phase of rehearsal will vary according to the individual. The average student probably should rehearse somewhere between two and ten times a five-minute talk to be given in a public speaking class. If the speech is longer or the situation more demanding, the number of repetitions may be increased. *However, never over-practice so that spontaneity is injured.*

(6) Use your rehearsal as a final check on speech organization and content. You will be wise to avoid making any major changes in your speech at this stage. However, your rehearsal may indicate that some points need additional supporting material, that a touch of humor should be inserted, or that the speech may exceed its time boundaries. Usually such requisite minor changes can be made successfully by even the inexperienced speaker.

(7) Work systematically to improve both vocal and bodily delivery. If you have been criticized for possessing insufficient animation in previous speeches, here is the chance to practice giving life and vitality to your presentation. Do not be inhibited while rehearsing. Try to force yourself to be more dynamic. Loosen up your facial muscles. Attempt some gestures. If you have had poor posture in preceding speeches, try to stand erect during your practice. Unless you are unusual, your voice is not the supple instrument it should be. A dull, flat, uninteresting speaking voice will spoil even the most carefully prepared speech. In your practice ask yourself these questions: Is my rate of speaking flexible? Does my voice reflect the intellectual and emotional meaning of what I am saying? Does my voice indicate thought phrases satisfactorily? Do my words come smoothly and easily, or are there awkward interruptions in the flow of language? Is my pitch monotonously level? Does my voice lack emphasis? Does it sound strained and weak? Does it need more projection?

(8) Every time you rehearse, endeavor to vary your phraseology, vocal inflections, and gestures. *Do not let your speech become "canned."*

(9) Practice especially those portions of the speech which give you difficulty. Since you have mastered the sequence of the talk (fixing the speech in mind, pages 276–278) there is no necessity to continue to rehearse the entire talk each time. If transitions from

one main point to the next are troublesome, practice until they come easier. If you tend to ramble when presenting the Summary Step, practice this portion until your recapitulation is concise. If your attempt at humor seems flat, concentrate on putting a punch into it.

SUMMARY

As in other fields of endeavor such as sports, drama, and concert work, practice is essential to the public speaker. Intelligent rehearsal should make your delivery smoother and more forceful. Although there are a wide variety of suitable places for practice, a private room at home will probably be most satisfactory. If possible, at least one practice period should be held either in the room where the speech is to be given or in a similar location. The rehearsal period should not begin until the outline has been finished and all materials gathered, and should be completed before the beginning of the program at which the speech is to be given. The actual rehearsal consists of two basic phases: (1) fixing the speech in the mind, and (2) polishing the delivery.

EXERCISES AND ASSIGNMENTS

1. Interview several persons who speak frequently in public so that you may discover their methods of rehearsal. Report your findings to the class.

2. Listen closely to speeches in class to discover which students have failed to rehearse sufficiently. Also, note which speakers have rehearsed too much.

3. Prepare a short speech for class in which you describe how some effective speaker in history rehearsed his speeches.

4. As soon as you have completed the outline for your next speech, and without any rehearsal, record the entire talk. Speak as effectively as you can. Even though you may stumble to a halt several times, go through the entire speech. Do not erase this recording.

5. A continuation of exercise 4: Practice conscientiously the "Preliminary Phase in Rehearsing"; then record the speech once again. Do not erase this recording.

6. A continuation of exercises 4 and 5: Carefully follow the rules for the "Second Phase in Rehearsing" given in this chapter. When you think

your delivery has attained maximum effectiveness, record the speech for the third time. Play back and compare the three recordings.

7. Prepare for presentation in class a "canned" speech. Memorize not only the exact words to be used but also facial expressions, gestures, and set patterns of pitch, time, force, and vocal quality. In the judgment of your instructor and the class, how does this presentation compare with your customary extempore delivery?

Adapting Basic Techniques to Various Speech Situations

Essential Purpose of Section IV: to enable the student to apply the basic techniques of effective speaking to various speech situations.

CHAPTER 14

Speeches to Inform, to Entertain, and to Persuade

We have treated the basic types of speeches (to inform, to entertain, and to persuade) concurrently in Chapters 1 through 13, because we feel that this method gives a more unified picture. However, now that we have presented the fundamental techniques of speech preparation and delivery, some students might profit by a recapitulation in terms of the specific needs of the three fundamental types of speeches. In this chapter we shall bring together in summary fashion the most salient points to remember when preparing a speech to inform, to entertain, or to persuade. Page numbers will be given for references to pertinent materials previously discussed in Chapters 1–13. By referring to the indicated sections, a more complete background may be secured.

THE SPEECH TO INFORM

A. Purpose of the speech to inform. Probably a majority of the speeches made today are concerned with the giving of directions, lectures, or reports (Chapter 2, pages 37–39). Such talks, basically informative in character, are designated as speeches to inform. Practically every speech contains informative material in the form of explanation, definition, narration, and so on. However, the speech to inform is a distinct type of public address because its primary, if not sole, purpose is to impart knowledge, to make clear, and to secure understanding. The informative speaker is not a persuader concerned with changing convictions or stirring an audience to action. Rather, he is an objective-minded conveyor of information.

Retention and *understanding* by the audience are the ultimate goals of the speech to inform. While it is desirable that the listeners remember the signal ideas of any speech, such retention is the *essential* purpose of *only* the informative speech. If the purpose of a speech is to entertain, that primary function has been attained by providing the audience with enjoyment. The design of the persuasive speech has been accomplished upon convincing, stimulating (impressing), or actuating the audience. On the other hand, the speech to inform cannot be considered a success if the audience fails to remember the instruction or understanding it has received.

B. Selecting the Specific Speech Purpose of the speech to inform. Plan your talk carefully to facilitate assimilation and retention by the audience. Such preparation begins with the selection of the Specific Speech Purpose (Chapter 2, pages 37–39). In order to determine a specific, limited goal which you can accomplish in your talk, consider the interests, capacities, and attitudes of the audience, the physical and psychological characteristics of the speech occasion, the time limits for the speech, and your own backgrounds and interests (Chapter 2, pages 25–36). The effective speech to inform gives instruction about something: how to build a particular type of bird house; how to get to a certain fishing hole; how to operate a micrometer; what happened at a Junior Chamber of Commerce convention. Here are some sample Specific Speech Purposes: to have my audience understand the provisions of universal military training; to inform the class about the new grading system to be used this semester in the adult division; to explain to my listeners the basic principles of the turbo-jet engine.

C. Developing the Introduction of the speech to inform. After selecting the Specific Speech Purpose, plan the content and organization of the speech so as to attain your purpose with a minimum of effort on the part of the listeners. Most speeches to inform can be divided into an Introduction, Discussion, and Conclusion.

Ordinarily the Introduction should contain both a Favorable Attention Step and a Clarification Step (Chapter 7). Many a lecturer on geopolitics, industrial safety, or on countless other subjects has discovered that he placed too much reliance on the belief that people will be attentive because they *"ought* to be." Sometimes speakers erroneously assume that an audience will be anxious to receive information merely because the subject is interesting to the speaker. Typically, such a person, ignoring the interests, attitudes, and capacities of his audience, states in his opening remarks that he selected the subject because *he* is interested in it. The informative speaker is a *salesman* in that he helps stimulate his auditors to listen, to learn, and to remember. (Naturally, if the audience is actively interested in the subject, you can omit the Favorable Attention Step.) Of the nine methods for securing favorable attention in the Introduction, perhaps the most important is to point out to the listeners the significance of the subject to their lives (see Chapter 6, pages 153–155, 156–159, and Chapter 7, pages 164–166). If you cannot find a direct application to the needs of your audience, choose a different topic.

The Clarification Step is of vital importance in the informative speech because by preparing the audience for the Discussion you are facilitating learning and retention. Until you have acquired considerable experience, always state the POINT of your speech in the Introduction. If there are important steps, stages, or procedures which constitute major divisions of the Discussion, and which must be remembered by the listeners, you may list them after stating the POINT. The Clarification Step should also include any necessary background material such as definitions, historical development, or general explanations which will enable the audience to follow the speech more easily.

D. Developing the Discussion of the speech to inform. The arrangement and development of the main heads of the Discussion should be planned to facilitate the comprehension of the audience. Too often a speaker crowds such a mass of factual information into his address that the audience receives a jumbled impression instead of a clear mental outline. While you should follow all the rules for the organization and partitioning of materials given in Chapters 4 and 5, several considerations are of special significance. (1) Group your materials under two to five main heads. Do not expect your auditors to remember more than five major points. (2) Make certain that a logical relationship exists among the main heads with no overlappings. After studying your audience and your material, select one of the six basic sequences or patterns of organization (Chapter 5, Parts II and III). If you are giving directions, explaining a process which involves a chronological order of steps, or describing the historical development of an institution, a Time Pattern for arranging the main heads may be used. If describing a battlefield, a factory area, a city park, or the furniture arrangement of a room, you might utilize a Space Pattern. If your speech does not fit either a Time or Space Pattern, it can usually be constructed as a Topical Pattern (a conventional or natural division of main heads). When using the Topical Pattern, place the most important and most interesting heads first and last, unless the subject is difficult or technical. In that case, arrange the major topics or heads in the order of understandability—from simple to complex. (3) It may be advisable to plan a brief summary at the completion of each main head. (4) Indicate the logical relationships among the primary points by using transitional phrases. A sergeant instructing recruits at rifle practice might link together the main divisions of his discussion in this way: "Now that we are acquainted with the techniques of firing from the standing and kneeling positions, let us move on to a consideration of the prone method of firing." Sometimes it is helpful to use obvious signposts such as: "First . . ."; "In the second place . . ."; "The next step is . . ."; "The third point to remember . . ."; "The last stage is . . ." (See Chapter 13, pages 268, 269). Perhaps the following schematic outline will help to explain points 3 and 4.

    I._____
        A._____
        B._____
        C._____
            1._____
            2._____
        D. SUMMARY OF MAIN HEAD NO. I

TRANSITIONAL PHRASE(S) CONNECTING MAIN HEAD NO. I WITH MAIN HEAD NO. II

    II._____
        A._____
            1._____
            2._____
            3._____
        B._____
            1._____
            2._____
        C. SUMMARY OF MAIN HEAD NO. II

TRANSITIONAL PHRASE(S) CONNECTING MAIN HEADS NO. I AND II WITH MAIN HEAD NO. III

    III._____

(5) Supporting materials must reinforce or clarify their immediately superior headings. Any strained or artificial connections between the amplifying material and its superior head will make understanding and retention by the audience more difficult.

In the selection of supporting elements always consider the needs of the listeners, their interests, backgrounds, and capacity to understand. Let us summarize briefly the salient points discussed in Chapter 6 ("Discovering and Using the Supporting Materials"). (1) Use a sufficient amount of supporting material to make each head easily understandable to the audience, without belaboring any topic. (2) Appeal to the eye as well as to the ear by means of charts, graphs, diagrams, pictures, maps, motion pictures, and slides. By combining appeals to the visual as well as to the auditory sense your information will be more vivid and more easily remembered. (3) Define any important terms which may be unfamiliar to the audience. (4) When possible, explain the unknown by means of the familiar. Attach the new information you are presenting to something already understood by the audience. In an address on foreign policy to the American Society of Newspaper Editors, President Eisenhower made persuasively clear the cost of military preparedness:

This world in arms is not spending money alone. It is spending the sweat of its laborers, the genius of its scientists, the hopes of its children. The cost of one modern heavy bomber is this: a modern brick school in more than thirty cities. It is: two electric power plants, each serving a town of 60,000 population. . . . We pay for a single fighter plane with a half-million bushels of wheat. . . .

To mention the number of board feet of lumber in a giant Sequoia would be meaningless to the average person; convert the unknown into the familiar by explaining how many seven-room houses this amount of lumber would construct. (5) Supporting material must be presented in such a concrete and specific manner that the audience will be able to construct a mental picture of what the speaker is saying. Avoid vague and generalized phrasing. Instead of "statistics prove," say: "Our university marketing department has just completed a survey in which 3,500 Chicago housewives were interviewed . . ." Utilize visual, auditory, olfactory, kinaesthetic, tactile, and gustatory imagery. Of course, in order to stir up word pictures in the minds of the auditors you must first

have an accurate image in your own mind. (6) Keep the supporting materials interesting. Occasionally lighten the speech by touches
of humor or figures of speech. Make liberal use of vivid illustrations
and figurative and literal analogies. Keep statistical information
vivid and meaningful by rounding off figures to even numbers, by
explaining the significance of the data, and by comparing the statistics to knowledge familiar to the audience. Promote involuntary
attention through the use of Factors of Interest: proximity, vivid
concreteness, significance, variety, and humor. If your audience is
not listening, it is not learning—and you are not communicating
effectively.

E. Developing the Conclusion of the speech to inform.   The inexperienced speaker should always plan a Summary Step for the
Conclusion (Chapter 8). If the speech is short, or especially clear,
a mere restatement of the POINT may be sufficient. Usually, however, in addition to stating the POINT, you should either relist the
main heads, or review informally the essential ideas. Sometimes a
quotation, comparison, or illustration will be helpful as an indirect
summary. You may wish again to direct attention to the significance
of the information you have presented and to suggest that the listeners continue their new-found interest in the subject. Since the
speech to inform does not demand action from the audience, no
Action Step is required.

F. Delivery of the speech to inform.   Your manner of speaking,
which should be guided by the suggestions given in Chapters 9–12,
will depend upon the nature of your audience, the occasion, and
your subject. We should like to re-emphasize the necessity for you
to be *enthusiastic* and to *think* during your presentation of the
speech. Maintain a lively sense of communication by keeping alert
and by being vigorous. Be sincerely eager to communicate your
knowledge, and your audience will reflect your enthusiasm by paying better attention. Watch the faces of your listeners carefully to
determine how successfully you are putting across your information.
Public speaking is not one-way communication. The audience is
constantly telling the speaker how it is receiving his message by
changes in facial expression, smiles, frowns, averted glances, shifts
of posture, yawning, nodding of heads, moving of feet, and cough-

ing. If some listeners look confused, perhaps you should review briefly the material already presented, define a troublesome word, or introduce additional explanation. If your auditors look uninterested, perhaps you should use a bit of humor, or increase your volume or animation. Be sensitive to the difficulties of understanding experienced by your listeners. When presenting difficult or technical material, you may need to reduce your rate of speaking. Do not expect others to remember a new name or term the first time it is mentioned; instead, repeat any important term at least twice in close approximation, and, if possible, accompany it with a picture, poster, actual object, or some other visual aid. In short: by being alert to audience reaction and by being enthusiastic you will be able to apply effectively the principles of delivery discussed in previous chapters.

THE SPEECH TO ENTERTAIN

A. Purpose of the speech to entertain. Sometimes at social gatherings such as dinners, smokers, fun nights, club meetings, and parties, a speaker's primary purpose may be to afford a pleasant diversion for his listeners. In such a case the giving of information or the persuading of an audience is secondary to the providing of entertainment. While it is probably true that most effective speeches contain elements of entertainment, only the speech to entertain has as its *primary* purpose the amusement of the audience. The entertaining speech may be completely without serious purpose, such as a series of side-splitting jokes at a convivial banquet. More frequently, however, it will have the secondary purpose of giving information. For instance, many lectures, which have as their major design the providing of recreation, also contain considerable information. The speech to entertain may be directed at a wide gamut of possible responses ranging from raucous laughter to quiet contemplation. Its basic intent is to serve as a pleasant distraction from routine problems and obligations.

B. Organizing and developing the speech to entertain. Unlike the general speech purposes to inform and to persuade, the general purpose "to entertain" cannot be constricted to a limited, more specific objective (Chapter 2, page 40). Pleasure and relaxation are mainly states of bodily feeling and mental attitudes; hence you have achieved your speech goal upon providing a refreshing diversion. Some sample Specific Speech Purposes might be: to entertain my audience with a description of the marine life found on the Great Barrier Reef of Australia, or to amuse the club by telling about my unsuccessful attempt to climb Mount Whitney.

Careful organization is less important for speeches to entertain than for those to inform or persuade. Since the audience is not expected primarily to retain factual information or to accept or reject courses of action, there is usually less need for summaries, transitions, and a careful amassing of supporting materials. Frequently no clear-cut division into Introduction, Discussion, and Conclusion is necessary. When an Introduction is used, its only purpose is to prepare the audience to be entertained. If present, the Conclusion ordinarily should contain no formal summary, but should serve merely to bring the talk to a graceful close. Usually the Discussion can be developed around a simple Topical or Time Pattern. Avoid complicated arrangements of evidence or systems of thought. A Time Pattern could be used for such speeches as "My boat trip down the Amazon," "My first and last boar hunt," or "Two days at a sales conference." A Topical Pattern would be a convenient plan for a speech on "Things to do and sights to see in Montreal" or for an amusing talk on "How not to build a house." If you wish to divert your listeners with a description of your professors, you might use a sequence like this:

I. The "pacer" type
II. The "bifocal" type
III. The "man-about-town" type
IV. The "introvert" type
V. The "big-wheel" type

The content of the speech to entertain should be buoyant rather than heavy, graphic rather than complicated, lively rather than exact, sanguine rather than pessimistic. It should be fresh and not hackneyed, bright not somber, genial not sarcastic. Avoid wearisome statistics, dull analysis, banal humor, and laborious descriptions.

C. Delivery of the speech to entertain.   Although you should follow all the canons for effective delivery, perhaps the most important is to demonstrate to your audience that *you* are enjoying the speech. If you are not at ease and are not having a good time, your audience will reflect your state of tension. The frozen face, the stiff, awkward posture, the averted glance, the forced grin, the inhibited gesture, and the flat, uninteresting voice are especially to be avoided. Be gracious, genial, good-natured, and relaxed. Since your intention is to divert your listeners from their problems, maintain a cheerful air of optimism. Pessimism, gloom, and depression have no place in the entertaining speech. In brief, you should reveal yourself to the audience as a friendly, animated speaker who is completely in harmony with the mood of the audience and the speech occasion.

THE SPEECH TO PERSUADE

A. **Purpose of the speech to persuade.** The persuasive speech aims at inducing the audience to think, feel, or act in a manner desired by the speaker. While the speech to persuade may contain entertaining or informative material, such content is only a means to the end—persuasion. The speech to persuade attempts to *form* rather than *inform*, its purpose is *persuasion* rather than *education*. Unlike the informative speaker, who is an objective conveyor of knowledge, the persuasive speaker is an advocate. He wishes his listeners to take a stand on the information he presents. Rarely will the pleader present a candid discussion of both sides of a question. Instead, he will utilize only that evidence which strongly supports his position.

B. **Selecting the Specific Speech Purpose of the speech to persuade.** Persuasive speaking is customarily divided into speeches to convince, to stimulate or impress, and to actuate. A careful analysis of the audience, the occasion, and yourself as the speaker is necessary in order to select the suitable general persuasive purpose and the Specific Speech Purpose (Chapter 2, pages 25–36, 41–48). Whenever a controversial subject is presented to an audience, the attitude of each auditor toward that proposal will fall somewhere on this diagram.

Diagram of Audience Attitudes
Toward Controversial Issues

If a preponderance of the audience is receptive to the speaker's recommendations, his task is to deepen or to make more intense the existing belief. Such a speech might have as its Specific Speech Purpose to stimulate the audience to a deeper feeling of gratitude for the sacrifices of our troops in Korea. If, however, a significant portion of the audience is opposed to his proposition, or is neutral because of insufficient interest or information, the speaker must change the mental set from one of inertia or opposition to one of agreement. For instance, let us suppose that a preliminary investigation has indicated that much of the audience will be uninformed, undetermined, or opposed to admitting Alaska to statehood. In such a case the Specific Speech Purpose might be to convince the listeners that Alaska should be admitted to the Union as the forty-ninth state. An accurate understanding of the distinction between the general purposes to convince and to stimulate is essential. Each type demands a different development in terms of the selection of materials and of vocal and physical delivery.

The basic purpose of the third type of persuasive speech is to move the audience to action. Such an actuating speech may be directed to any audience, whether favorable, neutral, or hostile to the speaker's program. Of course, the less favorably disposed the audience, the more difficult will be the speaker's task. When speaking to people who are opposed to your opinions, usually you must first remove their objections and prove the acceptability of your argument (convince), and then so stimulate or impress them with the desirability of your plan that they will be receptive to a request for action. A Specific Speech Purpose for the speech to actuate might be to persuade the audience to sign a pledge to give a pint of blood to the Red Cross Blood Bank. The signal difference between speeches to actuate and those to convince and to stimulate is that the latter types aim only at intellectual and emotional response, with any desired action only a possible eventuality. Definite and fairly immediate action is sought in the speech to actuate.

C. Developing the Introduction of the speech to persuade. Plan the organizational structure and the speech materials in terms of *psychological* as well as *logical* needs. Since your purpose is to mold · and lead public opinion, your speech must be *audience-centered* rather than subject-centered. You are talking to people, not to unemotional machines. You are attempting to influence mental and emotional states of being. Therefore, your speech must present a tightly woven appeal to both intellect and emotions, and should not be a dull, exclusively logical treatise.

As in the case of the speech to inform, the normal structure of the speech to persuade consists of an Introduction, a Discussion, and a Conclusion. Except when addressing a highly polarized audience, every Introduction should contain a Favorable Attention Step. Many centuries ago Cicero pointed out that the purpose of the Introduction is "to render the audience well-disposed toward the speaker, attentive toward his speech, and open to conviction." Occasionally the listeners may be hostile to you personally. Since such antipathy may color their reaction toward your proposals, attempt to reduce such hostility at the outset. If your auditors regard you as a "stuffed-shirt," reveal yourself in your opening remarks as being unassuming and free of ostentation. Perhaps telling a brief joke at your own expense will relieve antagonism. If your listeners believe you to be egotistical, probably you should avoid personal material in the Introduction. Instead, concentrate attention on your proposals, and demonstate by style of content and delivery that you are modest and unpretentious. If your auditors feel that you are intolerant or radical, indicate in your first sentences (and throughout the speech) that you are friendly and considerate, and that you understand and respect their convictions.

Any of the nine methods discussed in Chapter 7 may be used for securing the favorable attention of listeners either neutral or favorably predisposed toward the speaker's proposals. However, when speaking to a critical group the most effective method for winning a more objective reception will probably be to stress common beliefs, interests, and feelings. The hostile audience has been psychologically conditioned not to believe. Therefore, in order to gain a fair hearing, you must establish a common ground of understanding and objectives. Emphasize the areas of agreement and minimize existing differences. Demonstrate that you and the audience desire similar objectives even though some variance may exist on the means of achieving them. Use the "Yes" technique; by stressing points of accordance give the audience no opportunity to think "No" before you come to a presentation of your arguments.

Until you have gained considerable experience, always use a Clarification Step in the Introduction. Somewhere in the Introduction state the POINT of your speech in a simple declarative sentence. Occasionally in speeches to convince or to actuate it might be necessary also to list the major arguments you intend to present. Thus your listeners are prepared to follow your evidence more easily and to remember your main points. If necessary, provide an explanation about the background and recent history of the subject. Define any confusing terms; avoid the possibility that some of your listeners may be opposed merely through misunderstanding. (Experienced speakers occasionally develop persuasive speeches according to the method of *implication*. Instead of telling the audience what he is endeavoring to prove, the veteran speaker may present his material in such a skillful manner that the auditors are gently guided to the "correct" judgment through their own reasoning. Although highly successful at times, in general such a procedure is too risky for the average beginning speaker.)

D. Developing the Discussion of the speech to persuade (Chapter 5, Parts II and III). The Discussion should be carefully planned for maximum logical and psychological effectiveness. (1) A basic theme, or sequence of thought should connect each of the main heads. Any persuasive speech can be organized according to a Problem-Solution Pattern or a Proposition of "Fact" Pattern. An examination of the Specific Speech Purpose will reveal whether your intent is to propose a plan, a program, or an alteration of existing conditions. If so, your speech is basically problem-solving, and your material logically will fall into a presentation of the Problem and its Solution. Frequently, your Specific Speech Purpose may not involve the recommendation of a program or course of action; it may seek to establish the truth or validity of an assertion or viewpoint. In such a case, your talk can be organized according to the Proposition of "Fact" Pattern, in which you determine standards of measurements and then match the statement in question against the criteria. The Discussion may also be organized by Topical or Cause-and-Effect Patterns. (2) Frequent summaries should characterize the speech to the neutral or hostile audience. In some cases a summary should follow each main head. (3) Especially in the speech to convince, keep before your audience the major lines of your case. By linking the main heads together with smooth transitional phrases, you can show how each new point helps move your argument toward your goal of persuasion.

Much of the success of the persuasive speech depends upon the skill with which you develop the main heads of the Discussion. In re-emphasis of the suggestions made in Chapter 6, let us examine the following points. (1) Develop each major point in terms of the knowledge and attitude of the audience toward that issue. Avoid thinking solely of building a logical argument. Slant your material to meet the needs of your audience. For example, an uninformed, undetermined, or critical group will demand more explanation and documentary evidence and will respond less readily to emotional appeals. (2) Use a sufficient amount and variety of supporting materials to make your arguments persuasive. Buttress each major contention with enough proof to satisfy the audience that you have built a solid argument and to give the impression that you have carefully selected your data from a vast abundance of available evidence. If a preliminary examination of the audience has indicated various specialized fields of interest, draw your corroboration as closely as possible from those areas. (3) When addressing a neutral or critical audience, be vigilant to select only those supporting materials which closely reinforce their superior headings. Critical listeners will be only too eager to discover awkward links in your chain of logical association. (4) Apply the rules given in Chapter 6 to test the accuracy of your reasoning, i.e., from specific instance, analogy, deduction, causal relationships, etc. (5) Sometimes it is necessary to demonstrate that your evidence is representative of a preponderance of available data and is not isolated or extraordinary.

(6) Explain the importance of all major supporting materials to your Specific Speech Purpose. All of your elements of "proof" will not be of equal effectiveness. Therefore, highlight your most telling points so that the audience will appreciate their import. (7) Since most behavior is based upon certain motivating forces, largely emotional in nature, make judicious appeals to the basic drives discussed in Chapter 6. (8) Apply the Factors of Interest to keep your material vivid and compelling. (9) When possible, use visual material to strengthen your contentions. Would it not increase the effectiveness of his lecture on reckless driving for a judge to compel traffic violators to view hulks of wrecked automobiles and to visit accident victims in their hospital beds? (10) Except when talking to a definitely favorable audience, you should be courteous and conciliatory toward opposing beliefs. Be especially polite and gentlemanly toward other speakers on the program who may differ from you. Sarcasm is a double-edged sword which might be turned against you. (11) In order to use the various forms of support persuasively, you must keep in mind their uses and limitations. For instance, the literal comparison is better logical proof than the figurative analogy, although the latter possesses splendid attention-getting qualities and at times is unexcelled in giving clearer insight or perspective. Factual illustrations are more convincing verification than are hypothetical examples, but fictitious examples may permit a closer application to the individual members of the audience. Statistics are difficult to remember and are inherently dull, but can be compelling evidence if interpreted in terms of the audience's experience and interest. The use of testimony has intrinsic deficiencies as logical proof because such quotations represent subjective human judgments and not facts, and because a little research can uncover numerous attestations on either side of most controversial issues. However, if both the quotation and its source are acceptable to the audience, testimonial endorsement is persuasive.

E. Developing the Conclusion of the speech to persuade. The novice should plan a Summary Step for the Conclusion of each persuasive speech (Chapter 8). In unusual circumstances a mere restatement of the POINT of the speech will be sufficient. Customarily, however, you should review the arguments you have presented in the Discussion. Brief quotations, comparisons, and examples may also be used for the purposes of adding interest and of summarizing indirectly. Occasionally, if it is essential that the audience remember each point, you may list "formally" the main heads of your case. In speaking to neutral or hostile groups the summary usually should consist of a factual, logical summation with only a limited resort to emotional pleas. In general, the more favorably disposed the audience, the more liberal can be your use of emotional appeals. Of course, any address to the emotions must be sincere, in good taste, and in accord with the mood of the audience and occasion. Only the speech to actuate requires an Action Step in the Conclusion. Such a step is a direct logical-emotional plea for observable response and should state clearly the action desired, and how, when, and where the act is to be performed.

F. Delivery of the speech to persuade. The customary elements of effective delivery, discussed in Chapters 9–12, should serve as your guides in presenting the persuasive speech. In particular, we would like to direct your attention to the following suggestions. (1) During your early speeches you may need to follow your outline closely. Then, as you gain experience, you will become increasingly skillful in observing audience reactions. Subtle signals emanating from the audience may suggest to you the advisability of deviating from your prepared organization. After all, you planned your talk in terms of *anticipated* audience response. Frequently, despite the most careful analysis, your listeners will react differently from what you expected. Therefore, you must be able to adapt both content and delivery to meet the exigencies of the moment. Your organization should not be rigidly set, but should be sufficiently flexible to permit minor modifications upon the platform. For example, if the audience obviously agrees with one of your arguments, perhaps you should omit further discussion and move on to the next point. On the other hand, if significant numbers appear unconvinced after you have exhausted the supporting heads listed in your outline, and if the topic is vital to your case, perhaps you should introduce additional explanation or evidence. If some of the auditors look bored, possibly you should make the application of the material closer to their needs, or insert some relevant humor.

• (2) Adjust your vocal and physical delivery to the attitudes of the audience. By watching the listeners carefully you will be able to judge how much to gesture, what level of volume and animation to use, and so on. When addressing a neutral or critical audience, avoid any tendency toward bombast. This does not imply that you should avoid showing sincere intensity of feeling—but it does mean that your feelings should be evidenced by a quiet, well-controlled intensity. Any extreme emotionalism, such as shouting, banging the lectern, or gesturing wildly, may easily alienate the unconvinced. Remember that oratory is not a bull-whip. As long as your listeners possess the freedom to accept or reject, they cannot be driven into agreement. Of course, when you are addressing a group receptive to your proposals, your presentation may be more forceful. (3) Especially in speeches to stimulate and to actuate, endeavor to attain a climax or high point of attention near the close. Such a climax depends partly on the nature of the speech materials used, but perhaps to a greater extent upon magnetic delivery. (4) Avoid the extremely rapid staccato delivery so frequently used by high-school and college debaters. Human beings are not adding machines which total up the points a speaker crowds into a limited time span. Your rate of speaking should never become excessive, and your style should never approach neurotic ranting. (5) Our final suggestion is that the aspiring student should study carefully this definition written some two thousand years ago by the great teacher Quintilian: "An orator is a good man speaking well." The qualities of sincerity, courtesy, human understanding, honesty, and common sense, when combined with experience and an intelligent application of the suggestions contained in this book, should make any average student a persuasive speaker. Neither character nor speech skill alone is enough to make a speaker effective. In these days of decision, America needs men of integrity and honesty of purpose who can speak well.

SUMMARY

The purpose of this chapter is to apply specifically to speeches to inform, to entertain, and to persuade the fundamental principles of speech preparation and delivery. We hope that it will serve as a recapitulation of the three basic types of speeches, and that it will refocus the attention of the reader on the particular problems encountered in developing each.

Exercises and Assignments

1. Read several printed speeches for practice in determining the general speech purpose, i.e., to inform, to entertain, or to persuade.

2. Prepare a five-minute speech for class presentation in which you discuss the major differences in organization between the speech to inform and the speech to entertain.

3. In a five-minute talk analyze the differences in purpose, organization, and content between speeches to stimulate and speeches to convince.

4. Give a five-minute talk in which you show the similarities and the differences in the style of delivery for speeches to inform, entertain, convince, stimulate, and actuate.

5. Explain to the class the importance of audience retention in speeches promoting long-range influence as compared with that in speeches designed to produce immediate action.

6. In five minutes explain to the class the basic differences between an "audience-centered" speech and one which is "subject-centered."

7. Discuss before the class the use of basic drives in the speech to entertain.

8. In a short report to the class, contrast the role of "implication" in the speech to inform with its usage in the speech to persuade.

9. Make a brief talk explaining your answer to the question: "Is the 'Yes' technique as used in persuasive speeches unethical?"

10. Which of the three basic types of speech is the most difficult to prepare and to deliver? Prepare your answer to this question in the form of a short talk and give it in class.

CHAPTER 15

Speeches of Special Types

PART I. THE IMPROMPTU SPEECH

Almost everyone is called upon at some time to face an audience without opportunity for preparation. In fact, the more widely known a speaker becomes, the more often he will be asked "to say a few words." Conceivably, when a preceding discussion has been stimulating and the speaker has been called upon to discuss a familiar subject, his speaking may exhibit a spontaneity and fluency not characteristic of his prepared talks. Such effectiveness depends primarily upon a favorable combination of circumstances. The inexperienced speaker who has felt a pleasurable glow as the result of having spoken impromptu with success or even brilliance should not be misled into a reliance upon inspirations of the moment. Impromptu speaking is usually unsatisfactory. Many a speaker who is thoroughly competent when he has had an opportunity to plan and rehearse, finds that the task of thinking through a speech while on his feet is difficult, if not impossible.

As we have indicated in Chapter 9, there are suggestions which will help the average speaker to meet successfully an impromptu situation. First, if you suspect that you might be called upon, pay close attention to the discussion from the floor and from the platform. If you can do so unobtrusively, jot down a few salient notations of the proceedings. Observe that you disagree with a point some speaker has made, that an erroneous conclusion has been drawn, or that obvious arguments are being overlooked. In this way you are gathering speech materials and are organizing your thinking.

Second, utilize the brief interim between the call to speak and your first words to control your emotions and to plan what you are going to say. Do not waste emotional energy with feelings of fear or despair. Recognize that a rush of adrenalin into the blood stream is inevitable. Such is nature's way of preparing the body for an emergency. Be grateful that you are so stimulated; without such motive power you probably could not meet the occasion adequately. Control this surge of energy. Relax by taking several deep breaths and by making a conscious effort to ease muscular tension. Rise to your feet calmly. If you are expected to speak from a podium, walk deliberately without hesitation or undue haste. Before beginning your impromptu talk, look at the audience, address the chairman, take a full breath, and start to speak.

At the same time that you are preparing yourself physically, you should also be planning what you are going to say. Almost any impromptu speech can be organized according to the following plan:

I. POINT Step (Tell the audience in a clear statement what you will attempt to establish in your speech.)
II. Reason Step (State a reason why your POINT is valid.)
III. Evidence Step (Support your reason by means of illustration, comparison, quotation, or statistic.)
IV. Restatement of POINT Step

This schematic organizational plan represents the minimum demands upon the impromptu speaker. Ordinarily, you should be able to think of *more than one reason* why the audience might accept the POINT you are attempting to make. Actually, this simple outline represents nothing new to the reader. According to the tripartite method of development (Introduction, Discussion, and Conclusion), such a plan would have the following heads:

Introduction:
I. State the POINT of your speech
Discussion:
I. Give a reason why your POINT is valid
A. Offer some evidence to support your reason
Conclusion:
I. Summarize the gist of the speech by restating the POINT

Now, let us see how this plan would operate under various circumstances. (1) Upon being asked a question, you might repeat the interrogation and then answer it in one sentence. Your answer, of course, is the POINT of your talk. Give a reason or reasons why you have answered the question as you have. Back up your reason(s) with supporting evidence. In conclusion, restate your answer. (2) If you believe that an important argument has been omitted in the earlier discussion, state as your POINT that the particular argument has been overlooked. Tell why you think this new point of view is important or germane. Support your reason(s). Then, as a summary, say that you feel the argument merits the consideration of the group because of the reasons given. (3) To persuade your listeners that a particular proposal should be rejected, state as your POINT that you believe the argument to be invalid. Point out as your reason(s) that those who have supported the measure have used faulty reasoning, misleading statistics, untrustworthy testimony, or atypical examples; explain and support your reason(s); and restate your POINT. (4) A careful study of the elements of problem-solving, discussed in Chapter 5, will be of considerable aid in meeting many impromptu situations. For instance, if the seriousness of a problem under discussion has been exaggerated, state as your POINT that you feel the problem is not as severe as has been presented. Give reasons with evidence why this is so. Then restate your POINT. Follow this basic procedure when you believe that important causes of a problem have been overlooked or distorted, and when it seems evident that the proposed solution would not solve the problem, could not be put into effect, would create additional severe problems, or is not the best solution.

PART II. THE MANUSCRIPT SPEECH

Many persons in business, government, and the professions choose to read the majority of their speeches rather than to deliver them extemporaneously. Several factors may account for the frequent use of the manuscript speech. If a speech is broadcast or telecast, it must be timed very carefully; furthermore, radio and television stations often ask for the right to examine the text of a speaker's remarks prior to the broadcast. The possibility that an address may be quoted in whole or in part prompts many speakers to read rather than extemporize in order to assure exactness in language. Many who are faced with frequent speaking obligations have had little if any training or experience in extemporizing from notes, and are too busy to undertake a program to develop this skill. Distrusting their ability to extemporize, they choose to read from manuscript, particularly if the speaking occasion is an important one.

Is it a wise decision to read rather than to talk? Many authors of texts in public speaking advise students not to read from manuscript, except in situations where exactness in language or timing is demanded. Such authorities offer two primary objections to the manuscript speech. The first of these is that a manuscript imposes severe limitations upon flexibility, with the result that adjustments to the audience and occasion are difficult to make during the presentation of the speech. When reading a manuscript, the speaker finds it difficult, if not impossible, to make changes in word choice, phrasing, or content. If the manuscript speech is to be broadcast or telecast, straying from the written words invites trouble in concluding the speech on time. Only the experienced speaker dares take such liberties with a radio or television speech (see Chapter 16). However, in defense of the manuscript speech, we should point out that if the situation permits and the speaker is sufficiently skilled, some flexibility may be achieved by omissions, extemporaneous amplifications, and word substitutions.

The second common objection to reading a speech is that it often results in ineffective oral and physical delivery. Such a criticism is undoubtedly based upon the valid observation that most persons are unskilled at oral reading. It does not follow, however, that because the majority of us do not read aloud with skill the manuscript speech is to be avoided; by such reasoning, another large group of speakers who lack the ability to extemporize well would be advised to avoid the extemporaneous mode!

We believe that it is unrealistic to demand that speakers shun the manuscript speech. Many who extemporize with skill deliberately choose to read their speeches on frequent occasions. They do so because they recognize certain advantages to be enjoyed by the speaker who can read well. One advantage is the polish in style attainable in a carefully prepared manuscript. A well-written speech possesses clarity, conciseness, vividness, impressiveness, and other language attributes to a degree which can be equalled only by a few extremely effective extemporizers. Not only does such a polished style evoke favorable audience response; it also permits the speech to stand the scrutiny of those who may later study and analyze a published text of the remarks.

Effective manuscript reading, while posing some genuine problems, offers certain advantages to the speaker. By acquiring skill in both reading and extemporizing, one is free to choose that mode which seems better adapted to a given situation.

The remainder of this section will discuss the ways in which the fundamental principles of speech preparation and delivery (Chapters 1–13) may be adapted to facilitate the effective composition, rehearsal, and presentation of the manuscript speech.

A. Preparing the manuscript speech. It should be clear at the outset that the manuscript speech cannot be classified as a *special type,* in the same sense as the other types of speeches treated in this chapter. A manuscript speech may seek to inform, persuade, or entertain (although the last-named type is seldom read). With the exception of the impromptu speech, the special types discussed in this chapter may on occasion be read, although some of them are usually more effective when extemporized. The manuscript speech may not be characterized, therefore, on the basis of general or specific purpose; rather, it is differentiated from other types of speeches essentially by certain characteristics of preparation, rehearsal, and delivery.

In preparing the manuscript speech, the following sequence may be helpful: (1) *develop your outline;* (2) *write the first draft of your manuscript;* (3) *revise your first draft;* and (4) *prepare your final copy.*

1. *Develop your outline.* The initial phase in your preparation will be identical with that of the extemporized speech. You will choose your subject (Chapter 2), gather materials (Chapter 3), and develop an outline (according to the rules prescribed in Chapter 4) which will contain main heads (Chapter 5), supporting materials (Chapter 6), an Introduction (Chapter 7), and a Conclusion (Chapter 8). Do not attempt to write your first draft until you have developed a complete outline.

2. *Write the first draft of your manuscript.* Before beginning to write, it may be wise to re-examine Chapter 12 ("Using Language in Delivering the Speech") to remind you of the characteristics of good oral style. In particular, be aware of the necessity of choosing words which are clear, objective, vivid, and impressive. Avoid long, complicated sentence structure, and exercise economy in the use of words. *Do not write an essay.* Make certain that your manuscript is written in language meant primarily to be heard, rather than to be read. It may help to dictate to a secretary, if one is available; by so doing, your composition may acquire more of the qualities of oral style.

Keep your outline constantly before you to guide the organization and development of your speech. A complete, well-developed outline will simplify the task of writing.

When you have finished the first draft, read it aloud to check the over-all timing and the degree of ease with which the individual words and combinations of words lend themselves to oral reading.

3. *Revise your first draft.* The extent of revision necessary will obviously depend upon how closely the first draft adheres to time limits, and to what extent it reflects the previously noted attributes of effective oral language.

Strict timing must be achieved if the speech is to be broadcast or telecast. If the manuscript is too long, delete words, phrases, and sentences until it is no more than one-half minute longer or shorter than the prescribed time. It is safer to be too short than too long. Although timing need not be as precise in face-to-face speaking, do not vary significantly from the time allotted you. Careful revision will enable you to adhere closely to time limits.

Revision should also be guided by your knowledge of the principles of effective language. Do you find awkward and complicated sentences? Break them up into shorter, simpler units. Is your language overly wordy? Cut out unnecessary words and phrases, or restate entire portions more concisely. Does every word clearly express the meaning you intend? Eliminate vague and inaccurate terms. Are important points adequately developed? Amplify ideas which seem to need further emphasis. Have you made liberal use of appropriate figures of speech, parallel structure, and other techniques for achieving vividness and impressiveness? Take the time needed to develop these language attributes during revision. Are you guilty of too frequent use of favorite words and phrases? Find substitutes to break up excessive repetition.

Occasionally, revision may turn a speech into an essay. In attempting to polish the first draft, do not sacrifice those qualities of language which tend to establish a direct and personal relationship between speaker and audience, and which provide for instant comprehension of meaning.

Most of the changes you decide upon may be made on the copy of the first draft. However, if deleted portions, crossed-out words, and written-in sections are abundant on certain pages, retype or rewrite them at once (unless you plan to begin the final draft without delay); later on, such pages may be incomprehensible.

4. Prepare your final copy. The concluding step in preparing the manuscript speech is to write the final copy for use in delivery. *Do not practice delivery with the marked-up revision; only the final copy should be used for rehearsal.* In order to promote maximum audience contact and to facilitate rapid comprehension when glancing at your manuscript, you must become familiar with the particular copy you intend to use in delivery.

Observe these rules when preparing the final copy: (1) *Use reasonably stiff paper.* Paper without sufficient body may curl when placed on a lectern or table, or may be difficult to control when held in the speaker's hands. Heavy bond paper or note cards will prove to be better choices. (2) *Use paper or cards of the proper size.* For most persons, paper of the popular 8½″ by 11″ size is slightly too large to permit easy holding of the manuscript and facile turning of the pages. More usable is the 8½″ by 5½″ size derived from cutting the former sized page horizontally in half. If you perfer, use note-cards instead of paper. (3) *Use only one side of the paper.* To use both sides of a card or sheet of paper is to invite disaster. Not only does it require added effort to turn over each sheet, but the process may confuse you during delivery; you may not always be sure whether you are reading the first or second side of a given sheet of paper. (4) *Number your pages.* Numbering will facilitate rapid rearrangement if an improper sequence is discovered during delivery. The number should appear in the same place on each page—probably the upper right-hand corner is most convenient. (5) *Type your manuscript with double or triple spacing.* Unless your handwriting is unusually legible, have your speech typed to insure easy reading. Exclusive use of capital letters will aid those who find small letters difficult to see. Double or triple spacing between the lines tends to prevent confusing one line with another during delivery. (6) *Arrange your material into short paragraphs.* Short paragraphs are easier for the eye to encompass, and facilitate keeping one's place on the page. (7) *Maintain neatness.* Unless absolutely necessary, avoid such last-minute changes as crossed-out passages, interlinear insertions, and erasures. If your final copy is to possess maximum readability, it must be clean and neat.

B. Rehearsing the manuscript speech. The primary purpose of rehearsing the manuscript speech is to establish sufficient familiarity with the ideas, phrasing, and wording to enable the speaker to read it with a maximum of spontaneity, meaning, directness, and enthusiasm. Effective delivery may be accomplished by observing the following sequence of procedures.

(1) Read the speech aloud a number of times, keeping your eyes on the manuscript as much as necessary, in order to familiarize yourself thoroughly with the meaning you wish to convey, the structure of your sentences, the words you wish to emphasize, and important pauses you wish to make.

(2) Mark your script to indicate emphasis, pauses, and vocal phrases, *if you find it useful.* Some speakers find that such markings make them excessively word-conscious and tend to destroy spontaneous delivery; others rate these markings as unusually helpful during presentation. During rehearsal you might experiment with script markings and compare the results with those obtained with an unmarked script. It would be helpful if someone would aid in evaluating your performance in this experiment. If you decide to use markings, underline words which should receive special emphasis; use a diagonal line (/) to designate points at which a short pause would be appropriate, and a double diagonal line (//) to indicate the need for an extended pause.

(3) Practice to reduce dependence upon your manuscript. Your goal should be to maintain eye contact with your audience about 80 per cent of the time. Contrary to the opinion of many people, this can be accomplished without memorizing. By acquiring close familiarity with the script, as previously discussed, you will reduce dependence upon it; by practicing to increase the number of words you can encompass in a glance, the frequency with which you need

to glance at your paper will be cut down. First, look at the page and concentrate; then, deliver as many words as possible without looking down; finally, consult the page again and repeat the procedure. By rehearsing, you will gradually increase your visual span until you can grasp long phrases and sentences in a short glance and deliver them without hesitation or looking down. However, if you take a manuscript to the stand, you should read from it rather than recite most of the speech from memory.

(4) Practice to acquire ease in handling the manuscript. Placing it on the speaker's stand, as is usually recommended, will free your hands for gesturing, but will tie you closely to the lectern. Holding the papers in your hands will permit unrestricted movement about the platform, but will limit hand gestures, will attract attention to the manuscript, and will pose special problems in handling the manuscript. During rehearsal, if you decide to hold the script, keep it at the proper level; you should not be compelled to bend your head down, nor should the pages conceal your face from the audience. When you have completed the reading of a page, move it easily to one side and place it under the pile. Awkward hesitation during this change can be avoided by sliding the page down an inch before removing it; this will reveal the top few lines of the next page.

C. Delivering the manuscript speech.   In addition to observing the fundamental principles of good delivery (Chapters 9–11), consider the following suggestions. (1) Endeavor to *rethink* and *recreate* the speech at the time of presentation. While the extemporaneous speaker is forced to think of his ideas in order to choose his words, the manuscript speaker is seemingly relieved of this necessity to think—his words are before him. To neglect thinking of ideas, however, makes the speaker word-conscious, and usually results in a dull, monotonous, lifeless presentation. Concentrate on meanings, therefore, rather than words, if you are to speak with appropriate emphasis, proper phrasing, and enthusiasm. (2) Be particularly conscious of rate. While you may have established an appropriate rate in rehearsal, the tendency during delivery is to accelerate perceptibly. Relieved of the necessity of "finding" words to express your ideas, you will be tempted to increase your rate, particularly if tense and anxious to finish. Excessive speed is frequently accompanied by inadequate emphasis, slurring, and mumbling. (3) Do not attempt to conceal your manuscript or apologize for the fact that you are reading.

If you establish in rehearsal the pattern of procedures suggested earlier and follow them during delivery, and if you endeavor to recreate the speech while reading it, your presentation of the manuscript speech will be successful.

PART III. THE AFTER-DINNER SPEECH

The after-dinner speech is one of the most common of the various types of occasional speeches. Probably all civilized and barbaric peoples engage in after-dinner speaking. Once, following a meal of roast pig, the famed explorer, Frank Buck, sat around the campfire in interior Africa with his native hosts. After Buck had solicited their aid in the preparation of a motion picture, several natives offered constructive suggestions. There, in the pristine wilderness of Equatorial Africa, a program of after-dinner speaking was taking place. From Moscow to Teheran and from Toronto to Osaka, men and women engage in public speech over dining tables. In America, particularly, we seem to be habituated to the after-dinner speech.

Despite its frequent occurrence, the after-dinner speech is the most difficult to define of all the types of occasional speeches. Almost any original oral communication lasting long enough to be considered a speech, and taking place after some meal, may be termed an after-dinner speech. Other writers have pointed out that the after-dinner speech is not actually a *type*, but rather a *class*, of speeches. A talk following a dinner might range from a serious, dignified presentation of a problem to a hilarious selection of anecdotes.

A. The serious after-dinner speech. A majority of after-dinner speeches are basically serious. Dinners, lunches, suppers, and even breakfasts often serve as the occasion for serious transactions. Top drawer executives frequently engage in policy determination over the table cloth; Community Chest committees meet at dinners to plan campaigns; fraternities pay tribute at banquets to the founders of their orders; representatives of labor and management gather in dining rooms to discuss the probable effects of some recent federal legislation. Speeches delivered at such occasions might seek to inform, convince, stimulate, or actuate. In preparing the serious after-dinner speech you should follow the suggestions given in earlier chapters. The essential principles remain the same, whether the speech is presented in a restaurant or in a labor hall. However, in some respects, an after-dinner audience is easier to please. The auditors have eaten a meal together in pleasant surroundings and have engaged in congenial conversation. Usually they feel comfortable and relaxed. The occasion itself has produced a friendly in-group feeling. In some ways, however, such an audience presents a more difficult challenge. Everyone experiences a "logy" sensation after a heavy meal with a corresponding decline in mental and physical efficiency. If serious speeches are in order, they must be developed in a vivid, sparkling, interesting manner. Long chains of logical reasoning, detailed arguments, dull statistics, and the like will drug most after-dinner audiences into sluggish apathy. Do not let your speech drag; make greater use of illustrations and analogies than usual; use a liberal sprinkling of relevant humor; speak with animation and warmth; let your manner reflect congeniality and sincerity. Do not permit your speech to become heavy or otherwise unpalatable. Above all, *do not be dull.*

B. The entertaining after-dinner speech. In planning the diverting after-dinner talk, follow the procedures suggested in Chapter 14 for the speech to entertain. Fortunately, the after-dinner audience is in a mood to be entertained. Relatively little stiffness or unyielding dignity is present in most situations where entertaining speeches are appropriate. Almost everyone is having a good time, and your speech is expected to be consistent with the general mood of relaxation and congeniality. Since the format of the typical entertaining after-dinner speech is based upon humor, review the rules prescribed in Chapter 6 for the satisfactory use of humor, i.e., recall that humor should be relevant, appropriate, fresh, compact, and pointed. A diverting after-dinner speech needs to be planned as carefully as a serious one. However, you should keep your organization sufficiently fluid to be able to make on-the-spot adaptations to the speaking situation. Listen carefully to the conversations at your table during the meal and to the other speakers. Frequently, some chance remark or unusual happening, when incorporated into the speech in the appropriate place, can serve as an extremely effective source of humor. When the chairman introduces you, listen thoughtfully with the expectation of tying in your speech with some facetious comment he may have made. Once a petite woman was introduced by a jovial six-foot toastmaster with the remark that the speaker was so small he could put her in his pocket. Upon arising, the lady won a terrific response from the audience by her saucy retort: "In that case, Mr. Toastmaster, you'd have more brains in your pocket than you have in your head." Such repartee, while perfectly appropriate in a jocular situation, might be out of place at a more dignified occasion. Like all humor, playful digs at the chairman should always be in good taste.

In order to be effective the entertaining after-dinner speech must be well planned and rehearsed, be appropriate to the speaker, the audience, and the occasion, and must possess charm in content and presentation.

PART IV. THE SPEECH OF GOOD WILL

The extensive growth of public relations departments in business and industry in recent years reflects a growing sensitivity to public opinion. Business executives are now conscious that mounting profits, unrestricted expansion, and favorable legislation are more easily achieved when public opinion is friendly and sympathetic. Modern advertising promotes friendship as well as sales. The United States Steel Corporation, for example, appears almost as interested in promoting good will as in selling steel. Interest in securing the good will of the public is also evidenced by non-profit organizations, community projects, pressure groups, educational and religious institutions, and governmental agencies.

Most public and private institutions are aware of the power of the spoken word as one means of achieving successful public relations. Many of these groups encourage their officers and administrative personnel to appear publicly on behalf of the company; some have organized speakers' bureaus to arrange public speaking engagements for employees; still others schedule company-sponsored courses in effective speaking for interested personnel.

If you presently hold, or someday hope to secure, a responsible position in business or government, or if you are reasonably active in volunteer work in your community, you will probably be asked to prepare and deliver speeches of good will on behalf of your organization.

While any speech seeks a favorable attitude toward the speaker and his subject, the good-will speech has as its primary goal the winning of friends for the speaker's organization, project, or cause. Ultimately, this friendship may result in money for a project, increased patronage, favorable legislation, or votes. The *apparent* purpose of the speech of good will is to inform the audience about the speaker's organization or cause and to indicate how it performs valuable services for the listeners and their community; the *implicit* purpose is to persuade the audience to lend its friendship and support to the organization. The persuasive techniques employed to achieve the implicit purpose must be *unobtrusive* and *indirect*. Overt persuasive devices have no place in the speech of good will; using them puts an audience "on its guard." If you openly exhort your audience to give money, buy products, or vote for a candidate, your primary purpose is to secure action, not to seek good will; if you plead for belief in a principle or directly attack your opposition, your primary purpose is to convince rather than to secure good will. Thus, a speech of good will on the subject of the Red Cross might trace its history, outline its functions, and offer its services, but would not include an open plea for financial support. A speech on behalf of the Central Power and Lighting Company might review its superior service record, offer its special free consulting service for proper indoor illumination, and conclude with a demonstration of new lighting techniques. Omitted, however, would be any derogatory reference to public ownership of utilities or any overt plea for support of legislation favorable to private utilities.

Among the most common occasions for the speech of good will are luncheon meetings, service and social club gatherings, school and college assemblies, and convention programs.

With some adaptations, the following formula for the development of the good-will speech should fit almost any subject and occasion:

I. *Your Introduction should arouse curiosity about the institution or cause you represent.*
(You may open by referring to the importance of this opportunity to speak, by complimenting the audience, or by using any of the other

attention-getting devices discussed in Chapter 7. To arouse curiosity, you might present a few unusual, startling, or novel facts concerning your organization, such as its amazing growth, volume of business, service record, etc.)

II. *Explain how your organization is designed to meet the needs of the community.*

(Here you will need to explain something of the background, development, and organization of your cause. These facts should be as novel and interesting as possible. Since you are an employee or representative of your institution, you may be in a position to reveal information not commonly known. Your audience will appreciate hearing the "inside story." Stress the services your group offers to the community. Do not boast about its financial success, its nation-wide reputation, or its superiority to competitors or similar organizations. Do not ask for approval or argue for support. Assume that your audience is already favorable to your group.)

III. *Indicate in what way your organization can directly benefit your listeners.*

(Your speech of good will may conclude by your offering special services to the audience. Obviously, the specific method used will depend upon the nature of the service. You may demonstrate a model of an ideal kitchen; you might pass out literature or distribute coupons entitling the signer to visit the company's plant or attend a demonstration; or you may explain precisely where and when your organization makes its services available, and what steps may be taken to secure them. Be sure that your offer of services is specific as to *time, place,* and *nature.* Avoid leaving your listeners with the vague impression that somewhere and sometime you hope to be able to serve them. Do not conclude with obvious pleas for sympathy, understanding, patronage, contributions, votes, or membership. Your conclusion should stress what your organization can do for the audience, not what the audience can do for your organization.)

The fundamental principles of effective delivery for all speaking occasions (Chapters 9–12) apply in presenting the speech of good will. The following characteristics of speech personality are particularly important: (1) Be *genial.* Avoid seeming overzealous and polemic. You may defeat your purpose by forcing the issue or debating with your audience. A friendly, easy-going approach is essential. (2) Be *enthusiastic* and *lively.* Without overdoing it, demonstrate that you are "sold" on your organization or cause, and that you are pleased to discuss its functions and services. Your audience may catch some of your spirit. (3) Be *modest*. Do not let your enthusiasm for your cause lead you to adopt a superior, arrogant manner. Beware of overselling yourself or your organization. Nobody likes a braggart. (4) Be *tolerant*. Your manner, as well as the content of your speech, should show tolerance and magnanimity, particularly toward competing organizations. Should reference be made to competitors in a question period following your speech, your attitude should be one of politeness and courtesy.

PART V. THE SPEECHES OF COURTESY

A. The Speech of introduction. If you are reasonably active in the social and civic affairs of your community, undoubtedly you will be asked some time to present a speaker to an audience. At first glance such an assignment would seem exceedingly simple. Unfortunately, far more ineffectual speeches of introduction are given than good ones. With inexcusable frequency speeches of introduction say too much or too little, are too long or too brief, embarrass the guest speaker with flattery, or deaden audience anticipation with hackneyed, insipid comments. The following discussion should enable you to avoid these typical errors and to deliver a speech of introduction with felicity and ease.

The basic purpose of the speech of introduction is to stimulate a favorable attitude toward the speaker and his subject. You are a salesman in the limited sense that you are exciting a feeling of anticipation, a desire to hear this particular speaker on this particular subject. Here are five rules to help you prepare an introductory speech.

1. *Analyze the audience, occasion (see Chapter 2), the guest speaker, and the nature of his speech:* It is patent that your introduction should be skillfully adjusted to the nature and mood of your audience, the character and purpose of the meeting, the personality and status of the guest speaker, and the general tenor of his speech. When possible, you should consult the speaker himself to ascertain what *he* would like to have you say or, equally important, what he might prefer your *not* saying. Check the accuracy of the data you plan to use with the speaker himself.

2. Be brief but adequate: Usually, a speech of introduction should last at least twenty seconds, but should not exceed two minutes. Ordinarily, the better known the speaker is, the shorter the necessary introduction. In 1915, Shailer Mathews set the prototype for future presentations of the nation's chief executive by this concise introduction of Woodrow Wilson: "Ladies and gentlemen, the President." For most situations, however, such an introduction would be abrupt, almost to the point of rudeness. In most cases you should help arouse interest in the speaker's subject and in the speaker himself.

3. Exercise good taste: (1) Subordinate yourself and your speech in order to focus proper attention upon the speaker and his address. Any unnecessary discussion about yourself or your ideas on the subject helps defeat the purpose of your speech. Remember that you are not competing for attention with the main speaker. On the contrary, the more attention you steal, the poorer your introduction. (2) Do not embarrass the speaker by extravagant praise. Tell only enough of his exploits to establish him as a person of character and stature, and to stimulate audience anticipation. Do not compliment him so profusely that he will be unable to live up to expectations. On the other hand, be certain to do him justice. Indicate that there is much that you could say if time permitted. Avoid such unflattering remarks as: "I don't know very much about this man," or "Our speaker has been somewhat successful in business." The anticipation of hearing a personnel expert was diminished instead of increased for one audience because of this discouraging introduction: "The next speaker is a former school teacher who quit his job because he got tired of teaching. It seems like teachers and farmers are chronically dissatisfied. After he quit teaching he got a job in our personnel department. To be truthful, I don't know what he does. I talked to a couple of people in the personnel office this afternoon and asked them—and they didn't know either. However, let's hear a few words from him. O.K., Doctor _____, that's your cue." (3) Do not make the speaker's mission more difficult by calling attention to his speaking ability. A chairman once mentioned to Robert Ingersoll, one of the finest speakers in the history of American public address, that he intended to introduce him as the world's greatest orator. Ingersoll is said to have exploded that he would rather be presented as an atheist than as an orator. He did not want the attention of the audience distracted from his message to his techniques of delivery. (4) Provided it is used in good taste, humor is unexcelled for producing an atmosphere of congeniality. It serves to put both the speaker and the audience at ease. But humor must fit the speaking situation, the speaker you are introducing, and his speech. It is always poor form to make a goat of the speaker or to belittle either his subject or the occasion. (5) Good taste demands that you avoid trite expressions such as: "Our speaker needs no introduction," "It is an honor and a privilege," "We are indeed fortunate to have with us," or "A person who is an outstanding pillar of society."

4. *Plan your comments in a climactic order:* With some variations, the following organization will fit any speech of introduction:

I. *Address the audience*
   (If the audience is unusually large or distinguished, if it has endured inclement weather to attend, if it is especially enthusiastic, etc., you might make an appropriate compliment. If suitable, you might make a brief reference to the occasion or purpose of the meeting.)
II. *Direct favorable attention toward the speaker*
   (Tell briefly and modestly of the background of the speaker which qualifies him to speak on the subject. Build a friendly feeling toward him and stimulate a desire to hear him speak.)
III. *Direct favorable attention toward the speaker's subject*
   (Mention briefly the significance and the appropriateness of the subject. Do not say too much because you might infringe upon the speaker's address. Attempt to arouse an interest in the subject so as to make the speaker's task less difficult.)
IV. *Announce the speaker by name*
   (Authorities recommend the withholding of the name of the speaker until the final sentences. With a slight increase in force and volume, make a formal presentation in some such phrase as: "It is with pleasure that I present to you, Dr. Edward B. Hopkins. Dr. Hopkins"; "I give you the honorable Robert L. Warner. Senator Warner"; or "Here he is, ladies and gentlemen—the greatest football coach in America—Paul Brown.")

5. *Speak sincerely and enthusiastically in the extemporaneous mode:* As in most other types of occasional speaking, avoid using notes in the speech of introduction. Also, since such speeches place a high premium upon spontaneity, verbatim memorization should seldom be used. If you use the organizational pattern suggested in the preceding paragraphs, and if you rehearse adequately, you will have little difficulty remembering what you wish to say. Your delivery should be adapted to the dignity or informality of the occasion. Use adequate volume and projection to insure easy audibility for all. Address the audience rather than the speaker. Reduce your rate of utterance somewhat from that of ordinary speaking. Enunciate clearly, especially when announcing the speaker's name and his topic. Let your manner indicate that *you* are awaiting the speech with pleasant anticipation.

B. The speech of presentation. Many organizations utilize public observances to present awards, gifts, and memorials. Industrial concerns award diamond stick-pins to employees with thirty years of service; Boy Scout troops give waterproof match boxes to the boys who sell the most tickets to the annual jamboree; universities distribute scholarships on honor days and bestow honorary degrees at commencement programs to prominent citizens; sports writers present trophies to outstanding athletes; civic groups present statues to the community. At each such event appropriate speeches must accompany the awarding of the gift. Such presentations should be well suited to the audience, the donor, the purpose of the meeting, the recipient of the gift, the gift itself, and to you as the speaker. Your talk should be brief, usually under five minutes. Carefully prepare your speech to accomplish the following points.

I. *Tell why the presentation is being made*
(Direct attention to the achievements, services, or qualities of the recipient which warrant the presentation. If a contest was held to determine the winner, such as a popularity poll or a beauty contest, explain the nature of the contest briefly. In the case of a memorial, tell something of the character and qualities of the person or group of persons being honored. Praise should always be genuine and sincere, without straining for effect. If the recipient has been selected to accept a gift as a symbol for a group, praise the ideals, purposes, or services of the group as well as of the donee.)

II. *Express the satisfaction felt by the donor in making the presentation*
(Identify the donor, if different from the group in attendance. Express the sincere sentiments with which the gift is presented. Let the

recipient realize that the donor considers it an honor to be able to offer the present. If the gift has intrinsic merits, it might be advisable to point them out. However, you should indicate that the gift is basically a symbol of the esteem in which the donor regards the recipient.)

III. *Make the actual presentation*

(Save the actual presentation until the last. Up to this point you have been speaking to the audience, but now turn toward the donee and address him directly. With sufficient volume for all to hear make a formal presentation in some such way as the following: "It is with a deep sense of appreciation that the Alpha chapter of Phi Kappa Tau presents to you this beautiful silver vase. We shall never forget your loyal, devoted service as our housemother.")

C. The speech of acceptance. When a person receives a gift in a public presentation, he is expected to express appropriately his appreciation. Such speeches are called those of acceptance. They follow and grow out of addresses of presentation. The acceptance speech must be well adapted not only to the audience, occasion, donor of the gift (if different from the audience), and the gift, but also *to the preceding speech of presentation*. The subject matter as well as the mood is suggested, if not determined, by the speech of presentation. If the manner of the presenting speaker has been solemn and dignified, your remarks in acceptance must be likewise sober. However, if the presenter has been especially congenial, you must respond in an appropriate vein. The length of such a speech varies somewhat in different circumstances, but is usually short. Whereas a mere "thank you" is sufficient in some cases, a twenty-minute address might be expected from the speaker who accepts a monument for a community. It is difficult to give advice on the preparation of the speech of acceptance; much of such a talk is necessarily an impromptu adaptation to the total speaking situation. However, by using the following sequence you will be able to plan, at least, tentatively what you are going to say.

I. *Express appreciation for the gift*

(Express genuine sentiment to indicate that you appreciate the gift for its own value and because it serves as a symbol of the group's regard. Refer specifically to the gift. Be simple and direct, without straining for effect.)

II. *Minimize your own services and magnify the services of your associates*

(Be modest but not self-depreciating. Pay sincere tribute to those who have helped you achieve your success. For example, a half-back receiving a trophy as the conference leader in total yardage gained might state that he never forgot that he had ten men blocking for him and that most of his long gains were the result of key blocks by teammates. He might even relate the stories told of Knute Rockne, who once became disturbed by the egocentric attitude of his famous backfield of the Four Horsemen. Wishing to teach his ball carriers a lesson, Rockne asked his varsity to vote on the question: "Which is more important to a football team, a backfield or a line?" The result was, of course, 7 to 4, with the linemen, called by sports writers the "seven blocks of granite," all voting against the backfield. To deflate the ego of his Four Horsemen still further, Rockne let the regular linemen warm the bench while a line composed of substitutes blocked for the Horsemen. After consistently failing to gain, the backfield learned the lesson that a ball carrier is only as effective as his line permits him to be.)

III. *Pay tribute to the donor*
(Express your recognition of the merits of the group awarding the gift. As an example, if a representative of a civic committee for traffic safety has awarded you a loving cup at a public dinner for being the safest driver in Trenton, you should in your acceptance direct deserved attention to the outstanding work of the committee. Usually such people serve faithfully as a civic duty, with little or no compensation. Briefly indicate how much you and other citizens appreciate their efforts to reduce the maimings and fatalities due to accidents.)

IV. *Conclude by accepting the gift*
(You may tie your speech together and attain a climax by saving a formal acceptance of the gift until the close of your talk. During your comments of formal acceptance you should probably look at the gift, turn toward it, pick it up, or in some way give recognition of its presence. A professor who had completed a series of lectures to the graduate students of another university was presented with an expensive set of books. The formal acceptance portion of his speech went something like this: "Let me thank you again for solving most of my recreational problems for the next few months. This beautiful two-volume set of Davidson's *Life In America* will be my evening companion for weeks to come. Every time I pull a volume out of its box, I will remember this and many other expressions of your kindness during my week's sojourn with you.")

D. The speech of welcome. The reception of a distinguished visitor, group, or convention at a public occasion necessitates an appropriate address of welcome. The speech of welcome must extend a sincere greeting which makes the recipient feel appreciated and at ease. Such speeches should be short, well-planned, cordial, gracious, and in good taste. Unlike the speech of introduction which serves to present *a guest speaker and his speech,* the speech of welcome is concerned only with welcoming a *newcomer* to the organization or to the community. The occasion for the speech of welcome is usually more dignified and serious than for the speech of introduction. Frequently, as in welcoming returned veterans, the occasion may have emotional overtones. Because of the wide variety of possible types of speaking situations, only general suggestions can be offered for the organization of such a speech. However, with some alterations the following sequence should be satisfactory for most circumstances.

I. *Identify the group extending the welcome and the recipient of the welcome*
   (Here are some sample opening sentences: "The city of Rochester is honored to welcome home its Medal of Honor winner and native son, Thomas Higgins." "The University of Houston is pleased to welcome to this campus the eminent physicist, Dr. John Sievers." "This evening the Baptist Training Union has the unusual opportunity of experiencing the fellowship of our state director, Bess Frockton.")

II. *Make complimentary remarks about the individual or group you are welcoming*
   (Mention some of the outstanding accomplishments or services rendered by the visitor(s). If you are welcoming a convention, call attention to the significance of the meeting, and to the purpose, importance, and history of the group.)

III. *Explain the reason for the visit*
   (Tell why the guest(s) is (are) visiting the organization or community, i.e., for scientific investigation, relaxing at the beach, engaging in athletic competition, or visiting relatives. If you are welcoming a convention which has selected your locality for particular reasons, you might mention such reasons.)

IV. *Mention the mutual benefits which will occur through the association*
   (Sometimes it is fitting to direct attention to the contributions the

guest(s) will make to the welcoming organization, or to society at large. Perhaps your community or welcoming organization will be able to aid the recipient in various ways. For instance, when welcoming a new member into a fraternal organization you might show briefly the mutual benefits of this new association.)

V. *Conclude by specifically extending the welcome*
(Only one or two sentences are needed to sum up the gist of the entire speech in a congenial expression of appreciation at being able to extend the welcome. For instance, a representative of the Los Angeles Chamber of Commerce might close a welcome to a visiting dignitary in this way: "And so, Mr. Ambassador, the city of Los Angeles and the entire State of California extend a most cordial welcome. We hope that you will stay with us for many weeks, and that the California sun, beach, and surf will offer you relaxation and pleasure."

E. The speech of response to a welcome. Usually some remarks of appreciation must follow a speech of welcome. If a convention is being welcomed to a community, some representative of the group will make an appropriate response. If an individual is so honored, he will be expected to say a few words. Such a speech of response should be brief and well adapted to the speaking situation and to the preceding speech of welcome. Like the speech accepting a gift, the speech of response must of necessity be largely impromptu. However, if you know you will be called upon to make such a speech, you can tentatively plan your remarks under the following main heads.

I. *Identify for whom and to whom you are speaking*
(If responding to a speech of welcome as the representative of an organization or convention, you should mention the group by name. Recognize immediately the source which has accorded you the honor. A Rotarian visiting a lunch meeting of that organization in another state might begin his remarks of response in this way: "I appreciate this opportunity to visit the Denver Rotary Club. . . .")

II. *Express genuine appreciation for being so honored*
(Sometimes, as the Rotarian did in the above paragraph, a simple statement of appreciation is sufficient. However, if a signal honor has been accorded, it might be well to explain why you value the courtesy. A veteran just returned from Korea might, upon being welcomed by a public reception, explain his gratitude for such a demonstration.)

III. *Make complimentary remarks about the group or agency extending the welcome*

(For instance, if you are the spokesman for a convention being welcomed to a city, refer briefly to the cultural, scenic, industrial, or historical significance of the community. If a particular organization has welcomed you as a guest, you might indicate that you are aware of the reputation, exploits, or services of the organization. Be gracious, tactful, and sincere.)

IV. *Mention that you are looking forward to pleasant experiences*

(If you or the group you represent are to be the guests of a community for a period, you could say that you are looking forward to an enjoyable and enriching visit. If you are a guest at a meeting, you might express an expectation of enjoying the proceedings.)

F. The speech of farewell. When a person leaves the employ of a company, moves to another locality, or goes into retirement, he may wish to express publicly his regrets about leaving. Frequently, such speeches take place at farewell dinners or parties, and are preceded by the awarding of a "going-away" present. In such a case, the speaker must thank the group for the gift, in addition to saying goodbye. The typical valedictory speech should cover the following points:

I. *Express genuine regrets about leaving*

(Tell why you are reluctant to leave. Say that you have enjoyed your work, and tell why. Dwell briefly on your pleasant associations with the members of the group. Reminisce over previous happy experiences. Indicate that you will take with you many happy memories. Plan this heading carefully, to avoid aimless rambling about past happenings.)

II. *Indicate that you hold the group in high esteem*

(Express genuine regard for the merit and quality of the group. Reveal that you have profited much from the association.)

III. *Predict future cordial relations*

(Express the hope that although you are leaving, you will still experience the friendship of the group and will enjoy many future contacts. If you are moving to another locality, tell your listeners that you anticipate seeing them at, let us say, the national sales convention, or invite them to call upon you in case they visit your new community. If you are planning a tour of Europe before retiring to Florida, you might promise to send post cards to the members of the group and, upon your return, to tell them of your experiences.)

IV. *Conclude by wishing the group farewell*

(Make this step short. Avoid dragging out a final expression of good-bye. If you can think of nothing else to say, you can rely on the often-used: "Good-bye and God bless you.")

SUMMARY

The successful use of the information contained in Chapter 15 depends upon a proper application of the fundamental principles discussed in the first thirteen chapters. This chapter has presented particular factors to be considered in presenting speeches of special types.

EXERCISES AND ASSIGNMENTS

1. Write a manuscript speech utilizing the advice given in this chapter. Read it to the class. Hand in the manuscript to your instructor for comments and criticism.

2. Deliver a good-will speech concerning your university to a high-school assembly program or to some other off-campus meeting. Report your experiences to the class.

3. Give an impromptu talk upon a topic selected for you by some member of the class or by the instructor. After studying this chapter, you should be able to think on your feet more effectively than previously, as in performing exercise 6, page 225.

4. Give an entertaining after-dinner speech based on the current political scene, international diplomacy, life in a college dormitory, scenes in the coffee shop, peculiar people, and so forth. If possible, this set of speeches by you and your classmates should be given in the college cafeteria or in some eating establishment off campus.

5. During the final week of the semester give a brief speech of farewell to the class.

6. Bring a visitor to class, introduce him, and welcome him to the group.

7. In the next series of speeches, introduce another member of the class and his speech.

8. In a short talk present an imaginary award to a classmate.

9. (In conjunction with exercise 8): Accept appropriately an imaginary award presented to you by a member of the class.

CHAPTER 16

Adapting a Speech for Radio and Television

If you are active in the affairs of your school or community, probably you will be asked from time to time to broadcast your ideas to the radio and television audience. Opportunities for the layman to make use of these media of mass communication have increased markedly in the past few years. The number of radio stations in the United States has doubled since 1945. Many of the new stations are low-powered, independent enterprises aimed at limited local audiences. Without network affiliation, these stations are making considerable use of local talent and are striving to align themselves as closely as possible with the interests of the immediate community. As a result, high school, college, and community programs featuring amateur personnel are finding their way into radio program schedules in larger numbers than in years past, when radio outlets were limited to a relatively few powerful stations committed mostly to network shows. Although the newcomer, television, has grown more rapidly than did radio in its early days, opportunities for the nonprofessional to appear on the TV screen have not been extensive. The "freeze" on the licensing and construction of new stations, not lifted until mid-year of 1952, prevented the unfettered expansion of television in early years. The construction of many new stations has now provided nation-wide coverage and makes possible increasing opportunity for speakers to reach the viewing audience.

With radio blanketing the nation, and with the rapidly growing television industry now assuming imposing size and immeasurable influence, today's speaker must be prepared to use these media when the opportunity or obligation to do so arises. In this chapter, we shall note the significant differences between speaking to the face-to-face audience and addressing the microphone or the TV camera.

326

Although these differences necessitate certain adaptations, it should be stressed that the basic procedures for effective speech preparation and delivery (Chapters 1–13) are essentially applicable to radio and television speaking.

Your purposes in speaking to the air audience will be the same as in any of the face-to-face situations noted in preceding chapters. Whether facing a live audience, a microphone, or a camera, speakers seek to inform, persuade, or entertain their listeners; they discuss and debate, introduce other speakers, pay tribute, and say farewell; they must choose subjects, find materials, organize and support ideas, and deliver them effectively. Knowledge of certain techniques and adaptations discussed in this chapter will enable you to make the best use of the fundamentals of speech preparation and delivery in radio and television speaking. We disavow any attempt to present a discussion of all the varying types of broadcast [1] programs in which speech is used. If you are interested in a specialized study of announcing, newscasting, audience participation shows, dramatic productions, sports shows or other types of radio and television programs, we advise you to consult one or more of the many books now available which treat these subjects at length.

UNDERSTANDING THE RADIO AND TELEVISION AUDIENCE

In keeping with our consistent emphasis on the audience as the focal point in speech preparation and delivery, we turn now to a discussion of the air audience as the first step in understanding the adaptations which should be made in content and delivery. Keep in mind these four distinguishing characteristics of the air audience in preparing and delivering a broadcast speech: (1) the broadcast audience is potentially universal, and almost certain to be more heterogeneous than a face-to-face audience; (2) the radio and TV audience is composed of many small, intimate groups or single individuals; (3) no circular response is possible with the air audience; (4) the broadcast audience is more difficult to hold.

A. The broadcast audience is potentially universal, and almost certain to be more heterogeneous than a face-to-face audience. It is obvious that the ticket to an air performance is access to a re-

---

[1] The term "broadcast" is used in this chapter to refer to either radio or television transmission or both.

ceiver located within transmitting range of a station. Thus, an audience may include individuals of various races, creeds, political beliefs, ages, occupations, and intellectual capacities. Their attitudes toward you and your subject may range from the strongly favorable to the strongly opposed. Members of a face-to-face audience, on the other hand, are likely to have more in common. Attending a speech requires more effort than tuning in a radio or TV receiver; in the former case, you must go to the speaker, while the broadcast speaker obligingly comes to you. Attending a speech involves travel time, possibly unpleasant weather, and occasionally some expense. In short, the added inconvenience of hearing a regular speech limits the audience, for the most part, to those strongly motivated through interest or duty to appear. Moreover, a "live" speech is often restricted to members of an organizational group and their guests. These factors tend to provide considerable audience homogeneity.

The potential universality of an air audience is, however, limited by *interest* and *opportunity*. Although anyone within range may sample your speech, only those sufficiently interested in you and/or your topic will linger until the end. Your audience will also be limited by the availability of listeners or viewers. During morning and afternoon hours, children are in school and men are at work, with the result that the audience is composed predominantly of housewives and shut-ins. Children clamor for their favorite programs in late afternoons and early evenings. The man of the house is likely to be in the audience only during evening hours on work days, although he is more generally available on weekends. Viewers of television are likely to diminish in numbers during the bustling activity of early mornings and at meal times; radio, however, holds up well during these periods. Morning and evening rush hours and pleasant Sunday afternoons find millions of listeners using car radios. Another limitation on the universality of the audience is that some stations obviously point toward specialized groups. Small urban stations may direct many programs to nationality groups; rural stations cater to farmers' interests; some broadcasters woo music lovers with a steady diet of classical records; and college-owned outlets specialize in educational offerings.

In preparing the broadcast speech it is imperative to keep in mind that for a potentially universal audience, appeals should be as universal as possible. On many occasions, however, your talk will be directed to a particular segment of your potential listeners and viewers.

B. The radio and TV audience is composed of many small, intimate groups and single individuals. When the President talks to 110,-000,000 or more people via radio and TV, he is actually entering the privacy of approximately 25,000,000 living rooms, automobiles, club rooms, and the like. Listeners and viewers in small groups are sufficiently influenced by their surroundings to expect a warm, intimate, informal, and conversational approach by the speaker; they will tolerate excessively vigorous projection and the more formal, oratorical approach only if they know it is a broadcast of a speech made before a face-to-face audience.

C. No circular response is possible with the air audience. The speaker who uses these two media has no way of discovering during his speech what response he is evoking from his audience. The visible audience responds to the speaker in many noticeable ways: by laughter, riveted attention, tears, fidgeting, nods of approval, "poker-faced" boredom, and falling asleep. If the response is generally favorable, the speaker is stimulated and encouraged by his apparent success; if it is unfavorable, he may make adjustments in subject matter and emphasis or perhaps change his manner of delivery. While the air audience responds in similar fashion, the speaker has no way of knowing its response and thus cannot adjust. Ignorant of the reactions of his listeners and unable to rely upon crowd psychology, the speaker finds it difficult to reach emotional climaxes. Later in this chapter we will discuss methods of compensating for a lack of circular response in broadcast speaking.

D. The broadcast audience is more difficult to hold. Members of an actual audience are reluctant to distract a speaker and audience by leaving while a speech is in progress. Moreover, the audience is sometimes a captive group forced to stay until the meeting is over. If attendance is not required, it is usually prompted by interest in the speech, the speaker, or the occasion, and possibly all three. The radio and TV listener, however, usually is not required to listen and is subject to no embarrassment if, by turning his dial, he abandons a speaker in the middle of his speech. Remember, also, that other programs are ever competing for his attention. You may be in competition with a lavish variety show produced on television at a cost of $175,000 weekly, a popular radio network comedian, or a telecast of an intersectional football game. If you succeed in stemming your listener's temptation to try another program, other distractions may make his attention difficult to retain. Crying babies, the noisy antics of young children, ringing telephones, buzzing doorbells, and the conversation of companions bid strongly for his attention. Such competitive factors make it imperative that the broadcast speech contain unusually high interest values.

In the light of this discussion of the nature of the air audience, we shall proceed to those adaptations in preparation and delivery which will enhance the effectiveness of the broadcast speech.

PREPARING THE RADIO AND TELEVISION SPEECH

The principles and techniques of speech preparation previously discussed (Chapters 2–8) apply for the most part to the broadcast speech. Preparation will necessarily include choosing a subject, finding materials, organizing and supporting main points, and devising an Introduction and a Conclusion. Certain principles, however, need to be emphasized in adapting preparation to the mass media. Although essential to effective public speaking, these principles are unusually important to the radio and TV speaker.

A. Content and organization.   Keep these four suggestions in mind when selecting and arranging material to be broadcast.

1. *Ideas and supporting material should be universal in appeal, easy to follow, and concrete.*   Although you may be primarily interested in reaching a particular group, remember that your audience may include many kinds of people. Illustrations, explanations, analogies, and other supporting material should be varied, "down to earth," and related to the experiences and activities frequently encountered by most persons. As in public speaking, ideas should be concrete rather than abstract; your audience will abandon you rather than attempt to follow the byways of complicated reasoning and vague theorizing.

2. *Use a simple pattern of organization.*   For most broadcast speeches, choose a simple Time, Topical, or Problem-Solution Pattern of speech organization (Chapter 5). Simplicity and clarity in organization are extremely important because the broadcast audience has no chance to ask questions and opportunity for clarification is limited. Regardless of the organizational pattern used, restricted time makes it wise to avoid tangents and overamplification of minor points.

3. *Emphasize factors of attention.* The elusiveness of the air audience requires that special consideration be given such attention factors as proximity, vivid concreteness, significance, variety, and humor to keep the listener until the final word is spoken (Chapter 6, Part III).

4. *Pay close attention to timing.* Unlike a majority of events, radio and television programs begin and end on time. If your speech is more than fifteen seconds too long, you may be cut off the air. Keep in mind, also, that a fifteen-minute segment of broadcast time will not permit you to talk the full fifteen minutes. The opening and closing, station identification, and the half-minute to full-minute break between programs will consume two or three minutes. This means you can speak no more than twelve or thirteen minutes on a fifteen-minute program. These limiting factors necessitate the most careful kind of preparation, including a degree of flexibility which will allow adding or omitting material as needs arise, particularly near the conclusion.

B. **Language.** Language should be simple and concrete, yet alive and colorful. Avoid pedantic and hackneyed expressions. Use provincialisms sparingly, particularly on a network broadcast, and employ slang with care. Sentence structure should be varied, but complicated periodic structures should be used only rarely. Simple sentences, reasonably short, should predominate. Move from one idea to the next with informal, varied, and clear transitions. Above all, be certain that your speech sounds like a speech and not like an essay (Chapter 12).

C. **Preparing manuscripts and outlines.** Since the majority of radio speeches are read from manuscript, we suggest reviewing the discussion of the manuscript speech in Chapter 15. In addition, consider the following suggestions. Time limits are strictly enforced; therefore, write and rewrite until every word counts. Allow for the possibility that because of nervous tension you may speak more rapidly than in rehearsal. Planned flexibility may be achieved by bracketing an optional section near the end, which can be retained or deleted as time permits. Obviously, the bracketed material should not be crucial to your speech.

If you wish, make use of markings to aid in emphasis, phrasing, and breathing. Since you will not be concerned with eye contact in the radio speech, unless in the presence of an actual audience, you will be free to give full attention to your manuscript. It should be typewritten, not handwritten, to insure legibility. If your eyes demand slightly larger print, type exclusively in capital letters. Instead of expensive bond paper and onion-skin, both of which tend to crackle noisily when picked up by the mike, use cheaper, pulp-like paper, which is relatively quiet when handled.

If your manuscript speech is to be televised, two additional suggestions should be heeded in your preparation. Visual aids, while helpful in any speaking situation in clarifying ideas and in securing and holding attention (Chapter 6), are particularly effective in television, where close-up shots reveal minute details. For example, although useless in an actual audience situation, words in a newspaper clipping held in the speaker's hand are clearly readable in a close-up shot on all but the smallest TV screens. Visual aids also relieve the probable monotony of looking at the speaker for extended periods. In fact, an entire speech may be built around a succession of visual aids. The following rules should be used when preparing visual material for TV: (1) Since a television screen has an aspect ratio of four units wide to three units high, visual aids with a vertical emphasis (a newspaper page, for example) are difficult to frame in the camera without loss of detail. Visual materials should approximate the 4–3 ratio, e.g., twelve inches wide by nine inches high, sixteen inches wide by twelve inches high, and so on. (2) Because of glare, do not use white cardboard, glazed paper, or glossy prints. Gray cardboard with a dull finish and black lettering should be used in preparing charts, graphs, tables, and the like. Pictures and printed copy from newspapers or magazines should be mounted on gray cardboard mats.

A second suggestion for preparing the TV manuscript speech is to become so familiar with the speech that you can deliver most of it without reading. Eye contact and personality are of such great importance, particularly in close-up shots, that it is desirable for the speaker to minimize dependence upon his manuscript. An occasional glance at your paper should suffice, thus permitting maximum visual communication. Of course, while the camera is trained upon a visual aid rather than upon you, you may read your manuscript. The Teleprompter, a mechanical device from which a televised speech may be read, relieves the speaker of handling his manuscript and allows him to look consistently in the general direction of his audience. Used by speakers at the political conventions in 1952, this machine is also occasionally in evidence at other important speaking events. Because of the expense involved, it is not widely used at this time.

From the manuscript speech, we turn to a discussion of the extemporaneous speech delivered from an outline. This method of preparation and delivery is not often used in radio. Most extemporizing on radio is done in discussion, debate, and interview programs. When a radio speech is to be extemporized (since many stations require a manuscript, be sure to get permission to extemporize), use in your preparation the advice on outlining presented in Chapter 4. Rehearse sufficiently to insure that you will not be hesitant in finding words, and resist the temptation to add additional material which may occur to you in the course of delivering the speech. A seasoned speaker may safely do this, knowing that he will be forced to cut or telescope some material near the end, but the novice should stick closely to his outline. A helpful device in timing is to record in the margin of the outline at various intervals the time which should have elapsed at a given point. An occasional glance at the studio clock will indicate whether you are on schedule. If you are off, make *gradual* changes in rate; do not speed up or slow down suddenly.

The extemporized speech is gaining favor in television, because it permits greater freedom of movement and improved visual personality, particularly in the matter of eye contact. Unusual care must be taken in planning for camera shots of the visual aids. Cameras are trained on visual materials on verbal cue from the speaker, in the absence of a manuscript in the control room. These verbal cues are usually memorized or read. The following outline was prepared and used by Warren A. Guthrie, a television news reporter who has used the extemporaneous mode of delivery with notable success.

YOUR SOHIO REPORTER [2]

STATE TV NETWORK (OHIO)
ORIGINATING FROM
WXEL, CLEVELAND, OHIO
DAILY, 11:00–11:10 P.M.
MARCH 9, 1953

Opening—(sound film)   (10 seconds)
Communism and Stalin still big story tonight.
    Body of Soviet leader laid to rest in Moscow.
    Silence and top-level Soviet speeches the accompaniment—
    generally conciliatory in tone.
Cue film→ "And perhaps one of the significant comments was made here
    in the U. S. by Secy. of State John Foster Dulles. . . ."
    Top Soviet brass at funeral—special place for Premier Chou
    En-Lai of Red China—next to Malenkov.
Chart—→ *Further major development in China*—Panyushkin back to
    Russia; Deputy Foreign Minister Kusnetsov to replace;
    Vishinsky home; Gromyko here.
    On the U. S. political scene—
    Hawaiian statehood in snarl—Southern Senators oppose; GOP
    still forecasts approval.
    Ike holds another bi-partisan luncheon—12 GOPs, 7 Demos.
Cue film→ "Ike continues conferences with Anthony Eden, who speaks
    briefly and non-informatively. . . ."
    In UN, secret sessions to pick Trygvie Lie's successor—Demo. block
    wants Lester Pearson of Canada.
    Debate, also, on Lie's loyalty program.
Chart—→ *In U. S., Chairman Velde* of UnAm. Act. Com. says group
    may probe churches; Velde under attack from prominent
    churchmen.
    Supreme Court to review Bridges perjury and conspiracy case;
    upholds some feather-bedding and gambling tax stamp law.
Cue film→ "Taft met today with Ike, and still hopes for amendments in
    T-H law. . . ."
    Patronage book out in Wash.—Vol. I notes 65,000 jobs for
    deserving GOPers.
    In Korea—
    No silence—barrage for Joe's funeral.
    Fighting stepped up in improved weather.

  [2] By permission of Mr. Guthrie.

US brings pressure to stop attacks by Chinese Nationalists on Burmese army.

Cue film→"Italians get NATO tanks. . . ."

Briefs—

Tito sneaks to England under heavy escort.

Jordan to get 3 million in British economic aid—Israel to object.

Atom-plant road argument in white-heat in Columbus.

"Plant Ohio" program forecasts 25 million new trees for Ohio in 1953.

Still flips—   (total of approximately 1½ minutes)

1. This is what millions of Russians and others have seen since last Friday—the body of Joseph Stalin, lying in state in an open casket.

2. And these are the top four men of Russia, watching as the late dictator is laid to rest. Left to right: Foreign Minister Molotov, War Minister Bulganin, Secret Police Chief Beria, and Premier Malenkov.

3. In contrast was this gathering of four persons at the White House for tea. Left to right: Mrs. Wellington Koo, Mrs. Eisenhower, Madame Chiang Kai-shek, and President Eisenhower.

4. Fifteen million dollars in damage and thirteen injured firemen—that was the toll thus far taken by a fire which burned the heart out of the main dock area in Wilmington, N. Car., and which raged for hours out of control.

5. A Daytonian, Harry N. Routzohn, was sworn in as Solicitor of Labor in Washington. An interested observer was Matthew Durkin, Secretary of Labor.

6. Ohio Congressmen and a brass band greeted George Murphy as he galloped into Washington, completing his ride begun last Tuesday at Chillicothe, which re-enacted a similar trip made 150 years ago to present Ohio's petition for admission to the Union.

Commercial—(live or sound film)   (45 seconds to 1 minute)

Chart→*Weather—*   (10 to 30 seconds)

*Closing—*sound film)   (10 seconds)

Explanatory Notes on the Outline

1. The preceding outline, which is representative of those used nightly in the newscast sponsored by Standard Oil of Ohio, was prepared in the course of a two-hour period preceding the broadcast. After studying news releases, available film clips, and "still" pictures, Mr. Guthrie

chooses his news stories and decides which may be accompanied by visual charts, graphs, caricatures, and other drawings. An artist then prepares appropriate visual aids. Meanwhile, the reporter determines the most effective sequence of stories and constructs his outline. Two camera rehearsals complete the preparation.

2. A total of six or seven different charts, graphs, drawings, and films is used, in addition to the six or seven "still" pictures near the end of the program. The first visual aid is introduced within the first thirty seconds of the program. From that point until the end of the program, no more than 1½ minutes are allowed to elapse without the use of new visual material. Obviously, the producers of this program are convinced of the importance of an abundance of visual material in television speaking.

3. Each important story or group of related stories is begun in the outline with a key word or series of words underlined to catch the speaker's eye. While a single glance at these words usually is sufficient to permit the speaker to extemporize the story without further reference to the outline, additional key words and phrases may be included in the event the speaker needs them.

4. The appearance of the word "chart" in the left margin of the outline reminds the speaker that a statistical table, graph, line drawing, or caricature is to be used in conjunction with the story. These visual aids are located on the wall in an appropriate frame. The reporter leaves his desk and delivers his story from a point at one side of the chart, pointing to the chart when necessary. Cameras may be trained on the visual aid in close-up.

5. Film cues are usually delivered in the exact words appearing on the outline to allow the operator to begin the film at the moment a key word is spoken. To remind the speaker that these cues should be delivered verbatim, they are enclosed in quotation marks.

6. "Still flips" refers to a series of photographs. Each remains on the screen during the delivery of the commentary appearing in the outline. Since the speaker is not "on camera" in this series, he may read rather than extemporize the commentary. For that reason, a complete text is included instead of notes.

7. The commercial consists of either a sound film or a commentary accompanied by visual material and delivered by the speaker.

8. The weather story serves as the reporter's "cushion." It is telescoped or expanded to fit the time remaining.

9. The newscast differs in some respects from the types of speeches discussed in this book, particularly in organization. Newscasts are organized as a succession of news stories, arranged according to im-

portance and interest; they are usually not built around a central theme, or main point, as is the typical speech. The preceding outline, however, illustrates the technique used in preparing an outline and providing for visual aids for extemporized television speaking.

Whether spoken from manuscript or outline, a radio or TV speech should be rehearsed until one is thoroughly familiar with the ideas and supporting materials. Give special attention to pronunciation, and check articulation for clarity and distinctness. If possible, make a recording and listen critically to the playback. You may wish to rehearse your TV speech before a mirror. In addition, ask a competent critic to check for distracting mannerisms, and then practice to eliminate them.

DELIVERING THE RADIO SPEECH

Shortly before the actual broadcast, you will probably be asked to do a brief audition on the mike. This usually consists of speaking for a few moments into the mike while the control operator checks your volume and your position and distance in relation to the mike. If he suggests that you speak louder or move closer to the mike, be certain to preserve that adjustment throughout the broadcast. In a larger station with greater facilities, you may be assigned a studio and a producer for rehearsal. If possible, rehearse the entire speech. It will give you an opportunity to check your timing and to profit from the professional advice of the producer.

An important delivery adjustment in radio involves the use of the microphone. The extreme sensitivity of the microphone means a number of things to the speaker.

First, avoid sudden unplanned changes in volume. The control operator can compensate for a shout if he knows it is coming. Otherwise, the overload may cause an equipment failure which conceivably may put you off the air. Move your head back from the mike or turn it slightly to one side prior to a sudden increase in volume.

Second, avoid swaying back and forth or from side to side; such action will result in noticeable variations in volume and quality. Since doubling one's distance from the mike decreases volume by four times, it is obvious that a normal voice pickup is possible only if distance is kept fairly constant.

Third, avoid extraneous noise. The sensitive mike picks up and amplifies drumming finger tips, smacking lips, heavy breathing, rustling papers, shuffling feet, an accidental bumping of the mike, and so forth.

Delivery also must take into account the absence of the visual code. In an earlier chapter we noted the importance of movement, facial expression, posture, and gesture in the effective communication of meaning. With these ruled out in radio speaking, your voice must carry the entire load. Emphasis, stress, pause, phrasing, pitch, inflection, quality, and other voice characteristics must be used to best advantage if one's voice is to compensate for the lack of visual stimuli. While these attributes of voice should be developed prior to a radio appearance, certain suggestions should aid you in delivering a radio speech. Keep in mind that it is unwise to project excessively in the manner of the agitated old-time orator. Your audience will expect you to be relaxed, intimate, and somewhat subdued in approach, though not dull. They want you to sound like an animated conversationalist sitting on the other side of the room. Relaxed, conversational voice production also will aid in placing your average pitch in the lower register. Although gestures and facial expression will not reach your listeners, do not hesitate to use them, if you wish. Often their use aids the voice in getting across meaning.

If an audience is present during your radio talk, as is the case with "Town Meeting of the Air" and similar programs, delivery should be like that used in any actual audience situation, except that you must maintain a fairly consistent position in relation to the microphone. When a radio speech is directed primarily at an actual audience, radio listeners do not expect an intimate, subdued delivery, and seem content to be "overhearing" a live audience speaking situation.

We have discussed the importance of exact timing in preparation. While delivering your radio speech, be aware of the constant passing of time. Do not let yourself be carried away by the speech to the extent that you neglect to check the time during convenient pauses, either by looking at the studio clock or at the producer, who will give you time signals and will also communicate by prearranged signals other pertinent information about the progress of your talk.

A word might be said at this point about stage fright. To some speakers, microphones and insulated studios are frightening. While such fear is usually alleviated by time and experience, the beginner should try to ignore the microphone, except for the physical and vocal adjustments previously mentioned, and think of his audience. Sometimes conjuring up a vision of a friend or acquaintance and imagining you are speaking to him will help. Do not be upset if your voice sounds weak or hollow to you; the cause is the construction of the studio, whose walls absorb rather than reflect much of the sound to prevent reverberation. Probably you will become accustomed to this acoustical phenomenon during the audition and rehearsal period.

DELIVERING THE TELEVISION SPEECH

In respect to the auditory aspects of communication, television speaking is much like radio speaking. In both cases, sound is picked up by microphone. While it is important in television, as in radio, to avoid sudden changes in volume without warning and to abstain from distracting noises, one difference in microphone adaptation should be noted. Whereas the radio microphone is nearly always in a stationary installation (occasionally a portable mike is used to permit movement about the studio), the sound pickup in television is usually made by a microphone attached to a boom, which can be moved around the studio during a program, if necessary. Adjustments in the directional pickup also can be made by the operator of the boom. This makes it possible for the microphone to follow the speaker and adjust to his movements. Therefore, the TV speaker does not have to be as particular about his distance and position in relation to the mike.

Obviously, the most important difference between radio and television speaking is that the latter makes use of the visual code. Whereas radio speaking lays the entire burden of communication upon the voice, television allows the use of movement, gesture, and facial expression to help make ideas meaningful, much as in addressing the face-to-face audience. However, one important difference should be noted. The face-to-face listener maintains a constant position and views you from a single angle and distance. The TV audience, on the other hand, may see you from a distance of forty feet directly in front, from an angle at a distance of twenty feet, a profile view at ten feet, or a close-up which brings you "near enough to touch." Furthermore, almost nothing escapes the searching eye of the close-up lens. The intimacy with which your audience sees you makes doubly important facial expression, movement, dress, and personality.

You will probably be asked to rehearse your television broadcast in much the same way that a radio speech is auditioned. The rehearsal period will serve to check camera locations, the placement of lights, your voice level, and any movements which you intend to make in the course of your speech. Find out how far you may move in any direction and still be in camera range, and where you are to sit; check on arrangements for the placement of visual aids and the cues to be used for training the camera on them. In order to make the most of your audition follow closely the suggestions and guidance of your producer. He is familiar with the equipment and facilities of his station; it is his job to see that your program goes off well.

Heed the following advice for adapting delivery to television. Because television production techniques constantly are changing and because facilities in different stations vary, suggestions cannot be specific. Your director and his technicians will help you in adapting to the particular situation at hand.

A. Make the most of the visual aspects of delivery. In television speaking, facial expression is one of the most important factors in the visual code. Make every effort to be expressive facially; avoid being a "dead pan." Let your face reflect the meaning and emotion you hope to convey. Since our faces do not always express ideas and feelings as well as they might, it may be helpful to practice in front of a mirror, as suggested in Chapter 10.

Movement and gesture will require certain adaptations. If your televised speech is being delivered to an actual audience, conduct yourself in the usual animated way described in the chapters on delivery, but do not overdo gesture and movement. When speaking exclusively to the TV audience, you will probably be seated at a desk or in an easy chair. Perhaps your only movement about the studio will consist of going to and from a blackboard or chart on the wall. Gestures may be plentiful, but not too great in sweep. Avoid sudden or rapid movements; if you are in a close-up, the camera cannot follow you effectively.

Mannerisms are particularly noticeable and distracting in the close-up picture. Make a special effort to avoid drumming on the table with your fingers, stroking your face or hair, and playing with buttons, necklaces, bracelets, or wrist watches. While such random activities may not always be noticeable in a distance shot, it is unwise to take chances; you will not know precisely at what moment the director will switch to a close-up picture.

Since eye contact is of paramount importance, it is better not to read a televised speech. Speaking from notes permits maximum contact with the audience. If your televised speech is presented to an actual audience, keep your eyes on them, for the most part; the TV audience expects to be secondary in such a situation. In the studio telecast, however, your audience is the camera; your eyes should be on it most of the time, unless you are talking to a guest, conducting an interview, or participating in a discussion (radio and television discussion is treated in Chapter 17). If more than one camera is in use, that which is "taking the picture" may be identified by a glowing red light on its face. By "following the red light" you will always keep eye contact with your viewers. Transfer of attention from one camera to another should not be sudden and jerky; when a camera light goes out, turn your head easily and slowly toward the newly activated camera and look at the lenses. If powerful floodlights and spotlights make it difficult to see the camera lenses, fix your eyes upon the red light, which is always easily seen.

Dress and appearance are of obvious concern to the TV speaker. Color television—in the experimental stage at this writing—necessitates carefully chosen color combinations. Black-and-white television reproduces only blacks, various shades of gray, and whites, thus making contrasts, patterns, and designs the major considerations in choosing apparel. Ties, suits, and dresses should present pleasing contrasts; pronounced plaids and extravagantly figured or striped designs, however, create a "busy" effect and are distracting. Because whites tend to reflect excessively under the brilliant lights, men should wear light blue or light gray shirts, and women should not choose white blouses or dresses. Tie clasps, metal bracelets, and other accessories which sparkle or shine should be omitted. Careful grooming is essential. Since the upper half of the body appears on the screen most frequently, particular attention should be given to hair, face, tie, shirt, blouse, suit jacket, and the like. Hands should be scrubbed and finger nails clean, since they may be under scrutiny in close-up shots when handling an object or pointing at a map or chart. Makeup may be necessary to soften facial lines, cover shiny noses and circles under the eyes, or to eliminate the unkempt look which heavily bearded men find difficult to avoid, even when freshly shaven. Although future technical developments may eliminate the necessity of observing some of these precautions, one should be aware of them at present.

B. Adjust vocal delivery. The suggestions given for vocal delivery in radio speaking also apply to television speaking. Some differences, however, should be noted. In TV visual aids, facial expression, movement, and gesture will communicate much of your meaning. Extended pauses, which leave "dead air" on radio, seem entirely natural at points in the TV speech, particularly when a chart or picture is the center of attention. As in radio, avoid "high pressure," bombastic, or overly emphatic delivery. Animation, vitality, and enthusiasm are important, but they can be accomplished without excessive projection.

SUMMARY

The modern speaker must be prepared to use the mass communication media. By presenting the opportunity to communicate with large audiences, radio and television enlarge greatly the potential influence of the spoken word. At the same time, these media present to the speaker a genuine challenge and a clear responsibility for their wise and effective use.

The basic principles of effective speaking are applicable to radio and television communication. With some adjustments, a good speech to an actual audience will be a good broadcast speech. The suggestions in this chapter should help the speaker to adapt more successfully his speech content and delivery to the requirements of radio and television.

EXERCISES AND ASSIGNMENTS

1. Carefully analyze a radio or television performance by some well-known speaker. Give particular attention to (1) his adaptations to his potential audience in terms of organizational pattern, forms of support (including visual aids, if on TV) and language; to (2) his vocal delivery if on radio, and his use of the visible code in delivery, if on TV. In class, compare your evaluation with those of others who listened.

2. Revise a manuscript which you had previously prepared for delivery to the class so that it will be appropriate for a five-minute television speech. Be certain that it is timed carefully enough to permit you to complete it in exactly four minutes and thirty seconds. Prepare one or more appropriate visual aids according to the rules in this chapter.

3. Prepare a speech of five minutes (four minutes and thirty seconds) for radio presentation. If your school has recording equipment, with a little ingenuity it is possible to deliver this speech at a microphone in an adjoining room for reproducton on a loudspeaker placed in the classroom. If your school has a radio studio, make use of these facilities for this assignment. Should neither an amplifying system nor radio studio be available, record this assignment for playback in the classroom. Instructor and class members should evaluate the speech as a radio presentation.

4. Prepare a five-minute (four minutes and thirty seconds) newscast for TV. Study your newspapers the day before the speech is to be given, choose from six to ten stories, and arrange them in the most effective order. Make an outline similar to the sample in this chapter and prepare two or three visual aids for use at appropriate points. Deliver the newscast extemporaneously. A clock or stop-watch should be available for timing your presentation during delivery. If your school has a television station or a studio equipped for television, attempt to make arrangements to use these facilities to lend reality to this assignment.

5. Either as individuals or as a group arrange to visit a local radio or television station when live programs are being produced. Pay close attention to the microphone and camera work, particularly as it is being planned in the audition and rehearsal periods. The next class meeting may be used for discussing what you have learned from the visit and how it may help you in future radio and television speaking performances.

6. Evaluate a series of regular appearances by a well-known "professional" radio or television network newscaster, commentator, or speaker, such as Lowell Thomas, Drew Pearson, John Cameron Swayze, Don Hollenbeck, Douglas Edwards, Fulton Lewis, Jr., or Bishop Fulton J. Sheen. What accounts for the continued success of such performers in the use of the mass media? Discuss in class.

CHAPTER 17

Group Discussion

Most of us like to "talk things over" before making an important decision or initiating a plan of action. Whether to take a job or enroll in college is a decision most of us arrive at with the help of our families. Whether to buy a new car or make the old one last another year may be the topic of an extended family conference. Discussion groups range in type and scope from the dormitory "bull session" on religion, politics, or the opposite sex to the deliberations of the Security Council of the United Nations. In the business world, executive meetings are held to pool information, weigh courses of action, and determine policy. Discussion is utilized for similar purposes by women's clubs, civic groups, churches, government agencies, the armed forces, and many other organizations.

Discussion is fundamental to the democratic process. In a government such as ours, decisions are rarely made without extended deliberation. Problems are analyzed, possible solutions are carefully weighed, the most advisable solution is adopted, and a program is set up for putting the plan into action. Unless a nation is to resort to government by decree and force, its people must acquire skill in the techniques of group discussion.

WHAT IS GROUP DISCUSSION?

Discussion is systematic, objective group deliberation for the purpose of investigating and solving problems. Let us examine this definition more closely. (1) *Discussion is systematic and objective.* Unlike informal conversation, discussion is systematic. Conversation usually exists without purpose, is governed almost entirely by interest, and proceeds without plan. Group discussion, however, is carefully planned and organized. Its goal is the investigation and solution of a particular problem. Group discussion also strives for objectivity. Participants attempt to keep biases and prejudices in check and to be receptive to new ideas and attitudes. There are always several sides to a question—a given participant may not have heard all of them. Snap judgments should be avoided and conclusions kept tentative until all evidence has been examined. Mental and vocal activities during group discussion should stem from intellectual rather than emotional behavior. (2) *Discussion is group deliberation.* Members of a discussion group have in common the desire to share ideas and information and to solve a problem. They are drawn together by the belief that the judgments of the group are more likely to be valid than those of any one individual. (3) *The purpose of group discussion is the investigation and solution of problems.* Individuals frequently share opinions and information in the group situation. If the group is to be more than a "bull session," however, its efforts must be directed specifically at the investigation and solution of a particular problem. This basic purpose also differentiates group deliberation from argumentative or persuasive speaking. The arguer or persuader has arrived at conclusions before speaking; his purpose is to influence others to accept his beliefs or to follow a prescribed course of action. The ideal discussant, however, possesses only tentative conclusions prior to the discussion; his task is to solve the problem, not to sell his ideas to others.

PREPARATION FOR GROUP DISCUSSION

Preparation for group discussion involves four tasks: (1) selecting the subject or problem, (2) phrasing the subject or problem, (3) finding materials, and (4) organizing the discussion.

A. Selecting the subject or problem. Conference groups are not always free to choose their subjects. Committees, boards, and study groups are presented with problems which must be resolved; rarely must they search for discussion subjects. Classroom groups, however, usually must select a problem. Make use of these criteria in selecting a subject: (1) *The subject should be worth discussing.* Personal problems of vital concern to the individual are often of only incidental interest to others. Pressing public questions are too numerous and time is too short to permit consideration of trivial or personal issues. The timeliness and importance of a potential subject may largely determine its value. (2) *The subject should be suited to* *your group.* Your topic should interest you and your colleagues. It should also fit the intelligence level, education, and experience of your group. (3) *The subject should present a problem.* Without a problem little excuse for discussion exists. Your subject should be at least two-sided, preferably multi-sided. If possible, avoid subjects presenting only two courses of action. Such topics virtually invite choosing sides and debating. The problem "Should the Taft-Hartley Labor Law be repealed?" invites debate "for" or "against." The question "What changes, if any, should be made in the Taft-Hartley Labor Law?" does not so readily provoke debate; furthermore, it offers the possibility of several courses of action. (4) *The subject usually should be capable of solution.* It is fruitless to discuss questions of preference or taste. Since they are incapable of proof, they tend to evoke only opinion and are insolvable. Also to be avoided are scientific questions beyond the grasp of the group or problems concerning which insufficient evidence is available. (5) *The subject should be a problem of fact, value, or policy.* Questions of fact deal with the existence of things or events, their sequence, or with the prediction of future facts. The question "Is Adolf Hitler dead?" is concerned with the existence of a fact. Future fact and prediction are involved in the problem "Will the Brooklyn Dodgers win the National League pennant?"

Problems of value appraise the goodness or badness, rightness or wrongness, effectiveness or ineffectiveness of persons, ideas, or things. An evaluation is clearly called for in the question "What does organized religion have to offer us?" A similar appraisal is required in the problem "Is our program to rehabilitate Western Europe a justifiable financial obligation?" Questions of value are similar to questions of fact, since both depend upon the discovery, classification, and evaluation of evidence in reaching a conclusion.

Probably most discussions deal with questions of policy. Such topics require the discussant to analyze the situation giving rise to the problem and, in light of this, to select the most tenable solution. Occasionally, the discussion group also may be charged with the problem of finding ways to put the solution into effect. Topics such as "How can we prevent further inflation?" "How can the parking problem in downtown Chicago be solved?" and "What revisions, if any, should be made in our college curriculum?" are questions of policy.

B. Phrasing the subject or problem. The following rules should guide you in putting your problem into words: (1) *A discussion problem should always be phrased as an impartial question.* A phrase such as "war and peace" cannot be discussed successfully. It does not raise a specific problem. The declarative sentence or proposition should not be used, because it invites debate. Also to be avoided are "loaded" questions which imply assumptions that may be unwarranted. The question "How can we improve the low moral standards of American youth?" implies, perhaps unjustly, that the moral standards of our youth are low. Omitting "low" from the question would lend impartiality. (2) *A discussion problem should be phrased to limit the field of inquiry.* Some committees attempt to cover in an hour's meeting a problem which, from the wording, would seem to require several days of deliberation. Phrase your problem so that it can be treated adequately in the time at your disposal. The problem "How can we achieve lasting peace?" can scarcely receive more than a sketchy treatment in a forty-five minute discussion. On the other hand, the subject "How can we encourage better attendance at meetings of the Junior Chamber of Commerce?" may be adequately covered in a similar period of time. (3) *A discussion problem should be phrased in clear, precise terms.* Avoid clichés, trite terms, and abstract words in phrasing your topic. "The American way of life," "urban centers," and "the greatest good for the greatest number" have general but not specific meanings, and will inhibit clear thinking on your problem. Substitute "cities with populations of 100,000 and over" for "urban centers," and reduce "the American way of life" to "freedom of the ballot," or some other more specific concept.

C. Finding materials. Poor preparation is one of the most common reasons for the failure of a discussion group. Some people believe that discussion can be engaged in with little or no preparation. Since the atmosphere usually is less formal than that of public speaking and may resemble that of conversation, some persons believe they can slide through with little or no knowledge of the subject beyond a few prejudiced and hastily conceived conclusions.

The four methods of gathering materials for public speaking may also be used in preparing for discussion. *Think* of what you already know about the subject and what you need to find out; *observe* your environment for what it may yield; *communicate* with others to discover what they know; and *read* judiciously those references which bear upon your problem (Chapter 3).

The next step is to put the material you have gathered into outline form to clarify your thinking and to make your materials readily available during the discussion.

D. Organizing the discussion. The organizational pattern for the question of policy usually consists of five steps: (1) *What explanations should be made?* Pertinent background materials should be presented and necessary definitions made. (2) *What is the nature of the problem?* Examine the situations which gave rise to the problem. What is the extent of the problem? How acute is it? What are the probable consequences if the problem is not solved? What are the causes of the problem? (3) *What possible solutions to the problem should be considered?* Suggest and examine solutions which may possibly alleviate or remove the causes and results of the problem. (4) *Which of the possible solutions is preferable?* On the basis of conclusions drawn from examining several possible solutions, choose the best one. (5) *How can this solution be put into action?* Suggest methods for carrying out the preferred solution.

Ordinarily in the question of value or fact you will need only three steps: (1) *Explaining the problem:* This may be done in the same way as in the question of policy. (2) *Setting up criteria for evaluation:* If you are attempting to evaluate the chances of the New York Yankees in the next pennant race, possibly you will consider hitting power, pitching, defensive ability, experience, and intelligent leadership as criteria for judging the potential of the team. (3) *Making the evaluation and drawing conclusions by measuring the facts against the criteria:* Marshall all available facts and judgments about the Yankees and decide whether they "measure up." It is obvious that your conclusions will be based partially upon a similar evaluation of those teams competing against the Yankees.

A discussion outline should be constructed according to the organizational pattern explained above. For a problem of policy, the skeleton outline which appears below may be helpful.

SUBJECT FOR DISCUSSION

I. What explanations should be made?
   A. What terms in the question need definition?

    B. What other terms or concepts which may arise should be clarified?

II. What is the nature of the problem?
    A. What facts or events prompted consideration of the problem by this group?
    B. What is the extent of the problem? Its acuteness?
    C. What are the major causes of the problem?
    D. What may be the future situation if the problem remains unsolved?

III. What possible solutions to the problems should be considered?
    A. Solution I:
       1. Advantages?
       2. Disadvantages?
    B. Solution II:
       1. Advantages?
       2. Disadvantages?
    C. Solution III:
       1. Advantages?
       2. Disadvantages?

IV. Which of the solutions above is preferable?
    A. Why is it superior to the others?
    B. Is it a practicable solution?

V. How can this solution be put into action?

A group outline of this type should be constructed by members of the group during the planning conference for use as a guide during the forthcoming discussion. It may be more detailed and complete than the skeleton form appearing above. If no planning conference takes place, it will be the responsibility of the leader or moderator to construct this outline. Each member of the discussion group should have a copy.

Each participant also should prepare a personal outline. In the case of the conference and the panel (see pages 354, 355), the personal outline should follow the form suggested for the group outline, and should contain all the evidence and sources of evidence uncovered in individual preparation. It will undoubtedly be longer and more detailed than the group outline. In the case of the symposium (see pages 355, 356), the speaker's personal outline should develop the particular phase of the discussion assigned to him.

The discussion outline should serve as your guide, not as your master. New evidence and ideas or an unexpected development in the progress of the discussion may necessitate departures from the outline. Deviations from the planned course of the discussion are fully acceptable, as long as extended tangents are avoided.

PARTICIPATION IN GROUP DISCUSSION

Preparation is completed when the discussants have conferred and developed a group outline, and when each member has gathered his materials and organized them into an individual outline. The group is then ready to begin discussion.

A. Leadership in group discussion. The ideal discussion probably would need no leader. It would proceed systematically through the analysis and solution of the problem without conflict or difficulty. In most cases, however, discussion needs leadership of the highest quality if it is to be successful. What qualities should the leader possess and what techniques must he exercise?

1. Qualities of leadership

a. THE DISCUSSION LEADER SHOULD KNOW HIS SUBJECT. Leadership is sometimes erroneously thought of as a simple job akin to that of the traffic cop. But the effective leader does not simply call upon the participants for information and ideas. Ordinarily he will need to clarify issues which have become clouded, restate concepts, ask questions, stimulate thinking, and make transitions and summaries. These duties are difficult to perform unless the leader is well grounded in the subject. However, he should carefully avoid the partisanship and dogmatism which sometimes result from extensive knowledge of a subject.

b. THE DISCUSSION LEADER SHOULD KNOW HIS GROUP AND HIS AUDIENCE. It is the responsibility of the moderator to know the qualities and limitations of each member of his discussion group. If the leader does not know his participants well, he should make the most of the planning conference to discover what can be expected of them. If an audience is to be present, it is the leader's obligation to analyze the group to facilitate adaptation.

c. THE DISCUSSION LEADER SHOULD BE SKILLED AT EXTEMPORE SPEAKING. Ad-libs, introductions, restatements, interpretations, transitions, summaries, and the conduct of the question-and-answer period will exact from the moderator considerable skill in extempore speaking.

d. The discussion leader should possess important personal qualities. The most important of these are enthusiasm, tact, open-mindedness, and a sense of humor. A listless, lackadaisical group may be enlivened by the energy and enthusiasm of its leader. Tact is important in resolving antagonisms, conflicts, and in adjusting to the sensitivities of the participants. Open-mindedness is a "must." One of the fundamental principles of discussion has been identified earlier as objectivity. If the moderator is not fair and open-minded, discussion will usually be futile from the beginning. A sense of humor will relieve tension, encourage friendly and active participation, minimize conflict, and enhance audience interest.

2. *Techniques of leadership*

a. The discussion leader must open the discussion. This may include stating the problem, giving necessary background information, explaining the procedures to be followed in the meeting, introducing the speakers, and starting the discussion.

b. The discussion leader must direct the course of the discussion. Although the group should not be excessively tied to the outline, the leader must be wary of extended tangents. Confusion, antagonism, and excessive disagreement must be minimized. Brief summaries and clear transitions will aid the group and the audience in realizing what material has been covered, what is now being considered, and what remains to be presented.

c. The discussion leader must know how to handle the participants. Equal quantity and quality of participation among the members of a panel or symposium are probably not possible, nor even desirable. Some may have more of import to contribute. However, reticent members should be gently encouraged to take a more active part, and loquacious participants must be dealt with tactfully but firmly. Interruption by the chairman may occasionally be necessary.

d. The discussion leader must "keep one eye on the clock." Timing the discussion is primarily the leader's responsibility, although he may be aided greatly by a keen awareness of time on the part of each of his colleagues. Over-all timing should adhere closely to previous plans. Only in rare cases should a discussion planned for a half hour extend more than five or ten minutes beyond that limit, particularly if an audience is present and a question period is anticipated. Of course, over-all timing is of greater significance if the discussion is to be broadcast or televised.

Timing or pacing the progress of the discussion within the over-all time limit is also important. Moderators occasionally find that they are unable to complete their agenda in the time allotted. On rarer occasions, the discussion is allowed to progress so rapidly that the group arrives at hasty or preheld conclusions with a considerable amount of time remaining at their disposal. Timing errors can be avoided by assigning a rough estimate of time to each phase or step to be covered. Although this need not be rigidly adhered to, it is wise to keep close to the estimate.

e. THE DISCUSSION LEADER MUST CLOSE THE DISCUSSION. When the allotted time has elapsed or when conclusions are reached, the discussion leader must make a concluding statement. Although the nature of this statement may vary, it should summarize briefly the progress and accomplishments of the group, including both agreements and disagreements. If an audience is present, the closing statement should stimulate listeners to active participation in the forum period to follow.

f. THE DISCUSSION LEADER USUALLY WILL CONDUCT THE AUDIENCE-PARTICIPATION PERIOD. Duties during the forum period include: stimulating participation by raising some provocative questions near the beginning, if necessary; assuming responsibility for recognizing questioners; insisting upon relevance in all questions; discouraging monopoly of the time by any member of the audience; clarifying questions by restatement, when necessary; referring to the proper person questions not directed to a particular participant; and terminating the meeting before interest has died.

B. Membership in group discussion. Many of the characteristics of good leadership are equally applicable to effective participation by members of a discussion group.

1. *Ability as an extempore speaker.* This is as important to the participant as to the leader. Participation in group discussion is largely extempore; although symposium speeches are often read, many of these also are extemporized. Intelligent listening is also necessary if one is to adjust his remarks to what has been said previously. Unfortunately, many discussants are far more concerned with "having their say" than with understanding the points of view of others and why they hold them.

2. *Characteristics of personality.* Like the moderator, a participant must cultivate enthusiasm, tact, open-mindedness, and a sense of humor. Identify your prejudices and admit to yourself that you have them. Do not permit them to dominate your thinking and your participation. Submerge your ego to the point that you can face frankly the fact that the work of the conference is more important than imposing your will upon the group; and remember that a discussion is not the occasion to exhibit your brilliance or speaking ability at the expense of the group activity. If you must disagree with someone, do so tactfully. Even though the discussion does not proceed as you had hoped it would, continue to cooperate enthusiastically with your colleagues in search of a solution to the problem at hand. A sense of humor will help immensely in such a situation.

3. *The relationship between participants and moderator.* Resist the temptation to usurp the prerogatives of leadership. Occasionally, you may disagree with the chairman's tactics or become impatient with his inept conduct of the discussion; however, he is the designated leader, not you. The moderator, nonetheless, is not a dictator, and one may tactfully suggest corrections, point out inaccuracies in his interpretations, suggest "getting on" with the discussion, or make other comments to facilitate the progress of the conference. A discussant can be of considerable aid to the moderator by keeping an eye on the clock, facilitating faster pacing when necessary, quieting an overly talkative person, or helping to draw out a shy colleague.

4. *Length and frequency of participation.* As we shall soon see, symposium speakers are usually assigned definite time limits. However, panel and conference discussants are often uncertain as to how often they should talk. Talk only when fairly certain of the importance and relevance of your ideas. Do not monopolize; on the other hand, do not be backward. Occasionally, discussants mistakenly believe they have nothing of importance to contribute. Such persons are sometimes best qualified to speak. The length of individual contributions will obviously vary considerably. Some authorities advise that the average length of single contributions be under one minute in the panel discussion. Rarely should any panel member talk for more than two or three minutes without interruption. In general, it is better to offer a considerable number of brief statements rather than relatively few contributions of extended duration.

TYPES OR FORMS OF DISCUSSION

Four common types of discussion and one adaptation should be noted: (1) the committee or conference meeting, (2) the panel, (3) the symposium, (4) the lecture-forum, and (5) the radio and television discussion. Each has its peculiar values and limitations.

A. The committee or conference meeting. This is the most intimate and informal among the common types. The group is usually limited to ten or fifteen persons, a formal leader is not designated in many cases, and an audience is not present. When the purpose is to investigate and learn, it is sometimes called a study group. On other occasions, the purpose for convening may be policy-determination. Committee and conference discussion is used widely in industry to convey information, exchange ideas, train employees, and to formulate policy. Many industries are enthusiastic about the value of discussion in preventing employer-employee dissatisfactions and in settling employee grievances.

B. The panel. Panel discussion in many respects is similar to committee and conference discussion. However, the group is usually somewhat smaller (three to six persons) and an audience is present. The atmosphere is a bit more formal, and time limits are more strictly enforced.

In presenting a panel discussion program, the customary procedure is for the panel to analyze the problem and attempt to resolve it. Then comments and questions from the audience are entertained. The audience-participation period may last as long as one half of the total meeting time.

The presence of the audience adds to the obligations of the group. To its purpose of problem-solving must be added the task of interesting listeners and stimulating them to think along with the group. Unless the audience can be drawn actively into group thinking and oral participation, the panel will not be a complete success.

The effectiveness of the panel depends to some extent upon optimum environmental conditions. The group should be seated either

GROUP DISCUSSION

around a table or in a semicircle. Each member should be visible to every other member and also to the audience. Ordinarily, the moderator will sit near the middle of the semicircle, facing the audience directly. If possible, the group should be close to the audience.

The public nature of panel discussion necessitates a planning conference, at which the group outline should be drafted under the leadership of the moderator. If the group has had experience in public discussion, the discussion should not be rehearsed. Classroom groups involving beginning students may profit from rehearsal, but one should be sufficient. Repeated practice tends to destroy spontaneity.

C. The symposium. When each discussant is assigned a segment of the problem upon which to present a short speech, the arrangement is called a symposium.

The subject may be partitioned according to the steps in the pattern of organization discussed earlier. The first speaker may explain the problem, the second may analyze it, and the remaining speakers may examine tentative solutions. Each will have from five to twenty minutes at his disposal. At the conclusion of the speeches the group probably will discuss informally the various solutions in an attempt to arrive at a preferred solution and a program of action. Eventually, the audience will be asked to join with questions and comments. The following example illustrates how a subject may be partitioned for a symposium:

HOW MAY THE QUALITY OF COLLEGE TEACHING BE IMPROVED?

Speaker I: "What are the characteristics of good college teaching?"
Speaker II: "An evaluation of current teaching practices in selected colleges."
Speaker III: "Will raising the minimum educational requirements for teachers improve instruction?"
Speaker IV: "Will increasing teachers' salaries raise the standards of college teaching?"
Speaker V: "Will reducing teaching loads improve teaching?"

The symposium begins with brief opening remarks by the moderator, which will include necessary background explanations, a statement of the procedures to be followed in the meeting, and an introduction of each member of the group. The first speaker is then presented. One of the more important of the chairman's duties is to integrate each speech with the others by making an effective transition from speaker to speaker. At the conclusion of the speeches, the moderator will conduct the informal discussion and the subsequent question-and-answer period.

The symposium gives the discussant the opportunity to present a carefully conceived and well-organized treatment of an aspect of the subject; he must be careful, however, to reflect the spirit of inquiry rather than that of advocacy.

D. The lecture-forum. This activity features an expert lecturer. Customarily his address is followed by an audience-participation period under the guidance of a chairman.

Care should be taken to secure a speaker who will examine the problem with open-mindedness and objectivity. He should be asked to observe time limits so that ample time will remain for audience participation.

Since the audience may be large and the atmosphere somewhat formal, audience participation may be difficult to get under way. The success of the forum period will depend greatly upon the ability of the chairman. His responsibilities in this situation have been discussed earlier.

E. The radio and television discussion. It should be made clear that broadcast or televised discussion is an adaptation rather than a type; any of the forms previously explained may be presented via these media. The problem, then, is to adapt discussion to the peculiar demands of radio and television.

While any public discussion should stimulate involuntary attention, it is especially important that radio and television do so. We noted in Chapter 16 that it is easier for an air listener to find another program or turn his set off than for an audience member at a public meeting to leave his seat and make his way from the hall; furthermore, the air listener is subject to a greater variety of distractions. Therefore, every attention-getting device at your command should be utilized. The vocal aspect of radio is obviously of paramount importance. Your program also should be paced quickly and must be carefully timed. Unless the participants are experienced, it is advisable to rehearse a radio discussion.

The TV discussant must always be aware of the fact that he can be seen, and frequently from a much closer vantage point than that of most listeners at a public meeting.

Televised discussion should be characterized by motion. Although visual variety will be achieved by camera shots from different angles and distances, strive for some physical animation. Move from your seat to refer to a visual aid, gesture occasionally, and be facially expressive; the immobile, statue-like discussant makes for rather dull "looking." Delivery should be animated, conversational, and in the extemporaneous mode. Notes may be used, of course, but reference to them should be kept to a minimum. The attention of most televiewers cannot be retained long by speeches read from manuscript.

When possible, visual aids such as charts, slides, films, pictures, and short demonstrations should be incorporated into televised discussion. Their use will help to hold the attention of your audience and will aid measurably in making your ideas clear. (Radio or TV discussants may find it helpful to review Chapter 16.)

Summary

Discussion is systematic, objective group deliberation for the purpose of investigating and solving problems. Skill in its techniques is essential to the citizen in a democratic society. Preparation for discussion includes: (1) selecting a subject or problem; (2) stating the problem clearly and accurately; (3) gathering materials; and (4) organizing the discussion. Essential to successful group discussion are the qualities and techniques of effective leadership and participation. Discussion usually takes one of several common forms: (1) the committee or conference meeting, (2) the panel, (3) the symposium, and (4) the lecture-forum. Discussion may be adapted effectively for radio and television presentation.

Exercises and Assignments

1. *Class Project I:*
   (1) Bring to class ten discussion problems carefully selected and phrased according to the rules in this chapter. Among them should be problems of fact, value, and policy. Include at least one problem from each of these broad areas: (a) international affairs, (b) domestic problems, (c) local issues, and (d) college problems.

(2) From the topics submitted, choose by vote the best topics for panel discussions by the class. Three to five persons should be assigned to each topic, and from each group a moderator should be selected.

(3) Following individual research and preparation, a class period may be assigned for planning conferences. At this session, each group should construct its discussion outline. The moderator will serve as a conference leader. Consult your instructor for guidance when necessary.

(4) Each panel should present a thirty-minute discussion. This may be followed by a ten- or fifteen-minute forum period, during which the rest of the class may ask questions of the panel members. The audience, the participants, and the instructor may spend the remainder of the class hour in evaluation of the performance. Consider content, organization, and techniques of leadership and participation.

2. Class Project II:
Repeat the procedure outlined in Project I with groups assigned to the preparation and presentation of symposiums. It is wise to reconstitute the groups and select different moderators.

3. Invite a well-known speaker from the community to address the class for twenty or thirty minutes on a pertinent, controversial subject upon which he is especially qualified to speak. Appoint or elect a leader from the class to conduct a forum period following his speech. At the next meeting, evaluate the speaker and the conduct of the forum.

4. Ask either the intercollegiate forensic group at your institution or a community group to present to the class a panel or symposium which has been given at intercollegiate discussion conferences or before community audiences. A forum period may follow. Reserve time at the end of the period for oral evaluation of the presentation; the group probably will appreciate your criticisms. Your instructor may ask for a written report of the proceedings.

5. Read and carefully analyze the printed proceedings of a University of Chicago Round Table (or a series of Round Tables). In a written report evaluate (1) choice of subject, (2) use of evidence and argument, (3) degree of open-mindedness and cooperativeness achieved, (4) organization (did they adhere to a logical pattern?), (5) language used, and (6) the validity of their resolution of the problem.

6. Record on wire or tape a radio or television discussion for playback in the classroom. Using the criteria in exercise 5, take notes during the presentation and participate in class discussion about the program.

INDEX